**THE WAR DIARY
OF THE U.S.S. HORNET (CV-12)**
March 18, 1945.
At 0528 hrs. the Hornet's
40-mm. and 20-mm.
guns hit a plane coming
in at about 500
feet altitude on the
starboard quarter
which splashed
700 yards astern.

Painting by
Dwight Shepler
courtesy of
Navy Combat Art

THE KAMIKAZE SUICIDE FORCE

"In *The Divine Wind,* Captain Inoguchi and Commander Tadashi Nakajima relive the tragic ten-month history of this unique Suicide Force . . . without doubt the most carefully documented and accurate account of the suicide fliers, their lives and thoughts."

—*Saturday Review*

THE BANTAM WAR BOOK SERIES

This is a series of books about a world on fire.

These carefully chosen volumes cover the full dramatic sweep of World War II. Many are eyewitness accounts by the men who fought in this global conflict in which the future of the civilized world hung in balance. Fighter pilots, tank commanders and infantry commanders, among others, recount exploits of individual courage in the midst of the large-scale terrors of war. They present portraits of brave men and true stories of gallantry and cowardice in action, moving sagas of survival and tragedies of untimely death. Some of the stories are told from the enemy viewpoint to give the reader an immediate sense of the incredible life and death struggle of both sides of the battle.

Through these books we begin to discover what it was like to be there, a participant in an epic war for freedom.

Each of the books in the Bantam War Book series contains a dramatic color painting and illustrations specially commissioned for each title to give the reader a deeper understanding of the roles played by the men and machines of World War II.

THE DIVINE WIND

JAPAN'S KAMIKAZE FORCE IN WORLD WAR II

By CAPTAIN RIKIHEI INOGUCHI
COMMANDER TADASHI NAKAJIMA,
FORMER IMPERIAL JAPANESE NAVY,
with ROGER PINEAU

Foreword by Vice Admiral C. R. Brown,
United States Navy

BANTAM BOOKS
Toronto / New York / London

THE DIVINE WIND
A Bantam Book

PRINTING HISTORY
Naval Institute Press edition published in 1958
Bantam edition / November 1978

Drawings by Tom Beecham
Map by Shelley Drowns

All rights reserved.
Copyright © 1958 by the United States Naval Institute.
Illustrations copyright © 1978 by Bantam Books, Inc.
*This book may not be reproduced in whole or in part, by
mimeograph or any other means, without permission.*
For information address: Bantam Books, Inc.

ISBN 0-553-12578-8

Published simultaneously in the United States and Canada

PRINTED IN THE UNITED STATES OF AMERICA

FOREWORD

Among those of us who were there, in the Philippines and at Okinawa, I doubt if there is anyone who can depict with complete clarity our mixed emotions as we watched a man about to die—a man *determined* to die in order that he might destroy us in the process. There was a hypnotic fascination to a sight so alien to our Western philosophy. We watched each plunging kamikaze with the detached horror of one witnessing a terrible spectacle rather than as the intended victim. We forgot self for the moment as we groped hopelessly for the thoughts of that other man up there. And dominating it all was a strange admixture of respect and pity—respect for any person who offers the supreme sacrifice to the things he stands for, and pity for the utter frustration which was epitomized by the suicidal act. For whatever the gesture meant to that central actor out there in space, and however painful might be the consequences to ourselves, no one of us questioned the final outcome of the war now rushing to its conclusion. This "Divine Wind," this Kamikaze, this Special Attack Corps, was just another form of banzai charge, made by men experiencing the bitterness of defeat and unwilling to accept that reality.

But why this suicidal tactic? How could, not one man, but several thousand men seek certain death? Did these men, in the words of Admiral Ohnishi, think themselves "already gods without earthly desires"?

It is certainly not that the enemy was more courageous than we. One of the earliest lessons one learns in battle is that courage is a very common human quality. Mute evidence is the story of our own Torpedo Squadron Eight at Midway, and the unforgettable picture I once observed on board the *Essex* when I watched the 20-millimeter gun crews stand unflinchingly to their guns until enveloped in flames, in an effort to beat off a kamikaze.

But there was a fundamental difference in the heroism of the opposing warriors. The Japanese resolutely closed the last avenue of hope and escape, the American never did. To the Western mind there must be that last slim chance of survival—the feeling that, though a lot of other chaps may die, you yourself somehow are going to make it back.

No one has yet successfully explained to the Western mind this Japanese phenomenon of self-immolation, and perhaps it is not given to the Westerner to understand it. Hence, as we read this dramatic, gripping story of the Kamikaze Corps as it comes from the lips of those who personally acted out the great tragedy, we seek vainly for the key to the enigma.

One of the Japanese authors makes the statement, ". . . No man welcomes death. . . . But it is more understandable if one bears in mind that, considering the heavy odds our fliers faced in 1944, their chance of coming back from any sortie against the enemy carriers was very slim regardless of the attack method employed." Yet the answer is not there. Neither is it in the letters to home and loved ones from those about to die, though these letters haunt one with their poignancy.

Sometimes these letters are utterly beautiful.

"We are 16 warriors manning the bombers. May our death be as sudden as the shattering of crystal."

Sometimes they are deeply touching:

"My greatest regret in this life is the failure to call you 'chichiue' (revered father). I regret not having given any demonstration of the true respect which I have always had for you. During my final plunge, though you will not hear it, you may be sure I will be saying 'chichiue' to you and thinking of all you have done for me."

And always they are tragic:

"I am a human being and hope to be neither saint nor scoundrel, hero nor fool—just a human being. As one who spent his life in wistful longing and searching, I die resignedly in the hope that my life will serve as a human document."

And:

"The world in which I lived was too full of discord. As a community of rational human beings it should have been better composed. Lacking a single great conductor, everyone let loose with his own sound, creating dissonance where there should have been melody and harmony."

Such are the fleeting glimpses of tortured souls that we catch behind the façade of this extraordinary history.

Any way one looks at the Kamikaze Corps, there is stark tragedy. For whatever the private motivations or official explanations for the kamikaze, and however fascinating they may be, the key question for the pragmatic military man must be—was it a successful tactic?

My answer is an unqualified *no*. True, the Special Attack Force—the Kamikaze—did tremendous damage. It sank a lot of ships and damaged a multitude of others. It killed and wounded thousands of men—inflicted more casualties in the U. S. fleets off Okinawa than the Japanese Army did to the invading troops in the long battle ashore. Typical of the nightmare it made of destroyer picket duty was the destroyer man on picket station who, with grim humor, painted an arrow on his deck pointing off to the side, with the huge letters, *"Carriers that way!"*

But by that time Japan was already hopelessly worsted, and even in its flaming sacrifice the Kamikaze Corps sank no U. S. warship of cruiser size or larger. That, in a way, is the real tragedy of the kamikaze, as far as its pilots were concerned—that this extraordinary tactic was not conceived until it was already too late for even the most desperate measures to stay the inevitable defeat of Japan.

C. R. BROWN
Vice Admiral, U. S. Navy

July 1958

けふ咲きてあす散る花の我身かな
いかてその香を清くとゞめん

In blossom today, then scattered:
Life is so like a delicate flower.
How can one expect the fragrance
To last forever?

BY OHNISHI,
KAMIKAZE SPECIAL ATTACK FORCE

PUBLISHER'S NOTE

The Japanese authors of *The Divine Wind* were with the Japanese Naval Special Attack Force (Kamikaze Corps) from its inception until its dissolution with the suicide sortie of the admiral in command. One served as the commanding admiral's personal representative for operations and the other as a flight operations officer for suicide attack units in the Philippines, Formosa, and the home islands.

Captain Inoguchi graduated from the Japanese Naval Academy in 1921, served on staffs of various cruiser divisions, instructed at the Naval Academy and performed a tour of duty in the Bureau of Personnel before World War II. In February 1944, he commanded the 153d Air Group and subsequently led it through the campaigns in Timor, New Guinea, and Peleliu. In July he was transferred as a staff officer for the 23d Air Flotilla at Kendari. The following month he joined the First Air Flight as the senior staff officer to Admiral Ohnishi, the originator of the kamikaze concept, and participated in the initial suicide operations conducted from the Philippines and subsequently from Formosa. In March 1945 he served in the home islands as a staff officer of the 10th Air Fleet from which he was transferred in May to the Naval Section of the Imperial General Headquarters. He is now retired from naval service.

Commander Tadashi Nakajima graduated from the Japanese Naval Academy in 1927. He attended flight training school in 1933 and was in command of an aircraft unit on the carrier *Kaga* in 1936. He commanded another air unit in China during the Sino-Japanese

Incidents and was transferred to command of the Tainan Air Group in 1942, stationed successively in Bali, Rabaul, New Guinea, the Solomons, and Guadalcanal. In 1943 he commanded the Yokosuka Air Group stationed at Iwo Jima. In 1944 he was the flight operations officer for the 201st Air Group, in the Philippines, selected by Admiral Ohnishi as the original unit for the initiation of suicide tactics as a deliberate weapon of policy. In 1945 he served on the staff of the First Air Fleet in Formosa and then on the staff of the Fifth Air Fleet in the home islands during the Okinawa suicide campaign. At the war's end he was commanding officer of the 723d Air Group. He is now a Major General in the Japanese Air Self-Defense Force.

Roger Pineau, an officer in the United States Naval Reserve, after a tour of active duty in World War II, was a member of the U. S. Strategic Bombing Survey in Japan and later worked as a collaborator with Rear Admiral Samuel Eliot Morison in the preparation of the authoritative *History of United States Naval Operations in World War II*. His knowledge of the Japanese and their language, together with his own naval background and extensive research experience, makes him particularly well qualified as co-author of this absorbing account.

U. S. NAVAL INSTITUTE

March, 1958

PREFACE BY
ROGER PINEAU

In 1281 Kublai Khan organized a mighty Mongol armada to invade and conquer the islands of Japan. The success of this venture was all but assured when a great typhoon off the Japanese coast destroyed or dispersed the Mongol ships. The Japanese people considered this fortuitous storm an evidence of heavenly protection and have ever since credited the salvation of the Empire to *Kamikaze*—the Divine Wind.

In late 1944, after a series of stunning American victories on land and sea, an overwhelming naval force was poised to wrest the Philippine Islands back from Japan. With the Philippines in enemy hands the home islands of Japan would soon be in grave jeopardy. Once again it seemed that only an intervention of fate could stem the tide of national disaster. There were a few scattered remnants of Japan's once-mighty Naval Air Force in the Philippines and they were authorized by Japanese naval leaders to form a unit which is unique in the annals of war—the Special Attack Force. It was anticipated that each member of this force would sacrifice himself with his plane in an attack against an enemy aircraft carrier. The objective was to deprive American ships of aerial protection at Leyte Gulf and thus improve the Imperial Navy's chances of victory in an all-out surface engagement. It was inevitable that this suicide unit, intended to levy a storm of destruction upon the enemy, should be named after its celestial predecessor—Kamikaze.

In helping to write this volume my goal has been to preserve the theme and mood of the original text, while clarifying obscurities, and to supply supporting factual information from all available American and

Japanese sources. In this endeavor I have reorganized the entire text, retranslated parts of it, translated the Appendices, and added footnotes. My work has been approved by the Japanese authors.

Dates and times given in the text are those at the scene of action. Boy and girl names parenthetically appended to Japanese plane types are the Allied code identifications.

I could no more have prepared this volume alone than I can acknowledge in full measure the assistance of those who have done so much to help me with it. Authors Inoguchi and Nakajima and our mutual friend and collaborator, Masataka Chihaya, have exhibited monumental patience and skill in producing answers to the innumerable questions which arose in the course of this work. In the past three years I have often wished that Clarke H. Kawakami had been sharing with me the labors of this book as he did with *Midway, The Battle That Doomed Japan.* Unable to do so, he has nevertheless given sage counsel which I deeply appreciate. Mr. Andrew Kuroda, of the Library of Congress, and Mrs. Lily Tanaka have given unstintingly of their great knowledge of the language and history of Japan.

The graceful calligraphy which introduces each part of this book is by Mrs. Keiko Moore, talented daughter of famed wood-block artist Un-ichi Hiratsuka. She took time from her busy days in the Hiratsuka Gallery of Washington, D.C., to make this artistic contribution.

Lastly, but not least, I wish to express gratitude and appreciation to my family for having endured my absorption in this effort; and especially to my wife, Maxine, who has profited me by her sound advice in this undertaking and has uncomplainingly typed this manuscript many times.

ROGER PINEAU

Bethesda, Maryland
15 March 1958

PREFACE BY
RIKIHEI INOGUCHI AND
TADASHI NAKAJIMA

In the course of World War II the Japanese Navy lost practically all of its ships and planes. We lost as well two supreme commanders, Admirals Yamamoto and Koga, who died in battle within one year's time. Figuratively speaking, we fought to our last bullet, a fact which betokens the extraordinary character of that war. World War II is sharply distinguished from Japan's earlier wars with Russia and with China in two major aspects:

1. This was a total war.

2. This was a predominantly naval war, and yet air forces were deeply involved.

Considering these two points, we can see that numbers and quality of fighting men were decisive factors. Our air forces and naval forces were both inferior to those of the enemy. Extreme measures were called for. Kamikaze attacks were inevitable.

Then what did the high command have in mind in embarking on such a war? Did they really have a firm assurance based on careful calculation?

Vice Admiral Shigeru Fukudome, who was Chief of the Operations Bureau of the Naval General Staff at the outbreak of the war, has written of the Japanese Navy:

On the eve of war there was a fear in Japan that revolution was imminent. Admiral Yamamoto maintained that while civil war would not be fatal to the nation, an external war that had no chance of success would spell disaster. Accordingly, he was vigorously opposed to the idea of going to war. At the same time he said that as a result of the domestic situation, the evolution toward war was inevitable.

When I explained the plan of operations to Prince Fushimi* at his palace he said, "If war breaks out, Japan will lose all that has been achieved since the beginning of the Meiji Era. But it seems that there is no way to avoid war. I am filled with anxiety."

It was the Navy's conclusion that, undesirable as it might be, there was no alternative; survival of Japan could be achieved only by resorting to war. In this decision the Navy was represented by Admiral Shigetaro Shimada, Navy Minister of the first Tojo Cabinet.

On the basis of military strength, preparedness, and the strategic climate, an early commencement of war was desirable. This was outlined by the Chief of the General Staff, Admiral Osami Nagano, in an Imperial Conference on September 6, 1941. Nevertheless, a way was left open on the chance that satisfactory diplomatic arrangements could be achieved without recourse to military means. Even if we could not win a military victory, it was incumbent upon us to resort to arms in order to remain loyal to the Japanese spirit, which had to be preserved at all costs.

After the agenda had been approved, Admiral Nagano, representing the high command, commented on this point: "It is agreed that if we do not fight now, our nation will perish. But it may well perish even if we do fight. It must be understood that national ruin without resistance would be ignominy.

"In this hopeless situation, survival can be accomplished only by fighting to the last man. Then, even if we lose, posterity will have the heritage of our loyal spirit to inspire them in turn to the defense of our country."

And he concluded by saying, "In war, soldiers ask only the chance to fight in support of the Emperor. We shall fight to the last drop of blood."

---

*Prince Hiroyaso Fushimi was Admiral of the Fleet from April 1932 to April 1941.

We who were actually engaged in combat knew nothing of the proceedings of this Imperial Conference until after the end of the war. We fought as the Throne commanded. As the war progressed, we felt the growing bitterness of defeat, but were determined to undergo any hardships in fulfillment of our obligation to the Emperor and our homeland.

With the war's end, our complete defeat confirmed Admiral Nagano's speculation. More than that, the Navy's recklessness in concurring in the war had brought about its own complete ruin.

It is paradoxical that the Pacific War, which ushered in the atomic age, should have seen resort to aerial suicide attacks. Indeed, it may seem ridiculous that these should even have been considered, let alone put into use, to combat the scientific weapons and tactics of modern warfare. It is understandable that many people should regard such attacks as an example of barbarity, if not insanity, and prefer to forget that they ever occurred.

However, the remarkable progress in destructive weapons of recent years has forced men—military and civilian alike—to realize that war gives rise to desperation. Since war and its weapons are a product of the human mind, it does not seem amiss to look into that mind. Further, since the desire to live is so basic to the human mind, it is of interest to study the kamikaze pilots who had to surmount that desire in order to perform their duty.

We might wish that the suicide pilots could speak to us today, but their voices are silenced. Accordingly we have collected all available data and sought to compile this record to speak for them. This book is not intended as a criticism. It is meant to be a record of, and a memorial to, the brave men who gave their lives in these "special" attacks. We sincerely hope that it may serve to point toward the better world to which each of these men thought he was contributing.

Kamikaze attacks shocked the world primarily because of their "certain death" aspect. History provides many cases of individual soldiers who fought under certain-death circumstances, but never before was such a program carried out so systematically and over such a long period of time. In the case of a do-or-die action, however great the risk involved, there is always a chance of survival. But the kamikaze attack could be carried out *only* by killing oneself. The attack and death were one and the same thing.

In the storm of criticism that broke after the war, the blame for kamikaze attacks was variously placed. Some denounced the minds that had devised the tactics. Others impeached the leaders who had planned and supervised the attacks. Still others leveled their charges at the individual pilots who carried out these attacks under orders—and died. There may be something to each of these points of view. We have no intention of questioning them here. We seek only to explain the circumstances under which kamikaze attacks came about and how they were performed.

It must be remembered that in most cases kamikaze pilots did not make their attack sortie *immediately after* volunteering or being selected. After their designation or acceptance as special attackers, most of them went on with their regular military duties. In some cases they continued thus for months, never knowing from one day to the next when their turn would come. Momentary enthusiasm could never have supported them under such prolonged suspense.

One thing is certain. For the effort, and for its purpose, the Kamikaze Special Attack Corps was organized under the right men. Although the term "kamikaze" was later applied to other self-destructive corps, such as suicide glide bombs and small suicide boats, strictly speaking the only real kamikazes were the aerial attack groups organized under Vice Admiral Ohnishi. The success of his organization is attributable to the bond of feeling and purpose which existed between the Admiral and his men. This unity was of utmost importance. Without it the attacks could never have been continued over so long a period, no matter how brave the men or how able their leader.

"We die for the great cause of our country"—this was the kamikaze pilots' watchword and their faith. It signified a constant and deeply grounded belief in their country and their Emperor, and a willingness to die for that belief. Lacking that, the kamikaze attacks would never have been made at all.

In saying this we do not mean to imply our approval of Admiral Ohnishi's decisions and actions. It is a fair question, in fact, as to how he was able to justify his decisions to himself. A fair question, but one that does not admit of a ready answer except insofar as revealed by his statements recorded in this book.

His pilots never questioned the responsibility of their commander. But then they never considered that they were going to do anything extraordinary. Their greatest concern seems always to have been to make sure that they would hit the target. By comparison, their death was to them a matter of very minor importance.

But this is not sufficient explanation for their meeting death with such composure. Subconsciously they must have had a firm belief in "life through death." This attitude is one that comes down through the long tradition and history of the people of Japan.

We pray that the brave souls of these men who gave their lives in this effort may rest in eternal peace.

RIKIHEI INOGUCHI
TADASHI NAKAJIMA

December, 1957

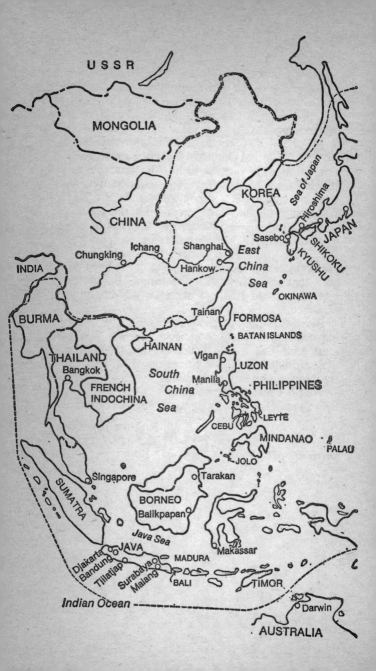

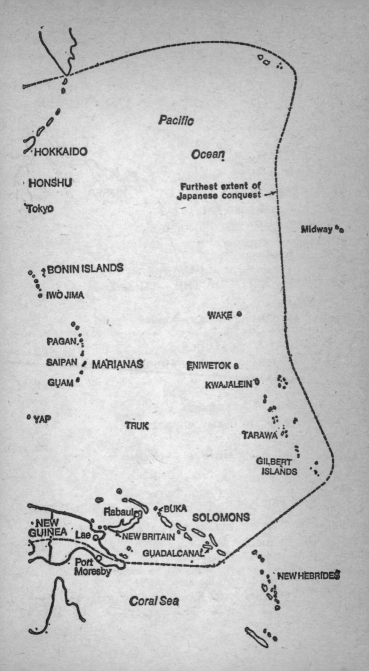

CONTENTS

PART FIVE:
THE DIVINE WIND

APPENDICES

PART ONE

BIRTH OF THE KAMIKAZE

"Life is as the weight of a feather
compared to one's duty"
—JAPANESE PROVERB

A kamikaze pilot receives his orders.

MABALACAT

BY INOGUCHI

THE 201ST AIR GROUP

The time was 19 October 1944; the place, Mabala-cat, on the island of Luzon, in the Philippines. The late afternoon sun was about to sink below the crestline of the mountains to the west of Mabalacat Airfield, which formed part of the sprawling Clark Base complex, some 50 miles northwest of Manila. Ground crewmen wearing the work uniform of the Imperial Japanese Navy Air Forces scurried here and there like ants, hurrying to conceal planes in revetments before dusk and to carry out attack preparations for the following morning.

I was sitting in the airfield command post, an old and tattered tent, talking with the executive officer of the 201st Air Group, Commander Asaichi Tamai. We were discussing the attack plan for the next day. Two days before, on 17 October, American ships had appeared off Suluan Island, at the mouth of Leyte Gulf, in such force as to indicate that a major invasion operation was about to begin. Yet the Japanese air forces in the entire Philippines area had fewer than 100 planes still in operational condition to throw into the breach. What could we do to check the enemy onslaught?

As Senior Staff Officer of the First Air Fleet, I had been sent from the headquarters in Manila to advise

3

the 201st Air Group.* I represented the top naval air command in the Philippines theater, while Commander Tamai represented one of the main tactical forces of that command. We two had been friends ever since our Naval Academy days, and the gravity of present circumstances brought us even more closely together than before. We spoke frankly of the difficulties confronting us, but we were at a loss to hit upon any plan that might offer a way out of the desperate situation.

Our gloomy discussion was interrupted by the approach of a black limousine which came from the highway in the gathering dusk. A yellow pennant fluttering at the front of the car indicated a passenger of flag rank. As we wondered who the unexpected visitor might be, the vehicle came to a halt near the command post, and a stocky figure wearing the uniform of a vice admiral emerged ponderously without any attendant ceremony except for the presence of a single aide. We promptly recognized the admiral as Takijiro Ohnishi, the new commander of Japanese naval air forces in the Philippines.

Vice Admiral Ohnishi had come from Tokyo only two days before, on 17 October, to assume command of the First Air Fleet and had barely had time since his arrival to complete taking over his duties from his predecessor, Vice Admiral Kimpei Teraoka. There must have been a host of urgent matters demanding his presence at Air Fleet Headquarters in Manila, yet here he was at Mabalacat.

Why had he come?

Commander Tamai and I sprang to our feet to greet him. He accepted a chair and sat silently for a few minutes, watching the activity of the airfield crews working feverishly in the fading daylight. Finally he turned toward us and said, "I have come here to discuss with you something of great importance. May we go to your headquarters?"

It was time to secure the command post for the day,

---

*A part of the Japanese Navy's First Air Fleet, the principal naval air organization in the Philippines at this time.

so Tamai and I joined the Admiral in his limousine. The squadron leaders and pilots followed us in other vehicles.

Mabalacat was a dusty Filipino town. Its two or three attractive western-style homes had been requisitioned for use as officer billets. The headquarters of the 201st Air Group was located in one surrounded by a low stone fence. The house was painted cream color, with green trim, which gave a pleasing, homey effect.

The outside appearance, however, totally belied the interior. All regular household furniture had been removed, and in its stead folding canvas cots covered all the ground floor area. Flight gear, towels, washing kits, and personal belongings were scattered everywhere. More than 30 officers lived in the main part of the house, while the Filipino owner and his family lived in two rear rooms. Though crowded, this was home to the officer fliers of the 201st Air Group.

On one side of the yard stood two open oil drums which served as bath and laundry. On the other side a small outbuilding housed the orderlies. Trees and shrubs grew lush and verdant, and there was a small patch of lawn. All in all, it was a pleasant billet.

Petty officers and men were quartered nearby in native homes. These rude dwellings stood about five feet off the ground. Their split bamboo floors, well suited to the climate, were cool at night. The men spread their blankets on the floor to sleep, but unless the cracks between the bamboo strips were very carefully covered, mosquitoes would swarm inside the mosquito nets and make life miserable. There was something comical about the helplessness of our veteran fighter pilots when pitted against the attacks of these bloodthirsty insects.

When our car drew up in front of the headquarters building, we dismounted and escorted Vice Admiral Ohnishi inside. While he responded to a phone call which came in just as we arrived, Staff Officer Chuichi Yoshioka, of the 26th Air Flotilla, and two squadron leaders of the 201st Air Group, Lieutenants Ibusuki and Yokoyama, were summoned. Then the six of us sat down around a table in a small room on the second floor, overlooking the yard. The door leading to the corridor was left open. Darkness hung heavy outside.

Admiral Ohnishi looked intently at the faces around him, as if seeking to read our thoughts. Then, quietly, he began speaking.

"As you know, the war situation is grave. The appearance of strong American forces in Leyte Gulf has been confirmed. The fate of the Empire depends upon the outcome of the Sho Operation*, which Imperial General Headquarters has activated to hurl back the enemy assault on the Philippines. Our surface forces are already in motion. Vice Admiral Kurita's Second Fleet, containing our main battle strength, will advance to the Leyte area and annihilate the enemy invasion force. The mission of the First Air Fleet is to provide land-based air cover for Admiral Kurita's advance and make sure that enemy air attacks do not prevent him from reaching Leyte Gulf. To do this, we must hit the enemy's carriers and keep them neutralized for at least one week."

The tremendous importance and difficulty of the task assigned to us were immediately and frighteningly clear. Only if the enemy's hard-hitting carrier task forces covering the invasion could be rendered ineffective for one week would Kurita's force—which included the mighty battleships *Musashi* and *Yamato*, but not a single carrier—have a chance of getting through to Leyte Gulf to destroy the enemy transports and thwart

---

*Plans for the Sho Operation had been completed in July 1944, after Japan's main defense line had been breached by U. S. forces in New Guinea and the Marianas. The Sho Operation was a defensive-offensive plan against the next enemy offensive. The Philippines were the most likely target for the Americans to choose, but Formosa, the Ryukyus, or even the Japanese home islands were possibilities, so all had to be considered. The Sho plan provided that no matter which area was first invaded by the enemy's main strength, that area would be declared the "theater of decisive battle" and all available forces would be rushed there to defeat the enemy. The decision to activate the Sho Operation was left to the judgment of Imperial General Headquarters. That activation took place at 1701 on 18 October with the first intimation of the American invasion at Leyte, and the Philippines was declared the decisive battle area.

the invasion attempt. The whole success of the Imperial Headquarters plan was thus keyed to our ability to fulfill our mission. *"Sho"* means "Victory," but if the First Air Fleet failed, Operation Victory would turn into irretrievable defeat.

Yet, at this moment, it seemed idle even to hope that we might succeed. In early September, we had been far stronger, but the enemy carrier forces had still been able to strike heavy blows at our bases throughout the Philippines, crippling our air strength. Since we had not been able to stop them then, how could we do it now when the Air Fleet's total fighter strength, concentrated in the 201st Air Group, was down to 30 planes in operating condition, and its equally meager bomber forces were dispersed from Zamboanga to central Luzon? True, the *Sho* plans called for the transfer of the Second Air Fleet from Formosa to reinforce us, but the Second Air Fleet had just been through a severe trial in the Formosa air battle against the enemy's far-ranging carrier force. Until it could regroup its depleted strength and transfer to Philippine bases, we stood alone—a handful of planes against hundreds!

As Admiral Ohnishi spoke, we sensed that he had come here for something more than just to repeat what we already knew was our mission. The question in all our minds was *how* we were to accomplish that mission against such overwhelming odds, and we waited for him to provide the answer.

I watched the Admiral's heavily lined face as he spoke again.

"In my opinion, there is only one way of assuring that our meager strength will be effective to a maximum degree. That is to organize suicide attack units composed of Zero fighters armed with 250-kilogram bombs, with each plane to crash-dive into an enemy carrier. . . . What do you think?"

The Admiral's eyes bored into us as he looked around the table. No one spoke for a time, but Admiral Ohnishi's words struck a spark in each of us. Indeed, "body-crashing" (*taiatari*) tactics had already been used by Navy pilots in air-to-air combat against big enemy bombers, and there were many fliers in the combat air units who had urged that the same tactics be employed against enemy carriers. This is, perhaps, hard to understand, for no man welcomes death. But it is more understandable if one bears in mind that, considering the heavy odds that our fliers faced in 1944, their chance of coming back alive from any sortie against enemy carriers was very slim, regardless of the attack method employed. If one is bound to die, what is more natural than the desire to die effectively, at maximum cost to the enemy?

The silence that greeted Ohnishi's words, therefore, bespoke neither consternation nor dread. It was finally broken by Commander Tamai.

"Yoshioka, just how effective would it be for a plane carrying a 250-kilogram bomb to smash bodily into a carrier's flight deck?"

Staff Officer Yoshioka answered, "The chances of scoring a hit would be much greater than by conventional bombing. It would probably take several days to repair the damage to the flight deck."

Commander Tamai undoubtedly knew this, but asked the question as a means of relieving the tension and gaining time to collect his thoughts. He then turned to the Admiral and said, "As executive officer I cannot decide a matter of such gravity. I must ask our group commander, Captain Sakae Yamamoto, for his decision."

Admiral Ohnishi answered curtly, "As a matter of fact, I have just spoken on the phone with Captain Yamamoto in Manila. His leg was broken in a plane crash and he is in the hospital. He said that I should consider your opinions as his own, and that he would leave everything up to you."

This brought Tamai to an abrupt realization of his personal responsibility. I wondered what his answer would be. Would this kindly and unassuming man accept such an attack method? We all turned toward him and waited tensely for his response, knowing that *we* would be the ones to carry out such attacks.

Commander Tamai was well aware of the grave war

situation which called for such an extreme measure; he also knew the innermost feelings of his pilots. After a long pause, he asked the Admiral for a few minutes to consider the matter. He beckoned Lieutenant Ibusuki to follow him, and left the room.

As Tamai later informed me, they went to his room and exchanged opinions about the pilots' probable attitude toward the prospect of crash-diving.

After hearing Ibusuki's views, Tamai rejoined the meeting and said, "Entrusted by our commander with full responsibility, I share completely the opinions expressed by the Admiral. The 201st Air Group will carry out his proposal. May I ask that you leave to us the organization of our crash-dive unit?"

I well remember Admiral Ohnishi's expression as he nodded acquiescence. His face bore a look of relief coupled with a shadow of sorrow.

Now that crash-dive tactics had been decided upon, it was necessary to form a special attack unit at once. The time for action was close at hand; it might even be tomorrow.

Admiral Ohnishi withdrew to get some rest. The historic meeting was over.

KAMIKAZE SPECIAL ATTACK CORPS

As soon as Admiral Ohnishi had left the room, Tamai set to work. From the first mention of a crash-diving unit, he had been considering which pilots to choose for such a mission. He had known these young men for many months. On completion of their basic training in October 1943, they had been assigned as fledgling fliers to his 263rd Air Group in Japan. Commander Tamai had held great expectations for them and he had put his heart and soul into preparing them for battle.

Their combat training had been only half completed by February 1944 when these youngsters had suddenly been ordered to the Mariana Islands for regular combat duty. Since that time, from Tinian through Palau to Yap, they had fought continuously, and against terrible odds. Many of them had fallen in battle, but the survivors had carried on. During the first week of August they had been moved to the southern Philippines and incorporated into the new First Naval Air Fleet, as the 201st Air Group. From his duty as commander of the 263rd Air Group, Tamai had come to the 201st as executive officer.

By this time the 201st was down to only about one-third of its original strength, but the grim experience of battle had refined the remaining pilots in heart and spirit, as well as in skill. They were now steel-fibered veterans and their morale was high. Commander Tamai, who had inspired them during their training period and had shared the hardships of uphill battles with them ever since their initiation into combat, was as deeply attached to these men as a father to his children.

It was his constant desire that these men be of supreme value to their country. The pilots, in turn, felt toward Commander Tamai as they would toward a parent, and expressed this feeling at every opportunity. So now it was natural for him to have them foremost in his thoughts.

Commander Tamai, after consulting with his squadron leaders, ordered an immediate assembly of all non-commissioned pilots of the air group. He reviewed the critical war situation when all 23 of the men were assembled and then explained Admiral Ohnishi's proposal. In a frenzy of emotion and joy, the arms of every pilot in the assembly went up in a gesture of complete accord. Tamai emphasized the necessity for strict secrecy, and when the meeting was ended, all the pilots retired to their billets.

It was past midnight when Tamai returned to the officers' quarters and told me of the pilots' reactions. "Inoguchi," he said, "they are so young. But though they cannot explain what is in their hearts, I shall never forget the firm resolution in their faces. Their eyes shone feverishly in the dimly lit room. Each must have been thinking of this as a chance to avenge comrades who had fallen recently in the fierce Marianas fighting, and at Palau and Yap. Theirs was an enthusiasm that flames naturally in the hearts of youthful men."

Thus, we were assured of pilots for the crash-dive unit.

To whose leadership should these fine young men be entrusted? We discussed various prospects, and I suggested that the leader should be a Naval Academy man. Tamai agreed, saying that Naoshi Kanno would be perfect for the job, but unfortunately Kanno was away on a mission to Japan. In deep thought Tamai murmured, "If Kanno were only here. . . ."

Several of the pilots had leadership qualifications, but for this important mission we needed the very best. The leader had to be a man of highest character and ability. Commander Tamai wrestled with the problem, and finally settled on Yukio Seki as standing out above the others.

Lieutenant Seki had trained for carrier-based bombers, not fighter planes. He had come to the Philippines about a month before, reassigned from Formosa. Commander Tamai, in his preoccupation with the daily task of sending his men off to attack the enemy and of coping with enemy air raids, had had little time to talk with Lieutenant Seki. But as the days passed, the young lieutenant had approached Tamai at every opportunity, fervently expressing his opinions on the war situation, and requesting a chance to participate in combat missions. This happened so repeatedly that, despite Seki's short time with the group, Commander Tamai decided that this man had something to offer.

I, myself, remembered Seki as a midshipman when I was instructing at the Naval Academy, and felt sure that he would be a good leader. So we agreed completely on this choice, and an orderly was sent to summon Lieutenant Seki.

The Philippine night was dark and quiet. We sat silently in the officers' lounge as the sound of the orderly's footsteps faded upstairs. I thought of Seki, deep in slumber, and wondered what his dreams might be. Quick steps soon descended the stairs and the tall figure of the lieutenant appeared in the doorway. It was evident that he had hurried, for his jacket was still not completely buttoned. He addressed Commander Tamai: "Did you call me, sir?"

Beckoned to a chair, the young man sat down facing us. Tamai patted him on the shoulder and said, "Seki, Admiral Ohnishi himself has visited the 201st Air Group to present a plan of greatest importance to Japan. The plan is to crash-dive our Zero fighters, loaded with 250-kilogram bombs, into the decks of enemy carriers, in order to insure the success of the *Sho* Operation. You are being considered to lead such an attack unit. How do you feel about it?"

There were tears in Commander Tamai's eyes as he ended.

For a moment there was no answer. With his elbows on the table, his hands to his head, jaws tight shut and his eyes closed, Seki sat motionless, in deep thought. One second, two seconds, three, four, five. . . . Finally he moved, slowly running his fingers through his long hair. Then quietly raising his head, he spoke, "You absolutely must let me do it." There was not the slightest falter in his voice.

"Thank you," said Tamai, simply.

Suddenly the oppressive atmosphere was dispersed and a brightness filled the room, as if clouds had cleared to let moonlight burst through. We talked of the next steps to be taken. The discussion was brief, but I observed in Seki's every word and gesture a strength of character which confirmed our choice of him as leader of the unit.

With the composition and leadership of the special attack corps decided, I said, "Since this is a special mission, we should have a special name for the unit." Tamai agreed and I suggested, "How about *Shimpu* Unit?" (*Shimpu* is another way of reading the characters for "kamikaze.")

"That's good," said Tamai. "After all, we have to set a kamikaze (divine wind) in motion with it."

I went upstairs where Admiral Ohnishi was resting,

to report that the organization of the unit had been completed. I knocked and then opened the door.

There were no lights burning in the room, but starlight filtered through the window and I could see a form on the canvas cot near the door. During the several hours since meeting with us Admiral Ohnishi had remained in the darkened room, alone with his thoughts and his anxieties.

He arose as I began my report: "There are 23 men for the special mission, and Lieutenant Seki, an Academy man, has been chosen to lead them. Since this is a special affair, we wish you to christen the unit. Commander Tamai and I suggest that it be called the *Shimpu* Unit."

Admiral Ohnishi nodded his approval. It was early in the morning of 20 October 1944, but an announcement was drawn up at once and posted as soon as the Admiral had signed it. In substance it said:

> The 201st Air Group will organize a special attack corps and will destroy or disable, if possible by 25 October, the enemy carrier forces in the waters east of the Philippines.
>
> The corps will be called the *Shimpu* Attack Unit. It will consist of 26 fighter planes, of which half will be assigned to crash-diving missions, and the remainder to escort, and will be divided into four sections, designated as follows: *Shikishima, Yamato, Asahi,* and *Yamazakura.**
>
> The *Shimpu* Attack Unit will be commanded by Lieutenant Yukio Seki.

In the meantime, Commander Tamai and Lieutenant Seki had continued their talk in the officers' room. They discussed all phases of the operations which might be called for in the approaching daylight. With this in mind, and the hour growing late, Tamai finally

---

**Shikishima:* a poetic name for Japan; *Yamato:* the ancient name for Japan; *Asahi:* morning sun; *Yamazakura:* mountain cherry blossoms.

suggested that Seki retire to get whatever sleep was possible.

Seki's thoughts as he went back to his room must have turned to his widowed mother and to his bride of only a few months. But Commander Tamai could not delve into Seki's private life. At this point he had to limit his concern to the task at hand and suppress his personal interest in this resolute young warrior.

MISHAP OVER MANILA

BY NAKAJIMA

The 19th of October 1944 is a day that I, too, will never forget. As flight officer of the 201st Air Group, I was busily engaged at our Mabalacat headquarters with my commanding officer, Captain Sakae Yamamoto, in the usual pre-dawn preparation for the day's activities. In accordance with the tactical orders for the *Sho* Operation, which had now been put in motion, the 201st Air Group had the duty of attacking the enemy forces off Leyte Gulf.

Day was just breaking when the captain was handed a dispatch. He scanned it, and turned to me. "Nakajima, it's from Admiral Ohnishi. He wants us to be at his headquarters in Manila by 1300!"

We had no more than realized the import of this message when the air raid alarm sounded. American planes were striking Mabalacat in an early morning raid. The ensuing damage and confusion delayed our departure, and it was not until the afternoon sortie had been dispatched, at 1400, that we finally left for Manila by car.

Being a flier, I seldom took a long automobile drive. I had flown over the area many times but had never traveled this route in a car. The many uninhabited stretches of road between Mabalacat and Manila were likely spots for guerrillas to lie in wait, and we were relieved to reach Manila at 1630. But we were embarrassed and disturbed to find that Admiral Ohnishi had already set out for Mabalacat by car. Unknowingly, we had passed each other on the road.

The Admiral's reason for calling us all the way to Manila must have been important, and we still had the job of attacking enemy ships next morning as ordered for the *Sho* Operation. We felt, therefore, that we should get back to Mabalacat. If we tried to return by car, night would fall before we reached our destination and we would be exposed to guerrilla attacks. So I telephoned nearby Nichols Field and asked that a fighter plane be made ready. With the captain's approval, I planned for us to fly back to Mabalacat.

Mitsubishi Zero

We hurried to Nichols Field and found a Zero drawn up on the apron. Mechanics were tinkering with the engine, which did not sound quite right. I ordered a change of spark plugs. When this was done, Captain

Yamamoto climbed into the space behind the pilot's seat. I got into the cockpit and gunned the engine. It still did not respond perfectly, but night was fast approaching, and after all it was only a 20-minute flight to Mabalacat. I decided we could surely make that, and took the plane into the air without giving the engine further thought. It was stupid of me to take off in a plane with a faulty engine, however, and I was promptly punished.

As soon as we were in the air I tried to retract the wheels, and found that the control lever would not budge. Captain Yamamoto reached over my shoulder to help, but it was no use. We would have to fly with the wheels down. This cut down our speed considerably, but was unavoidable. I circled over Nichols Field and headed to the north. The altimeter registered 400 meters as we started across Manila Bay—and then I smelled gasoline!

Gas fumes in an airplane are ominous. They indicate a gas leak which means that fire may break out at any moment. Just as I thought of this unhappy possibility and tried to decide what to do, the engine suddenly stopped dead. There was not even time to be surprised. I pushed the hand fuel pump and glanced at the pressure gauge. I tried all the switches. I tried everything, but the engine remained completely dead.

We could not make it back to Nichols Field, nor could we reach any other airfield. Alternative landing possibilities ran through my mind. It was either the sea or a rice paddy. With landing gear retracted it would have been safer to land in Manila Bay, but the wheels were still down. If we splashed, I could probably get clear, but Captain Yamamoto, jammed as he was in the back of the fuselage, would never be able to get out before the plane sank.

As soon as the engine stopped I had banked sharply to the right and headed back toward land. I could see the road along the right shore of Manila Bay below. If I tried to land on the road and the plane should veer to the left, we would fall into the sea, and Captain

Yamamoto would not have a chance. I decided to aim for a rice paddy.

To prevent the plane from stalling, I kept careful watch on my air speed. At the same time I tried to loosen the lock pins of my seat so the captain could escape quickly in case the plane caught fire after landing. I managed to pull out the right-hand pin, but my weight on the seat held the left one tightly in place. It was probably fortunate that this pin did not come loose, for, if it had, the seat might have wobbled and disturbed my control of the plane.

We lost altitude quickly, barely clearing the scattered buildings on the outskirts of Manila. Close below I saw a rice paddy—and then there was a jarring crash as the plane ground to a halt in a spray of muddy water. Miraculously we did not turn over, nor did the plane catch fire. The landing gear broke at the moment of impact, and the plane skidded about 20 meters to a stop. It was a lucky landing.

I quickly withdrew the remaining lock pin, removed the seat, and lifted Captain Yamamoto from the plane. His left ankle had been broken in the crash. I luckily had suffered nothing more than a few face scratches. We struggled to the nearest road and hailed a passing Army truck which brought us back to headquarters, looking like a pair of bedraggled sewer rats.

It was at headquarters that we learned for the first time that Admiral Ohnishi's purpose in calling us was to propose the formation of a special attack unit. When Captain Yamamoto heard this from Ohnishi's chief of staff, Captain Toshihiko Odawara, he immediately telephoned Admiral Ohnishi at Mabalacat to express his regrets for the forced landing. He added that, although confined to Manila, he was in complete accord with the Admiral, and gave his executive officer, Commander Tamai, responsibility on all matters at Mabalacat.

I returned by car to Mabalacat early the next morning, 20 October, and there found that 24 pilots had been chosen for a unit which had already been named the "Shimpu Special Attack Corps." Its members were prepared to sortie at a moment's notice. Commander Tamai gave me details of the selection of Lieutenant Seki as leader, and of the pilots' volunteering the night before, and I was happy to learn that the organization of the special unit had been carried out so smoothly.

3 (OCTOBER 1944)

"ON BEHALF OF YOUR HUNDRED MILLION COUNTRYMEN"

BY INOGUCHI

By the latter part of October the mornings and evenings are chilly in central Luzon. The Bamban River, which flows just north of Mabalacat, is so clear that small stones in the bottom of the shallow stream are clearly visible from the bank. White plumes of pampas grass sway in the breeze on both sides of the river and are reflected in the water. The graceful scenery made me think of Japan.

Here, surrounded by the pampas grass and close by the stony river bed that stretches to the foot of the cliffs, were a group of young men whose thoughts at that moment must have also been centered on the homeland, if they had taken the occasion to admire the landscape. They were members of the first special attack corps, commanded by Lieutenant Seki. Since dawn of this day, 20 October, they had been ready for the call to arms. Eager faces alight, they discussed various methods of attacking enemy carriers and the precautions to be taken.

Breakfast was announced and they ate, but the meal did not disrupt their animated conversations. As they finished eating, a call from headquarters summoned them to assemble for Admiral Ohnishi's first and final instructions. The 24 men of the *Shikishima, Yamato,*

Asahi, and *Yamazakura* Units lined up, with Lieutenant Seki standing a step ahead of the others. Admiral Ohnishi looked solemnly at the men before him. He was pallid, and his words seemed slow and troubled as he began to speak. "Japan is in grave danger. The salvation of our country is now beyond the power of the ministers of state, the General Staff, and lowly commanders like myself. It can come only from spirited young men such as you. Thus, on behalf of your hundred million countrymen, I ask of you this sacrifice, and pray for your success."

At this point his voice shook with emotion, but he continued. "You are already gods, without earthly desires. But one thing you want to know is that your own crash-dive is not in vain. Regrettably, we will not be able to tell you the results. But I shall watch your efforts to the end and report your deeds to the Throne. You may all rest assured on this point." There were tears in his eyes as he concluded, "I ask you all to do your best."

I have never heard such moving words. They were not intended merely to incite youthful ego nor to flatter youthful pride. Japan had in truth placed her fate in the hands of these young men who were willing to die to save their nation. It seemed almost impossible to crush the overwhelming might of the enemy and turn the tide of war. Our situation was beyond human wisdom. Our only chance for a miracle lay in reliance on these youths.

At their final briefing, I observed in these men a composure and tranquillity which comes only to those who are aware of their own significance and power. As I watched them go, it was impossible to suppress a feeling of protest against our country for having come to such dire straits, against the spirit of the young men themselves, against Admiral Ohnishi, and against my own involvement in these circumstances.

ADMIRAL TERAOKA'S DIARY

The high-level background of these bizarre developments is delineated in the diary of Vice Admiral Kimpei Teraoka, who recorded events at headquarters in Manila from the time he turned over command of the First Air Fleet to Admiral Ohnishi until Ohnishi's return from Mabalacat.

18 October 1944: *Sho* Operation activated.

Time is against us. Available airplanes are limited in number. We are forced to take the most effective method to fight in this operation. The time has arrived for consideration of Admiral Ohnishi's proposal to employ crash-dive tactics. Various opinions were frankly expressed:

"Ordinary tactics are ineffective."

"We must be superhuman in order to win the war."

"Volunteers for suicide missions will have to be reported to Imperial Headquarters before their take-off, so that they will feel secure and composed."

"Should we speak directly to the young fliers, or through their group commanders?"

"It would be better for future actions to have their group commanders present the proposition."

"If the first suicide unit is organized by fighter pilot volunteers, other units will follow their example. If all air units do it, surface units will also be inclined to take part. And if there is a unanimous response by the Navy, the Army will follow suit."

After exchanging these opinions, we arrived at the conclusion that suicide tactics were the only possible salvation for the nation. It was decided to let the new commander, Ohnishi, organize the special units at his discretion.

Admiral Ohnishi summoned Captain Yamamoto, 201st Air Group commander at Mabalacat, and his flight officer, Commander Nakajima, to Manila. When they failed to arrive at the appointed time, Ohnishi set off for Clark Field at 1600, hoping to meet them on the way. (Sunset at 1830.)

Captain Yamamoto, however, arrived at Manila a little after 1700, having remained at Clark Field to send off the afternoon sortie unit.

Yamamoto's executive officer, Commander Tamai, was on hand at Mabalacat to receive Admiral Ohnishi and to assure him of volunteers for suicide missions.

Twenty-four men volunteered for the first assignment, and the group was christened the *Shimpu* Special Attack Corps. It was divided into four units: *Shikishima, Yamato, Asahi,* and *Yamazakura*. These names were taken from the *waka* (poem) by Norinaga Motoori, a nationalistic scholar of the Tokugawa period. *Shikishima no Yamato-gokoro wo hito towaba Asahi ni niou Yamazakura-bama*—(the Japanese spirit is like mountain cherry blossoms, radiant in the morning sun).

Admiral Ohnishi was pleased to find that Lieutenant Yukio Seki, an Academy man, had jumped at the opportunity of leading the corps. The Admiral returned to Manila from Clark Field on the evening of 20 October. He was enthusiastic in telling about the Kamikaze Corps. "The fliers are eager, and have formed a good outfit. They asked permission to work out the organizational details by themselves, and I approved."

Ohnishi relieved me of command at 2000. I sincerely wished him good fortune with the new tactics, and he pledged his best efforts to achieve success. . . .

If, on his return to Manila from Mabalacat, Admiral Ohnishi's face bore a look of grim determination, it was understandable. Relieving Admiral Teraoka, he knew that his only hope of opposing the mighty enemy task force lay in the chance that the unprecedented tactics he sponsored might prove successful.

MARIANAS AFTERMATH

BY INOGUCHI

First Air Fleet Headquarters was in a two-story house, not far from Nichols Field, in the suburbs of Manila. On the first floor were two large rooms which served as the mess hall and conference room, and several smaller ones where the orderlies were quartered. Upstairs a bathroom and five good-sized rooms served chiefly as the sleeping and living quarters of the First Air Fleet commander and his staff officers. The yards, front and back, were small, but in each was an air raid shelter.

The structure itself stood out imposingly from surrounding homes. Its owner had been a man of means, and the contents of his bookshelves identified him as an intellectual. Next to the house was a building that apparently had been used for playing *jai alai,* and adjoining it were a number of hastily constructed barracks for enlisted men. One of these barracks served as the communications center.

A paved road and a breakwater separated these buildings from the sea. Standing by the breakwater I could look westward across Manila Bay at the antenna towers and chimneys of Cavite; and beyond, slightly to the right of Cavite, appeared Corregidor, in the middle of the bay entrance. Separated from Corregidor by a narrow strip of water, the Mariveles Mountains loomed from the southern tip of Bataan Peninsula.

Near at hand the Manila Hotel's hulk rose at the

southern end of the city. Facing the sea, this building added a touch of strange modernity to the scene. Nearer still, at the foot of Legaspi Wharf, stood the former U. S. Army and Navy Club, now the headquarters of the Japanese Southwest Area Fleet.

With the setting sun the reddish glow of the western sky shaded into purple, and then, with the mountains, islands, ships and buildings, into deepening gray. Watching the sun set behind Mariveles, silhouetted against the sky, I thought of the day's momentous events and of the cycles of history that had transpired here—and most especially of the abrupt change of circumstances that had brought Japan to the crisis that she now faced.

It was here at Manila Bay, almost 50 years earlier, that the American Commodore George Dewey had given his oft-quoted order, "You may fire when you are ready, Gridley!" His action led to the capture of Manila and added to the U. S. Navy's tradition of decisiveness and courage. More recently this place had seen momentous action in the opening battles of the Pacific War—Japanese naval air raids, mopping up operations on Bataan Peninsula, and the attack on Corregidor. American and Spanish warships had come and gone in these waters upon which now floated the ships of Imperial Japan.

These mountains had looked on complacently as General MacArthur had given up hope of defending the Philippines, boarded a small patrol boat, and escaped to Australia. Victory for Japan followed shortly in the Philippines, as it did throughout vast areas of the Pacific Ocean and its islands, extending from the Solomons to China, and from Australia northward. The Battle of the Coral Sea in May 1942 had brought Japanese military expansion to a stop for the first time, and Nippon was handed her first thumping defeat a month later in the Battle of Midway. But these checks did not prevent the establishment within the area of conquest of a great defensive perimeter which had suffered no major blow from the enemy until February 1944, a bare eight months back, when the Americans had occupied the central Marshalls.

After our loss of the Marshalls, the Japanese High Command had set up a new "absolute" defense line, stretching from the Ogasawara Islands, through the Marianas and the western Carolines, to western New Guinea. This line, the Army and Navy decided, would be defended to the death. Yet within four short months after the capture of the Marshalls, the very center of this line had crumbled.

Our naval air forces, which at the beginning of the Pacific War boasted absolute mastery of the air in all theaters of battle, found that from the middle of 1943 their Zeros were inferior to the new F6Fs, F4Us, and P-38s from the United States. As a result, lacking even

P-38 Lightning

minimum requirements of pilots and materiel, our air forces suddenly found themselves fighting against impossible odds.

Not only was there no better plane to replace the Zero, but the supply even of Zeros was insufficient to fill half the requirements of the fighting fronts. The gradual retreat of our forces from the Solomons, followed by the loss of the Gilbert and Marshall Islands and the eventual withdrawal of our naval air forces from Rabaul itself, had all resulted, in the final analysis, from the inability of our air strength to hold its own against the enemy.

The enemy's advance into the Marianas in June 1944 had led to activation of what Japan called the *A* Operation.* This was an all-out effort to prevent penetration of our defensive perimeter. Vice Admiral Kakuji Kakuta's land-based First Air Fleet and Vice Admiral Jisaburo Ozawa's Mobile Force there had sought and achieved an engagement with the enemy—but the long-sought encounter had resulted only in a crippling of our own fighting strength. In the two-day Battle of the Philippine Sea, 19-20 June, Japan had lost three aircraft carriers and more than four hundred planes and pilots. Upon retirement from this action there was not a single organizational unit left intact.

To cope with the situation following our defeat in the *A* Operation, our naval forces in the Philippines area had been reorganized. In the Philippine Sea engagement the First Air Fleet, main strength of the Japanese Navy's land-based air force, had lost half of its planes and men based on Tinian and Guam. The forces that remained were completely reorganized at the end of July, when the decision was made to transfer this organization to the Philippines. Command of the First Air Fleet, which had been directly under Combined Fleet, was now placed under the Southwest Area Fleet.

The commander of the First Air Fleet, Vice Admiral Kimpei Teraoka, was supposed to effect the speedy transformation of Philippine training fields into frontline air bases, but local deficiencies were too numerous to be overcome. Shortcomings were particularly apparent at bases in the central and northern Philippines.

To facilitate tactical operations and simplify the problems of training and maintenance, it had been decided to abolish the former system of small air units

---

*Pronounced "AH" in Japanese and usually called *"A-Go,"* meaning "Number A."

and form a large-unit organization based on plane types. Thus, all fighters were organized into the 201st Air Group, all bomber planes into the 761st, and all night fighters and reconnaissance planes into the 153rd.

When Admiral Teraoka arrived in early August, First Air Fleet had 257 fighter and bomber planes and 25 transports, and there were some 18 Army reconnaissance planes placed under his command, for a total of 300 planes. Owing to inadequate maintenance and upkeep, however, so few of the Navy planes were operable that even the task of defensive air patrols had to be entrusted to Army units.

Through a concentrated build-up program Admiral Teraoka had been able in the intervening months to bring his air fleet up to 500 planes, of which 280 could participate in tactical operations. However, the number of combat-ready planes had been cut in half by American striking forces, which threw heavy air raids at Davao on 9-10 December, and at Cebu, Legaspi, and Tacloban on 12-14 September. And the 21-22 September raids on the Manila area had inflicted still heavier losses. By the end of the month Admiral Teraoka had only about 100 operable planes left in his entire force.

Our greatest shortcoming had been in the establishment of air bases. The confusion following the First Air Fleet reorganization, the change in naval policy regarding the use of land bases, the dragging negotiations with the Army for the use of its bases, and difficulties of transportation were all factors which contributed to our lack of preparedness. The Navy's sorry air strength was further handicapped by the miserable condition of the land bases.

At the end of August the Navy's best organized bases had been at Davao and Cebu. Early in September, however, enemy attacks with land-based B-24s and P-38s from Morotai had mounted until it became impossible for us to station an air unit permanently in the Davao area. There were no nearby bases to which the planes could be transferred, and as a consequence the Navy had had to use some of its planes to fight off the enemy task force while the other planes moved to rear bases.

In mid-September it had been decided to hasten the build-up of Clark Field facilities, and vast quantities of supplies were channeled there. But the sands of time were running out and, when the Second Air Fleet was transferred to the Philippines, toward the end of October, bases there were still in a most unsatisfactory condition. It was for this reason principally that our land-based air forces were so slow to act and were later so ineffective in the Battle for Leyte Gulf.

As far back as late 1943 and early 1944, even while the Navy still had air forces at Rabaul, certain of the pilots, worried over the inferiority of our strength, had started to consider suicidal crash-dive tactics. Ensign Ohta, who later proposed the *Ohka** special attack plane, was one of these men.

Nothing is more destructive to morale than to learn of the enemy's superiority. Following the Battle of the Philippine Sea in June, the inferiority of our naval air strength had become even more marked. Captain Eiichiro Jyo, who commanded the light carrier *Chiyoda* of Vice Admiral Ozawa's Carrier Division 3 in the June battle, analyzed our fighting strength after the battle, compared it to the enemy's, and submitted to his superiors the following opinion:

> No longer can we hope to sink the numerically superior enemy aircraft carriers through ordinary attack methods. I urge the immediate organization of special attack units to carry out crash-dive tactics, and I ask to be placed in command of them.

Captain Jyo, who had served as a naval attaché in Washington as well as naval aide-de-camp to the Emperor, continued as *Chiyoda's* skipper and in that post

---

*The *"Ohka"* was a rocket-propelled suicide missile, carried by a bomber to the scene of attack and then released. This is explained later in detail.

was to participate in the Battle for Leyte Gulf as part of Ozawa's main force. On 24 October 1944, the day the first kamikaze plane crash-dived into an American ship, the *Chiyoda* was attacked and sunk by American carrier-based planes and Captain Jyo went down with his ship. But meanwhile his ideas had been taken up by another officer, equally dedicated.

In the summer of 1944 Vice Admiral Takijiro Ohnishi had been Chief of the General Affairs Bureau of the Aviation Department in the Ministry of Munitions. In that position he was fully aware of our inferiority in aircraft production capacity as compared to the enemy, and could see the dismal prospect. He gave serious consideration to opinions and suggestions from the fighting fronts, since he was seeking a solution to the future role of naval aviation in the steadily worsening war situation.

Early in the war, as chief of staff of naval land-based air, he had exercised personal command in air actions in the Philippines and in the sea battle off Malaya. From such experiences the Admiral now knew that with ordinary tactics Japan no longer had any chance of stopping the American forces, let alone defeating them. Hence he was influenced by the opinions of Captain Jyo.

On 17 October, the very day that Admiral Ohnishi arrived to take up his new post in Manila, the spearhead of the American invasion forces had landed on Suluan Island, at the entrance of Leyte Gulf. In the forefront of the invader his great carrier task force rampaged about the Philippine seas like a mighty typhoon. To the rear stood the American invasion armada in full array, ready for the reconquest of the Philippines. Thus the fateful day of 17 October had marked a new and graver crisis in the war situation for Japan—a situation far different from that of early 1944.

I was suddenly startled to find that twilight grays had darkened into night. My brief musings had spanned from memories of the glorious past to realities of the ominous present. Heavy of heart, I left these reveries to return to headquarters and the problems of the hour.

RISE OF
THE KAMIKAZE SPIRIT

BY NAKAJIMA

In my position as flight officer of the 201st Air Group, I knew better than anyone else that the Kamikaze Special Attack Corps had not sprung full blown overnight. I knew that it was but the climax of an ever ascending fighting spirit in men finally confronted with insuperable odds. For I knew that this build-up of spirit and dedication had already manifested itself long before any kamikaze units were ever organized.

For instance, on 21 September—the month before —when hundreds of enemy airplanes bombed and strafed Manila all day, 45 fighters of Rear Admiral Masafumi Arima's 26th Air Flotilla at Nichols Field had attacked them and shot down 27 enemy planes, with a loss of 20 of our fighters. And on the following morning, Lieutenant Usaburo Suzuki had led 15 fighters of the 201st Air Group in a sortie against the whole gigantic U. S. carrier force itself, making five direct hits* and shooting down three Grumman Hellcat interceptors against the loss of only five of his own planes.

But long before that—as early as midsummer—the high morale of the Japanese pilots had been demonstrated in another way. This time it was the develop-

---

*No bomb hits were scored on ships of U. S. Task Force 38 this day.

ment of the technique of skip bombing by fighter planes.

F6F Hellcat

At that time—August 1944—the 201st Air Group (fighters) was supposed to be working with the 761st Air Group (bombers). The 761st possessed 16 Type-1

("Betty") and 35 Tenzan ("Jill") bombers, but less than half of them were operational, and most of the pilots were hopelessly inexperienced. These two air groups had been coordinated with the idea that fighters would escort the bombers to their targets. But a fighter plane unit which is used only for interception or bomb-

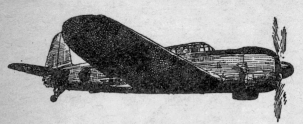

Nakajima B6N2, Tenzan ("Jill")

er escort work cannot remain at peak efficiency, no matter how high the morale of its pilots, and the pitifully few bomber planes we had would be ineffective against the mighty American task forces. To achieve results and maintain morale in our air units, some effective retaliation must be launched against the enemy. Under these circumstances it had been decided that fighter planes might be used to attack enemy warships.

Our small Zero fighters were unable to carry the great weight of a torpedo, so that weapon was not considered. They could, however, with slight alteration be fitted with a 250-kilogram bomb. Studies and tests showed that such a weapon was most effective when delivered to the target by skip bombing.

Of the many problems involved, the most difficult one was the selection of pilots for the skip-bombing unit. Practically every fighter pilot volunteered, but commanding officers were reluctant to risk their best men on this form of attack in which chances of survival were so slight. The best pilots—those who would stand the best chance of surviving—were the very ones needed most desperately for escort and interception missions.

In skip bombing, the attacking plane skims low over the water at full speed, and approaches to within 200 to 300 yards of the target ship before releasing its bomb. If properly aimed, the bomb skips, bounces from the water, and strikes into the side of the target with the effect of a torpedo. This, however, is more easily said than done. To begin with, the height to which a bomb will skip is determined by the level at which it is released, so the drop must be made at a level below the target vessel's deck—a most difficult task. Flying at high speed over water, it is almost impossible to differentiate an altitude of 60 feet from one of 30 or even 15, especially if the sea is fairly calm. One method of achieving proper drop altitude is to keep the deck of the enemy ship and the horizon at eye level during the approach to the target. But the smoke of battle, or heavy weather, may prevent visual alignment of the horizon, and then the solution is pure guesswork.

Another difficulty in this method of attack is to get the plane safely clear after dropping the bomb. If the fighter continues in a straight line toward the target after release, the bomb may bounce up and strike the plane, or the plane may be damaged when the bomb explodes at the target. The pilot must therefore change his course by a rapid acrobatic maneuver as soon as he drops the bomb. A second's error may mean the loss of plane and pilot. Fighter pilots, probably because of their extensive practice in split-second maneuvers, did well in this part of the training.

The practice area for skip bombing was in Bohol Strait, near the Cebu base. To conserve the larger ammunition, small bombs of 30 or 60 kilograms were used in training. These skipped erratically but the pilots practiced patiently and, as their skill improved, they soon advanced from fixed to moving targets. Though good progress was being made, the entire program came to a sudden halt with the enemy's devastating surprise attack on Davao in September, when half of the 201st Air Group was destroyed. So few planes then remained that kamikaze attacks alone held any chance of success. The response of volunteers for skip bombing clearly indicated the tremendous morale of our pilots—a morale which would make suicide operations possible.

There had been many individual examples of our pilots' high morale and devotion to duty. Typically valorous were the deeds of such men as Warrant Officer Nakagawa over Davao, of Lieutenant Kanno at Yap and elsewhere, and of Admiral Arima off Luzon.

Throughout all of August, Lieutenant Tadashi Minobe's night fighter squadron of *Gekko* ("Irving") planes at Davao had no luck against the almost nightly raids of enemy B-24s on that city. Inexperience of the *Gekko* pilots was to blame for our lack of success in shooting down these bombers. But Warrant Officer Yoshimasa Nakagawa and his observer, Chief Warrant Officer Isamu Osumi, set a new precedent of valor on 5 September when they knocked down a B-24 by ramming. The enemy raid had begun an hour after midnight. Nakagawa's plane rose to meet the attackers and was closing in on one of them when his cannon jammed, and it appeared that the enemy bomber would get safely away. Nakagawa shouted, "I'm going to ram it!" and headed for the port side of the enemy craft.

"Go to it!" came Osumi's unhesitating reply, and the propeller of the *Gekko* slashed into the bomber's fuselage. The big American plane started to fall immediately, while the small Japanese plane, with canopy shattered, miraculously continued to fly. Nakagawa's right eye was gashed by flying glass, and the blast of air in his face forced him to turn sideways in the seat, but he managed to keep the plane level. Their victim started just once to level off, and Osumi shouted for Nakagawa to attack again, but even as the *Gekko* dove, its victim faltered and plunged into the water south of Samar Island. Nakagawa's battered night fighter was then brought skillfully back to base for a safe landing, providing the rare example of a fighter plane's surviving a successful ramming attack.

Nakagawa and Osumi had come directly from flight

school to Lieutenant Minobe's unit, which was noted for its aggressiveness. But unquestionably the most colorful pilot to serve in the Philippines was Lieutenant Naoshi Kanno. His flying skill had been recognized even before he had finished flight training, and his early combat record was excellent. His reputation had really blossomed, however, in the summer of 1944 while he was based at Yap. He there engaged in combat with an American B-24 and, after several ineffective gunning passes, decided to ram the stalwart bomber. Figuring that the usual head-on ramming attack might prove fatal only to his own fighter plane, Kanno decided to destroy the big plane by shearing off its rudder with his propeller. He knew that in an approach from the rear he stood little chance of success against the bomber's concentrated gun power, and that his plane would probably be shot down before there was any chance to ram. He resolved, accordingly, to strike at the rudder by way of a head-on approach. The difficulty of this maneuver lay in keeping clear of his target's propellers and yet getting close enough to shear off its rudder.

His first and second passes failed, but he managed both times to pull clear of the B-24's deadly gunfire. On the third try he came in still closer, following straight down the body of the bomber, until his propeller gnawed into the huge plane's rudder with a shuddering crash. The shock of impact caused Kanno to black out momentarily, and when he regained consciousness he found his plane in a tight spin which compressed him into a corner of the cockpit. Still stunned, he responded automatically and pushed forward on the control lever while pressing slowly, ever so slowly, on the foot pedal until his plane pulled out of the spin and regained level flight. He watched the B-24 crash into the sea and then managed to bring his badly damaged plane back to Yap.

By late August, Kanno was in the Philippines with the 201st Air Group in time to volunteer for skip-bombing training. In my position as flight officer of the group, I had to choose from among the applicants, and because he was such a valuable asset to the unit, it was with great reluctance that I finally gave in to his insistent requests for training in this hazardous tactic. He was as delighted at the chance as he was chagrined soon afterward when skip-bombing plans had to be cancelled.

Japanese pilots in the Philippines needed but few belongings. The tropical climate made an extensive wardrobe unnecessary, and the frequent moves from one base to another made it undesirable. A change of underwear and towels, along with aerial charts, pencils, and a few personal items and mementoes, were the only requirements. These things could all be contained in a small bag. Every pilot had such a bag, clearly inscribed with his name. The inscription on Lieutenant Kanno's bag was unusual in that it read, "Personal effects of *the late Lieutenant Commander* Naoshi Kanno." It was the custom for Japanese servicemen to receive a posthumous promotion of one rank, and Kanno had written off any chance of his survival long before kamikaze operations were ever begun.

Toward the end of September the 201st Air Group learned that new Zero fighters would be available in Japan, as replacements for some of our many losses. We had to send pilots to receive the planes from the factory in Japan and fly them to our base in the Philippines. There was no problem about getting enough enlisted volunteers for this duty since they were all eager to return home, even for a few days, after long service overseas. Selection of an officer to command the group was not so easy. We decided to choose the officer having the longest continuous duty away from the homeland. This proved to be Kanno.

Contrary to what one might have expected, Kanno did not like this decision and was quick to voice his displeasure. "A major operation will soon be going on in these islands. If I go home I may miss the opportunity to take part in it. Please pick someone else."

His words were perfectly sincere, and coming from "the late Lieutenant Commander Kanno," were no surprise to us. But we had to be firm. It was true that whoever went to Japan at this time might miss the impending battle, but Kanno had been chosen and, finally ordered, he reluctantly went. Soon after he reached Japan, the enemy landed at Leyte.

Kanno's reaction was to cable the headquarters at Mabalacat requesting permission to return immediately. Our reply was that he should come back, as instructed, with the new aircraft. But the factory, as usual, was behind schedule, and Kanno did not get back to the Philippines until the end of October, after the kamikazes had been formed.

When we at Mabalacat learned that he was on his way back, one of the officers said, "When he gets here, I'll bet he says, 'The damned operation started, just as I said it would.' " As Kanno's flight of new fighters arrived at Mabalacat he must have wondered why his remarks were met with such a burst of laughter. Upon climbing down from the cockpit, the first words he said were, "The damned operation started, just as I said it would!"

It was this man Kanno whom Tamai had immediately thought of as the natural choice for a leader, when the kamikaze operations had first been formally proposed. I knew that if he had been present he would have insisted on commanding the first suicide unit. I was not surprised, therefore, when he sought me out upon his return from Japan and said in a tone of truly envious complaint, "Commander Nakajima, I wish I could have been in Seki's place!"

"Be reasonable, Kanno," I answered. "You will have chance enough. Whether one goes first or second is no matter. You have never looked for glory in the past; why do you now talk this way?"

"What you say is true," he replied, "but I still would have liked to be the first kamikaze."

He pressed eagerly and insistently, formally and informally, to join a suicide unit, but his applications and supplications were continually sidetracked. Fliers of his ability were too sorely needed for escort and interception work to be used otherwise.*

Admiral Arima's contribution was no less notable, coming, as it did, less than a week before Admiral Ohnishi organized the first kamikaze units.

Arima, commander of the 26th Air Flotilla at Manila, was the picture of dignity as a commanding officer. Precise and thorough, meticulous and formal, he was always in full uniform, even under the glaring sun of the tropics. Slender, gentle in appearance, and soft-spoken, he came from a family of Confucian scholars who for ages had served the feudal lords of Kagoshima in southern Kyushu. In his few spare moments he read a worm-eaten military classic whose cover had long since been worn off. To inquiring looks he would laugh and explain, "This is my grandfather's book on tactics." A customarily mild behavior gave no intimation of his last desperate action.

The 26th Air Flotilla headquarters at Manila had been established in a fine Western-style house where Admiral Arima had comfortable quarters. But he chose to live in a tiny shack, furnished with only a cot, near the Nichols Field command post. When there was no action at the field, his officers frequently suggested that he rest at his billet or come to the dining room for a meal. He would always reply, "The air is good here. I think this is the healthiest place for me."

Carrier-borne American planes struck Manila for the first time on 21 September. Because of foul-ups in our radar, lookout, and communication systems, the attack had taken Nichols Air Base almost completely by surprise. Admiral Arima was out on the field directing the departure of his fighters throughout the incessant bombing and strafing. He refused to leave the exposed command post until, toward the end of the at-

---

*Subsequently, Lieutenant Kanno was transferred to the 343rd Air Group in Japan for homeland defense. In June 1945, during the Okinawan battles, he was shot down near Yakushima, south of Kyushu, leaving a reputation for valor that had spread throughout the fleet, fanning the kamikaze spirit.

tack, one young officer insisted on standing as a shield at his side. Arima afterward explained wryly, "I had to go to the shelter because Ensign Kanamaru seemed determined to die for me."

The September enemy raids were but the prelude of heavier ones to come. By mid-October the high command was declaring, "The destiny of the homeland depends on the next great battle, and everyone is expected to do his best."

What does this mean? A pilot flies his plane into combat against the enemy and he is doing his best. But how does an admiral in command do his best? Tactical air operations are led by squadron commanders, who thus can do their best. But how does a flotilla commander do his best?

Admiral Arima knew his own heart's answer to that question. On 15 October an American task force was sighted to the east of Luzon. The decision was made to launch all available planes—Army and Navy—against this target. As planes of the 26th Air Flotilla were ready to take off from Nichols Field for the mission, Admiral Arima suddenly announced that he would lead them. While aides and staff officers tried to dissuade him, Arima removed all insignia of rank and boarded the lead plane of the second wave, composed of 13 Type-1 bombers, 16 Zeroes, and 70 Army fighters. At 1554 Arima spotted enemy warships in position distant 240 miles, bearing 065° from Manila, and he ordered all planes to attack. His own plane led the way by crash-diving into an enemy aircraft carrier.*

The war was rapidly approaching an inevitable and catastrophic end. A commanding officer must now fight with a spirit surpassing all ordinary demands.

---

*The USS *Franklin* (CV-13) was damaged this date at 16°29′ N, 123°57′ E by a Japanese horizontal bomber. One of the attacking planes was shot down by antiaircraft fire and when it splashed 100 feet from the *Franklin's* deck-edge elevator, a wing section from this plane ended up on the *Franklin's* flight deck. The pilot's intention will never be known. (Information from Captain Dwight M. Bradford Williams, USNR [Ret.] in letter of 27 December 1957.)

Perhaps that is what Admiral Arima thought in determining to go on his one-way mission.

Thus the Japanese morale, this kamikaze spirit, or whatever one wishes to call it, was widely evident in the autumn of 1944. It found its culmination in kamikaze attacks—a climax as violent as the circumstances which engendered it.

CEBU

BY NAKAJIMA

YAMATO UNIT ARRIVES

On my return to Mabalacat from Manila that morning of 20 October, I was immediately briefed by Commander Tamai on the organization of the new special attack corps. "Nakajima," he explained, "the *Yamato* Unit of the corps is being sent to Cebu this afternoon. You will accompany this unit, along with three other escort planes, and at Cebu you are to set up another special attack group."

By late afternoon, I was 400 miles to the south, flying the lead plane of eight Zero fighters. We were crossing the mountains which fringe the eastern shore of Cebu Island and were about to land at the naval air base located just north of the city of Cebu. As flight officer of the 201st Air Group at Mabalacat, I had been chosen to lead these planes to Cebu. So secret was our mission that the three other pilots flying with us were unaware that they were escorting the *Yamato* Unit of the newly organized special attack corps.

Maintenance men came running to tend the planes as soon as we rolled to a stop in the still bright light of the setting tropical sun. While removing my parachute I ordered an immediate assembly of all base personnel, and then radioed Mabalacat announcing our safe arrival.

The landing of eight Zeros had alerted everyone on the base to the fact that something unusual was afoot,

and word of the assembly spread rapidly. All officers
and men were soon gathered at the field command post.
To speak to them I mounted a stand improvised from
wooden boxes. My audience knew of the enemy landing at Leyte, separated from Cebu by only the narrow
Camotes Sea, and they must have guessed that my message would pertain to that landing. They knew that
our sudden arrival signified something important, and
their eyes sparkled in anticipation. Their eagerness
heightened my own tenseness, and I had to struggle to
keep my voice calm.

"The war situation is extremely grave," I began. "If
the enemy succeeds in establishing air bases on Leyte,

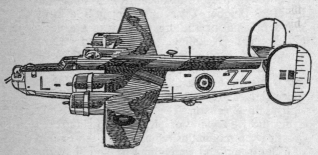

B-24, Liberator

the operational radius on his B-24 bombers will reach
across the China Sea to the mainland. Thus he would
jeopardize Japan's fuel supply from the south. Without fuel our ships will be immobilized and have no
chance to fight.

"The *Sho* Operation has been activated, and all our
warships are moving toward Leyte Gulf with the objective of wiping out enemy amphibious forces. These
forces in the Philippines area are exceedingly powerful, however, and our Navy will have to fight against
overwhelming odds. If American carrier planes attack
our ships on the way to Leyte, even the titanic guns
of our huge battleships *Yamato* and *Musashi* may be
silenced before they can reach the battle area.

"If the *Sho* Operation is to have any chance of success, it is up to pilots of the Japanese Navy to disable the American task force. But Japanese air strength in the Philippines is too hopelessly depleted to oppose the enemy effectively by orthodox methods of attack. The moment calls for the employment of crash-dive tactics. Admiral Ohnishi authorized such tactics last night at Mabalacat with the organization of the *Shimpu* (Kamikaze) Special Attack Corps. Four units—*Shikishima, Yamato, Asahi,* and *Yamazakura*—of this corps were activated at Mabalacat. Four of the planes that have just arrived with me constitute the *Yamato* Unit.

"I have come to Cebu to organize another special attack unit. Any non-commissioned officer or enlisted flier who wishes to volunteer will so signify by writing his name and rate on a piece of paper. Those who do not wish to volunteer will submit a blank paper. Each piece of paper is to be placed in an envelope which will be delivered to me by 2100 today.

"It is not expected, however, that everyone should volunteer. We know that you are all willing to die in defense of our country. We also realize that some of you, because of your family situation, cannot be expected to offer your life in this way. You should understand also that the number of volunteers required is limited by the small number of planes available. Whether a man volunteers or not will be known only to me. I ask that each man, within the next three hours, come to a decision based entirely upon his own situation. Special attack operations will be ready to start tomorrow. Because secrecy in this operation is of utmost importance, there must be no discussion about it."

The men listened in complete silence, and there was not the slightest stirring in the crowd. When I had finished talking, the coconut trees of nearby Mactan Island were black in the twilight.

VOLUNTEERS FOR DEATH

Base Operations at Cebu was located in a fine Western-style house on the brow of a low hill. The two-story building and its spacious garden had reportedly belonged to an American movie executive before the war. The operations room on the second floor served also as my bedroom. A large table in the center and a crude iron bed in one corner were its only furnishings.

Sitting alone in this room after leaving the airfield, I was suddenly aware of someone walking up the stairs. There was a knock at the door, and in came Lieutenant (jg) Yoshiyasu Kuno, who had flown one of the escort planes accompanying me from Mabalacat that afternoon. His face almost quivering with emotion, his eyes glittering, he strained to keep his feelings under control.

"What can I do for you?" I asked.

"I do trust that you will not exclude me from the special attack corps," he said, in a tone as casual as he could make it. But his forced casualness was contradicted by the unsubdued fire in his eyes.

Kuno had been sound asleep at Mabalacat the previous night when the first kamikaze unit was being organized, and it was through no fault of his that he had not been told of the decision. Because the organization had to be carried out secretly, only staff officers had been notified and they had passed the word individually to the men they considered likely to volunteer.

I knew Kuno personally as a modest man, reticent, but full of explosive fight. Had I not been absent from Mabalacat at the time, because of the plane crash near Manila, he would have been the first one I would have thought of notifying. Although organization of the special units had been kept secret, a mounting tension had been apparent at Mabalacat that following morning. Kuno had sensed the charged atmosphere and had remarked, "Something unusual is happening, Commander. What is going on around here?"

By that time the selection of special attack pilots had been completed and there was nothing that I could then tell him. But here at Cebu with the secrecy restriction now broken, I knew that Kuno would be among the first to volunteer. And here he was.

I looked squarely into his eyes and slowly answered, "One of the eight Zeros we brought here from

Mabalacat is reserved for *your* special attack mission." (It was with Kuno in mind that I had arranged for my plane from Mabalacat to be equipped also for carrying a 250-kilogram bomb.) He smiled broadly, saluted, and withdrew.

An orderly came to report that supper was ready in the officers' mess hall, located on the first floor of the house. Supper hour was usually a very social time at the base. After eating, the officers would read, play chess and checkers, or just sit around the big table and chat. There was an old piano in one corner of the hall. Lieutenant Kuno, an accomplished pianist, often played complicated pieces which I did not know.

On this particular night his performance was exceptionally good. The music was spirited, yet strangely melancholy. One officer, still at the table, suddenly stopped eating and sobbed aloud.

I retired thoughtfully to my room.

I was soon lost in deep concentration on how the special attacks should be effected next day. My solitary contemplation was undisturbed in the nighttime quiet. The stillness was broken only by the distant sound of engines being tested. The maintenance crews now worked night and day.

A sudden and more disturbing sound heralded the approach of Ensign Chisato Kunihara of the reconnaissance unit, who stamped abruptly into the room. He spoke out almost belligerently, trying hard to control his anger. "You invited the noncom fliers to volunteer for special attack, but made no mention of the officers. What about us, sir?"

I grinned up at him and said, "Why? What do you officers want to do?"

"We are all eager to join the corps!" he roared.

"Then, why should I bother to inquire whether you would volunteer?"

Kunihara's scowl turned slowly into a smile of understanding. He saluted, said, "Thank you, sir," and took his leave.

As Kunihara departed I returned to a chart spread before me on the table. It was almost 2100, time for

the written applications to be delivered. I heard someone approaching, quietly, so as not to disturb officers
asleep in the next room. A petty officer entered with
a handful of envelopes. He saluted, set the fateful bun-
dle before me, and withdrew as silently as he had
come.

I stared for some moments at the envelopes, hesitat-
ing to open them. I had not urged the non-coms to
volunteer, but had left the decision entirely up to
them. I had even offered a sincere alibi for those who
could not volunteer. What if they all declined?

That thought was disturbing, but there was no time
for delay. I reached for scissors in the drawer and
started the unpleasant task.

Of the 20-odd envelopes only two contained blank
pieces of paper. I learned later that the blanks had
been submitted by two bedridden pilots in sick bay.

I arranged the applications in a neat pile and went
out on the balcony. In the balmy night breeze the
mountains and sea blended in darkness. The sky
stirred with myriads of flickering stars.

The special attack corps had spread to Cebu.

Coming in from the balcony, I noted that the house
was completely quiet. Everyone seemed to be asleep.
While wondering what they dreamed, I fell into
thoughts of days past—those glorious days of New
Guinea in early 1942, when we were winning every
air battle. What a change!

My reverie was broken by the sound of a door being opened. Standing in the doorway was Ensign Ma-
sahisa Uemura. At Tokyo's St. Paul University he
had been captain of the football team. Direct from
college, Uemura had received a hurried flight training.
And now this handsome, aggressive young man stood
before me, sheepish and ill at ease. His coming to my
room at this particular time suggested that he was of
the same intention as Kunihara. I bade him enter.

He walked in, hesitated uneasily for a few moments,
and then asked several casual questions, none concerning special attacks. He listened to my answers,
backed gingerly out of the room, and was gone.

I was puzzled by his behavior but, with many things on my mind, soon forgot about him.

Next night, however, he was back. He came alone, almost stealthily, like a guilty man. A few pointless questions and he was gone again.

I felt that he wanted to join the Kamikaze Corps. But he did not volunteer. Why did he act so strangely? I could not figure him out.

When he came again the third night it was very late. I looked at his eyes, but he kept looking down awkwardly, apparently not knowing what to say. I wanted to help him. "You have come here alone on three consecutive nights . . . am I wrong in thinking that you wish to volunteer for the special attacks?"

He looked up furtively and answered in a low voice, "You are not wrong, sir. I keep coming here to volunteer, but simply cannot speak my thoughts because, as you know, I am the clumsiest flier in this outfit."

Overwhelmed, I searched for an answer, but he went on, "Just the other day I had a crack-up because of my clumsiness—and at a time when we suffer so from a shortage of planes. I know I'm not a good enough flier—but I simply cannot give up the idea of volunteering for the special attack."

He was on the verge of tears. I got up from my chair, patted his shoulder, and said, "Don't worry, Uemura. I'll find a chance for you. Stop worrying and go to bed."

I saw him smile then for the first time in three days. He bowed deeply and said, "Thank you, sir. I will be waiting."

PART TWO

KAMIKAZE OPERATIONS IN THE PHILIPPINES

"If you would shoot a general,
first destroy his horse"
—JAPANESE PROVERB

将を射んとする者
先づその馬を射よ

THE SHO OPERATION
AND EARLY SORTIES

BY NAKAJIMA

The *Sho* Operation, which was Japan's last hope for a decisive naval engagement, and which had been set off by the American invasion of the island of Leyte in the Philippines, was a three-pronged affair. Up from their anchorage at Lingga, south of Singapore, were to come the ships of Japan's First Striking Force. Vice Admiral Takeo Kurita's main body of this force, including the superbattleships *Yamato* and *Musashi*, was to slip through San Bernardino Strait in the Philippines and pounce on the American amphibious forces from the north at dawn on 25 October. Striking at them simultaneously from the south, through Surigao Strait, would be the cruisers and destroyers of Vice Admiral Kiyohide Shima's Fifth Fleet, coming down through the South China Sea from their base in the homeland; these would be joined for the attack by a force of old battleships, a cruiser, and some destroyers, detached for the purpose from Admiral Kurita's main body and placed under the command of Vice Admiral Shoji Nishimura.

It was unthinkable that these scattered ships, all that remained of Japan's fighting Navy, would be able to overcome the far more numerous carriers, battleships, cruisers, and destroyers of the U. S. Navy. Admiral Soemu Toyoda, Commander in Chief of the

Combined Fleet, realized this and so had provided that the remnants of the once-victorious carrier forces of Japan be used as decoys. There remained one heavy carrier, three light carriers, and two converted battleships with flight decks.* These ships, carrying their total of only 116 planes, all commanded by Vice Admiral Jisaburo Ozawa, were to come down from Japan's Inland Sea in an attempt to lure the enemy's fast battleships and carriers northward, away from the Leyte landing areas. This, it was hoped, would permit Kurita to pounce upon and destroy the unprotected American transports and amphibious forces—something which the Yamato's and Musashi's 18.1-inch guns would have an excellent chance of doing.

Sheer strategem was not the only tool to be used in the operation. The entire Second Air Fleet, consisting of 350 naval planes flown by the cream of Japan's surviving naval aviators, plus 50 bombers from the Army's Air Force, was in Formosa. It had been made into a mobile air force capable of striking anywhere. Upon activation of the Sho Operation, Vice Admiral Shigeru Fukudome ordered his Second Air Fleet to land bases in the Philippines. There they would stand prepared to strike at enemy carrier forces wherever they were sighted.

But these would be conventional attacks—fighters against fighters, bombers dropping bombs or torpedoes on enemy decks. And remembering what crushing defeats we had suffered both at Midway and at the Philippine Sea, when we had had far greater air forces to throw at the enemy, I wondered what chance our smaller forces would have in conventional attacks now.

By 20 October, Admiral Kurita's warships had reached Borneo en route to the Sulu Sea and Leyte. The other forces were similarly in motion. It was time

---

*These were the Ise and Hyuga. Following the Battle of Midway it was decided to remove their after turrets and install flight decks on the stern of these battleships. This conversion was completed in September 1943 and each ship was then capable of carrying 22 planes, but neither ship ever carried planes into battle.

for Admiral Ohnishi's idea of a special attack corps to justify itself, it ever.

Restless in my command post at Cebu, I waited tensely for the sortie of the kamikazes—the units first formed at Mabalacat and the later ones at Cebu.

The first report of the sighting of a worth-while enemy target came in the afternoon of 20 October, just hours after the first pilots had volunteered for the program. But the enemy forces sighted were too far away to the eastward in the Pacific—beyond practicable flying range for our planes. The decision was made to save our attack for a more favorable opportunity—a decision, I must say, that came as a great disappointment to the dedicated volunteers.

At Mabalacat, a 20-meter cliff rose just north of the western end of landing strip No. 1. At the base of this promontory a stream trickled past the shabby structure which served as a billet for the Mabalacat kamikaze fliers. The building stood within 200 meters of the airstrip and, shaded by the cliff, was a good place for pilots to rest undisturbed by enemy air raids. It was here that the attack fliers awaited their order to sortie. I was familiar with the setting and could readily visualize the scene when Tamai told me about it afterward, the first time I came back up from Cebu.

Despite the disappointment of the 20th, the *Shikishima* Unit fliers did not have long to wait for the sortie order. Scout planes reported the discovery of an enemy task force east of Leyte, at 0900 on the 21st. The alerted fliers, in full flight gear, jogged down a narrow lane to the command post. There was nothing in their attitude to indicate that theirs was anything but a routine mission. No somberness of demeanor betrayed the imminence of their departure to certain death.

Led by Lieutenant Seki, the pilots lined up for a farewell drink of water from a container left by Admiral Ohnishi. Their fellow pilots, standing by to see them off, took up the ancient song, a sad yet stirring air, whose words must have been especially haunting as they drifted out on the morning breeze:

> *Umi yukaba*　　　　(If I go away to sea,
> 　*Mizutsuku kabane*　　I shall return a corpse
> 　　　　　　　　　　　awash;
>
> *Yama yukaba*　　　　If duty calls me to the moun-
> 　*Kusa musu kabane*　　tain, A verdant sward will
> 　　　　　　　　　　　be my pall;
>
> *Ogimi no he ni koso*　　Thus for the sake of the
> 　*shiname Nodo niwa*　　Emperor I will not die
> 　*shinaji.*　　　　　　peacefully at home.)

Orders were given for the take-off. Turning from their comrades, the fliers headed toward their planes on the runway. The warmed-up engines were idling as each pilot climbed into the cockpit.

Lieutenant Seki's face was grim, but his eyes shone as he walked up to make his last report. His tired appearance was the result of a severe diarrhea he had been suffering the past three days.

"Please take care of this for me, Commander," he said, handing a small folded paper to Tamai, and then he ran for his plane. Later Tamai looked into the paper and found that it contained strands of Seki's hair —a traditional memorial from Japanese warriors which is sent home to their loved ones.

The planes flew eastward in close formation to the reported location of the enemy. A search of the area proved vain; for they found nothing there but the ocean, and all planes returned to Mabalacat. With tears in his eyes Seki apologized for his failure.

I could well understand the feeling of futility, for at Cebu, 400 miles to the south, we were having no better success.

The long, thin, north-south stretch of Cebu Island is spined by a narrow mountain ridge whose slopes everywhere reach almost to the shore. These mountains are not thick with jungle, as are those of New Guinea and New Britain, but resemble more the mountains of our homeland. Cebu seems like western Honshu in miniature.

Many narrow valleys near the coast afforded good protection for our Zero fighters, under cover of natural camouflage. In one of these valleys was the rest house for pilots of the newly organized *Yamato* Unit. The rest house was a mere shack, but it lay beneath glossy green mango trees whose leaves rustled in every breeze.

Waiting for the call to man their planes, the pilots passed their time in varied activities, as casual as those at any other base. Some read magazines long out of date. Others stretched out on the floor, lazily listening to popular Japanese melodies scratched out by a battered old phonograph in the corner—anything mechanical deteriorates rapidly in the tropics. Another small group, more professionally minded, studied air navigation charts. Boxed lunches and flight gear were close at hand. Nowhere was there any outward sign that these men were awaiting a call for their one-way mission.

Since before daybreak—this was 21 October—scout planes from Philippine airfields had been out searching the ocean to the east for the enemy carrier forces that were supporting the invasion of Leyte. Any report of an enemy surface force within range would be the signal to launch a special attack.

At 1500 on 21 October the telephone rang in the Cebu operations room. It was a sighting report: "An enemy task force built around six aircraft carriers has been sighted 60 miles east of Suluan Island."

Everyone sprang to immediate action. Mechanics rolled planes out while I compiled flight data for the pilots' briefing. The maintenance officer advised that it would take 40 minutes for three Zeros to be loaded with bombs and two fighter escorts readied to guard them against enemy interceptors. This was ten minutes longer than the average for readying a mission, but today the planes had to be hauled uphill some 500 meters to reach the airstrip, because they had been so carefully hidden away in forest revetments to avoid discovery by enemy planes.

Within ten minutes of the alert I was briefing the pilots—carefully and slowly this once, because there was time to spare. I had scarcely begun to speak, however, when, to my complete surprise, the maintenance officer came with word that all five planes were ready to go! This was not only embarrassing, it was a horrible shock. Planes on a runway are easy to spot from the air, and, in this most vulnerable position, are easily destroyed. I concluded the briefing and ran with the fliers to the airstrip.

My worst fears were confirmed as we approached the field. Fighter planes from enemy carriers were even then coming in over the mountains. There was no time for our planes to take off, nor was there opportunity to camouflage their stark outlines on the field. Brave men of the alert ground crew did, however, cut the switch of each idling engine just before the enemy planes began to strafe the airfield. I shouted for everyone to take cover and, followed by my assistant, ran to the dubious shelter of some piled sandbags. There we crouched and watched the strafing. The first few passes achieved no real damage since they were concentrated on the decoys we had scattered about the open field. Unfortunately for us, however, our real Zeros also drew enemy fire. My observations were interrupted by machine-gun bursts at our position. We ducked and circled around the sandbags to avoid the gunfire. The brief strafing attack seemed to us interminable.

When next I viewed the field, my heart sank. The planes which a few minutes before had been ready to sortie were riddled. Fuel spurted from some; others were afire. Bombs, ammunition, and fuel tanks in these planes might explode at any second. No sooner had the enemy's strafing fighters departed than his dive bombers arrived and the destruction continued. Bombs fell thick and fast and quite near, increasing our concern for bomb explosions in the Zeros. It was a miserable time for us, and we could do nothing but hide behind sandbags.

When the enemy finally left, our ready-to-launch Zeros were in flames. I ordered three more prepared at once, thinking that they might follow the enemy planes back to their carriers for a sure chance at a worthwhile target. Once more the ground crews worked with amazing speed, and in ten minutes two bomb-laden Zeros and an escort plane were ready on the field. By that time the first group of Zeros had all exploded.

The three-plane mission took off at 1625, led by Lieutenant (jg) Yoshiyasu Kuno. With them went our prayers for success. But they encountered bad weather and failed to locate the enemy.

Two of the planes returned—but not Lieutenant Kuno.

I remembered our conversation of the previous night, in which he had said, "In view of our acute shortages of planes, why send escorts along on our kamikaze sorties? We are not looking for publicity. We seek only to serve Japan and die for the Emperor. Please stop wasting escorts by sending them with us."

I had jumped at the chance to correct his misunderstanding. "They are not sent along for the sake of publicity. They are needed to observe results and to gather data that will be useful in future sorties."

"How about dismounting the machine guns from our planes then?" he had asked. "Certainly they serve no purpose in our tactics."

"Machine guns are still needed, Kuno, in case you meet interceptors on the way. Also, if you are forced to turn back without sighting a target, you need protection against pursuers. Without machine guns you would be easily destroyed. They must stay in the planes."

Kuno had finally nodded agreement, but added, "If I fail to contact the enemy at sea, I will go to Leyte Gulf, where there are sure to be many targets."

We had no witness to Kuno's final effort. But, knowing his ability and enthusiasm, I feel positive that he found a good target against which to crash his plane.*

Lieutenant Seki's unit at Mabalacat, as has been

---

*If he did, it was not a U. S. warship, for none was sunk or damaged by suicide attack on 21 October 1944.

said, was having no better luck. In fact, for three successive days, starting on 21 October, Japanese search planes located none of the enemy carriers which were to be the prime target for the special attack corps. The American amphibious forces landing the invasion troops at Leyte were readily located and Kurita's guns would take care of these, if he could only reach them. But Kurita would never arrive off Leyte unless the enemy carriers with their hundreds of planes were first put out of action.

When, on 23 October, our reconnaissance planes had not been able to locate any of the enemy carriers, we began to feel desperate. Admiral Kurita's force was advancing toward the San Bernardino Strait, well within range of the enemy's planes. And that the enemy's carriers were not the only thing to be feared was brought crushingly home on the 23rd, when over the air waves we heard the sickening news: U. S. submarines, ranging unchecked in the seas to the west of the Philippines, had sunk two heavy cruisers of Kurita's main body, *Atago* (the flagship) and *Maya,* and had disabled a third, the *Takao*. All this time the special attack corps, despite numerous sorties at every reported enemy sighting, had not succeeded in launching a single attack.

One reason for this failure was our lack of reconnaissance planes, since most of them had been lost in the destructive raids the enemy had made earlier on our airfields. But the weather also was to blame. In the tropics, towering cumulo-nimbus clouds cause frequent and sudden changes in the weather. Blinding rain squalls may be followed in ten minutes by the clearest and fairest of skies. For supplying precious drinking water and relief from sweltering heat, the rain squalls were welcome; but to our fliers they were a terrible hazard. Furthermore, they served the enemy as superb hiding places for his warships. Under cover of a rain squall his ships were safe from attack by our radarless planes. Our kamikaze sorties returned hopelessly day after day, largely because their assigned targets had found refuge in rain squalls.

No wonder that bitter tears filled Lieutenant Seki's eyes as, sortie after sortie, he had to report his failure.

The 350 planes of Vice Admiral Fukudome's Second Air Fleet, while flying south to their new Philippine bases, were just as unsuccessful in conventional attacks the few times they had located enemy carriers. But their arrival did provide sorely needed plane strength, and a 250-plane attack was planned against the enemy on 24 October.

As compared to these 250 planes, the entire strength of the new special attack corps consisted of but 13 planes, divided into four units—*Shikishima*, *Asahi*, and *Yamazakura* at Mabalacat, and *Yamato* at Cebu. Yet Vice Admiral Ohnishi, Commander in Chief of the First Air Fleet, seemed confident that the four units would be able to insure the success of the *Sho* Operation by sinking or damaging enough enemy carriers to enable Kurita's Force to destroy the enemy fleet in Leyte Gulf. Just before leaving for Cebu on 20 October, I had asked the Admiral if he really believed these four units would be enough.

"We have so few planes," he had answered, "it cannot be helped." It was his intention then, I was sure, to limit special attacks to these thirteen planes.

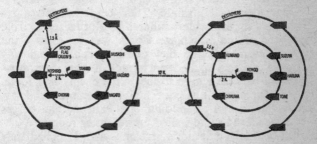

Antiaircraft cruising disposition of Admiral Kurita's force in the Sibuyan Sea. 0600-0647. 24 October 1944.

But, on 24 October, the situation became critical. That morning the weather was particularly bad, giving our scout and fighter pilots no end of trouble. The heavy 250-plane raid by Admiral Fukudome's Second

Air Fleet was launched as planned, but in the bad weather it succeeded in damaging only two enemy cruisers and three destroyers.*

A group of 14 Zero fighters was sent to give air cover to Kurita's ships in their passage through the Sibuyan Sea, but was driven off by heavy antiaircraft fire from the very ships they were supposed to protect. Against these now unprotected ships the enemy carrier planes, ranging from their carriers far to the eastward, struck with sudden, devastating force. Our hearts went sick as desperate radio calls for air cover came from Kurita's force—calls that produced successive shocks as the toll of enemy bombs mounted. One—two—three—four—all of Kurita's battleships had been hit by midafternoon. The heavy cruiser *Myoko* and superbattleship *Musashi* had been put out of action and were retiring westward escorted by two destroyers. To the south, in the Sulu Sea, the battleship *Fuso* of Admiral Nishimura's force, as well as a destroyer, had been damaged. Then came the most incredible blow of all; the unsinkable *Musashi,* mightiest warship ever launched, had been battered beneath the waves. And Kurita was reversing course to the west, complaining bitterly over the radio at the lack of air support which had left him open to crippling air attacks.

Our fliers were frantic. They held themselves responsible for every blow suffered by Kurita, for the sole purpose of the Kamikaze Corps was to destroy the enemy carriers before they could launch their deadly attacks. So far we had not struck a single carrier— had not been able even to locate the enemy task force.

Pressures and anxieties built up with each delay, each failure and disappointment. Patience and nerves became frayed as we waited for a sighting report.

Late in the afternoon it came, and I immediately alerted pilots and ground crews. This day's flight leader was Ensign Uemura—he who had come to my quar-

---

*The *Leutze* (DD-481), *Ashtabula* (AO-51), and *LST-552* were the only U. S. ships damaged in the vicinity by aerial attack on this day.

ters on three consecutive nights seeking assurance that he could be a kamikaze. Now I had to summon him to my desk for disappointing news. "Today's mission is so late in getting started that most of the flying will have to be done at night. Since you have had no training in night flying, you will have to be relieved."

The young man slumped into a chair and dismally shook his head. "I'm sorry to miss this chance. Please see that I am picked the first time that you deem me capable of the job."

Flight Sergeant Hiroshi Shioda grinned with delight when told that he would lead the mission. At the same time it was plain to see that he felt sorry for the disappointed Uemura.

Shioda's unit sortied, but was forced to turn back late that night when it ran into a torrential rain.

FIRST SUCCESSES

BY NAKAJIMA

LIEUTENANT SEKI

It was simple justice that Lieutenant Seki, who had been the first to volunteer, should be the first to succeed. On four consecutive days he had sortied, only to return each time in miserable disappointment. But it was different the fifth time—on 25 October—when his *Shikishima* Unit sortied from Mabalacat at 0725. The plan was to search for the enemy in waters east of the Philippines. If this proved unsuccessful, the planes were to strike at the enemy vessels in Leyte Gulf.

The alternative proved to be unnecessary. An enemy fleet was sighted to the east at 1010. Through a light rainfall the group was made out to be four or five U. S. battleships accompanied by more than 30 cruisers, destroyers, and other ships. They were headed north under a combat air patrol of about 20 planes. Another group was discovered at 1040, in a position bearing 085°, and distant some 90 miles from Tacloban, on the eastern shore of Leyte Island.

In Cebu, however, we did not then know the details of Seki's sortie. The first intimation we had of it was when three unexpected Zeros came in for a landing shortly after noon on the 25th. I was sitting in my rattan chair in the air command and flight control post where I had spent most of the last five days and nights.

The command post stood on a hillside at the edge

64

of a north-south runway. The building itself was of native construction—one of those high-floored tropical shacks which geography books show as typical of the area. Part of the space beneath the floor was used for storage; the remainder served as a shady rest spot for fliers awaiting orders.

In the command post was a large rattan chair which came to be reserved exclusively for me. It had been requisitioned from some American house in town and its former owner must have been a big man. It was far too large for me, so much so as to be really uncomfortable. It had been designed for use with several cushions. But the Japanese Navy did not supply mere commanders with cushions for rattan chairs.

The command post was well situated to overlook the runways. At night we could even see antiaircraft fire over Leyte, 60 miles to the east.

Being that close, we were a convenient stopover place for planes from other units after they had struck at enemy shipping in Leyte Gulf or the waters east of the Philippines. Also the excellence of our luncheon fare at Cebu had gained wide reputation. The quartermaster boasted that he served the best meals in the Philippines. In fact, so famous had Cebu food become that fliers from other outfits frequently landed there just to get a meal.

So when the lookout reported, "Commander Nakajima, there are three Zeros coming in," I thought they were just paying the usual lunchtime visit.

As the first plane set down, however, its battle-scarred appearance spoke clearly that this was no casual social call. The pilot jumped from the plane and came running toward the command post. I quickly recognized him to be Chief Warrant Officer Hiroyoshi Nishizawa, my flying comrade of two years before at Rabaul. There was a tense excitement about him as he approached. Others noticed it too, and they gathered around as he started to talk.

Nishizawa had come to report his observation of the first successful kamikaze mission. He had witnessed the special attack by Lieutenant Seki's *Shikishima* Unit. The five bomb-laden planes, escorted by four Zero fighters, had located an enemy carrier task force. Each pilot had selected his target, and at a banking signal from Seki, who was in the lead, their planes plunged. Seki's plane hit first, at 1045, striking squarely into a carrier. He was followed by another plane which hit the same carrier in almost the identical spot. Nishizawa said that the smoke and flame from the two hits rose 1,000 meters into the air. And the carrier sank.*

A third plane hit another carrier and set it afire. A fourth plane struck a light cruiser, which sank instantly. The fifth plane apparently failed to score.†

Cebu fliers were greatly cheered to hear this report. They were pleased not merely at Seki's success, but also because it dispelled a growing anxiety which had been bothering everyone. We had feared that when a plane plunged at top speed the pilot might instinctively close his eyes before crashing, and thus miss the target. This concern diminished when we heard of the successes reported by Nishizawa, and especially that two kamikazes had succeeded in hitting the same important target.

I promptly cabled the news to Manila. We later learned that Tokyo broadcast the report of this event in an epochal communiqué from Imperial Headquarters:

The *Shikishima* Unit of the Kamikaze Special Attack Corps made a successful surprise attack on an enemy task force containing four aircraft carriers at a point 30 miles northeast of Suluan Island at 1045.

---

*The U. S. escort carrier *St. Lo* (CVE-63) was sunk this date by suicide plane in position 11°10′ N, 126°05′ E.

†Ships damaged by suicide planes this date in this approximate position were the *Kalinin Bay* (CVE-68) and the *Kitkun Bay* (CVE-71) at 11°10′ N, 126°20′ E, and the *White Plains* (CVE-66) at 11°40′ N, 126°20′ E. Thus it is possible that all five of these kamikazes made hits, and that Nishizawa simply was not up on his warship recognition.

Two planes hit one carrier, which was definitely sunk. A third plane hit another carrier, setting it aflame. A fourth hit a cruiser, which sank instantly.

THE YAMATO UNIT FOLLOWS SUIT

We had waited so anxiously and long for a special attack to succeed that the *Shikishima* Unit's success was a matter of deep emotion. It meant a great deal to each of us who had played some small part in bringing it about. One can only imagine the feelings of Admiral Ohnishi, the promoter of this strategy. The success had its debit side, of course, in the extraordinary sacrifice of the fliers' precious lives, but this too was inspirational.

It was after 2200 on 25 October when I left the operations room to eat supper. The processing of cablegrams and plans for the next day's operations and other routine matters had taken much time. At the mess hall I was surprised, upon ordering my food, to be told that it had already been eaten. A very embarrassed orderly explained, "It was a chief warrant officer unknown to me. He came in and demanded your evening meal."

I was puzzled for a moment because it was unthinkable that a noncommissioned officer would demand and consume the meal of a senior officer without the latter's permission. Then I remembered my friend Nishizawa, who was capable of anything, and I had to laugh.

Nishizawa truly deserved the meal. That afternoon he had agreed to give me his Zero as well as the two planes manned by his wingmen. The *Yamato* Unit, having lost six planes on 21 October, was elated to have this contribution.

The enemy task force was reported by a scout plane still to be east of Leyte on the 26th. The *Yamato* Unit, having completed their preparations on the previous night, took off for these targets with great hopes and expectations. The unit was divided into two groups. The first, of two kamikazes and one escort, departed at 1015. The second, three kamikazes with two escorts, took off at 1230.

Nothing is known about planes of the first group, because none of them returned. One escort plane of the second group did come back, however, and the pilot was able to report their successes. An enemy force, which included four carriers, had been located about 80 miles east of Surigao. Our three attack planes had managed to pierce the wall of about 60 Grumman interceptors protecting these ships and to strike fatal blows. One carrier was hit by two planes and definitely sunk. The third kamikaze had struck and damaged another carrier.*

The successes of this day involved sacrifices and losses, however. There were the brave young special attackers, escort fighter pilots, and others, among whom was the great flying ace, my friend Nishizawa. After contributing their Zeros to Cebu, Nishizawa and his two wingmen had hopped a ride in a transport plane to return to Clark Field. American carrier-based fighters attacked this unarmed plane during the flight, destroying the transport with all its passengers.

Nishizawa had taken part in many air battles of the Pacific War and had scores of kills to his credit. A truly great pilot. But all his flying skill was useless when as a passenger he came under attack of the powerful enemy. His death was a great personal loss to me.

KAMIKAZE FORMATIONS AND PROCEDURE

In the initial stage of special attack operations, a standard sortie consisted of three kamikaze and two escort planes. This formula was devised on the theory that each formation must be kept small for maximum mobility. Sorties had to be surreptitious, while superior enemy air units were not in the vicinity, and the take-offs had to be made swiftly and surely. Once the

---

*The *Suwannee* (CVE-27) was the only U. S. carrier damaged by suicide plane attack on 26 October 1944. Her position when hit was 09°37' N, 126°53' E.

sortie was begun, each step had to be carried out with all possible swiftness.

A small group was better able than a large one to evade enemy interceptors and keep together under adverse weather conditions. "The fewer, the better," applied as far as speed and mobility were concerned, but there were other considerations which also set five planes as a minimum. A single plane, for example, could not be sure of dealing an effective blow against a ship the size of a carrier.

It was determined that five was the optimum number of planes for a sortie, and the pilot skill of the time dictated that three suiciders with two escorts was the best ratio. These numbers, of course, were not rigidly fixed. Depending on weather conditions, the enemy situation, and the availability of planes, the number in each sortie might be varied.

The two escorting fighters were very important. They had to ward off interceptors until the kamikaze planes could make their plunge at the targets. The fight against interceptors had always to be a defensive one. The escorts could not initiate air duels, nor could they seek a point of vantage if engaged. They had to stay at the side of the kamikazes. If attacked from behind, they could not retaliate, if to do so involved altering course. To deviate even briefly from the group's course would put an escort behind, with no chance of catching up. Escort pilots had to be able to dodge adroitly and bluff the enemy, rather than just shoot him down. An escort pilot's first duty was to shield the suicide planes in his mission, even if it meant the sacrifice of his own life.

It took men of superior skill and ability to fly escort. And thus the requests of our best fliers, like Lieutenant Kanno, to become kamikaze pilots had to be denied. Such men were so urgently needed to guard the suicide planes that they could not be spared to pilot them, despite their strong desire to do so. Many fliers of unit-leader rank flew escort for special attacks, and almost invariably they would volunteer as suiciders.

The procedure at our kamikaze bases followed a general pattern that was both simple and effective. A successful search plane would radio its findings to shore. The communications center relayed this information by telephone to the operations room near the airstrip where—at Cebu, for example—I stood by to alert and brief the pilots. After sounding the alert I would pinpoint the position of the enemy force, would estimate its strength, course, and tactical objective, and evaluate flying conditions en route to and at the target. Considering these factors I would decide how many kamikaze planes to launch, when they should take off, and what course they should follow. This done, I would run to the pilots' resting place—their last but one—where they would all be lined up. They would jot down essential information from my briefing and then be ready for departure.

Meanwhile, ground crews would have wheeled planes from their hiding places to starting positions on the airstrip, with bombs loaded, fuel supply checked and topped off, and engines warming up. The whole ordered routine is still a living picture for me. Pilots climbing into cockpits of readied planes . . . a farewell wave . . . engines roaring . . . and they are off, diminishing from view as they climb eastward above the indigo ocean until there is only water and sky.

Flying out to sea, the pilot in his last view of land sees the lush verdure of coconut forests clipped abruptly by a narrow strand of sparkling white beach before the land yields to the endless blue of ocean. Thoughts of such beauty must also yield, however, for there is work to do. The planes climb steadily to high altitudes, where chances are fewer that they will meet enemy interceptors. The pilots don their oxygen masks because the air gets thin at high altitudes.

Far ahead on the ocean tiny black specks spring suddenly into being. The lead plane heads straight for the enemy ships, which are now running full steam to the east. Clouds hide them sporadically from view.

Kamikaze planes boost their speed as they approach the target area, and the few escorting fighters take position to block enemy interceptors. Kamikaze pilots ready their bombs by removing the fuse safety pin.

Enemy fighters rise swiftly to intercept as our formation continues patiently toward the targets. The lead plane banks slightly and signals, "All planes, attack!" The raised arm of the leader is plainly visible and one can almost make out his broad smile. Each pilot selects his target, preferably an aircraft carrier, and plunges toward its most vulnerable spot—the flight deck elevator. Into the barrage of shipboard gunfire, into and through this wall of flying steel, each plane makes its hit. Each detonation raises flaring sheets of flame which spew up tall pillars of dense black smoke.

Back in the operations room, after every kamikaze sortie, I would thus hopefully reflect on the progress of the mission. Usually unwarranted though they were, the dream and hope always persisted.

WORD FROM THE EMPEROR

Even while kamikaze sorties continued and the enemy intensified his attacks against our base at Cebu, we learned that the Emperor had been informed of the *Shikishima* Unit's accomplishment. That news was followed by a message containing the Emperor's own comment about this feat. I gave instructions for all members of the base to assemble at the command post that evening to hear the Emperor's message. As they gathered I could see that their spirit and morale were high, despite the intense day-and-night effort demanded of them. Holding the cablegram in my hand I addressed them:

"I relay to you His Majesty's words to the Naval Chief of Staff upon hearing the results achieved by the Kamikaze Special Attack Corps."

Everyone snapped to attention, and I read the message from Admiral Ohnishi:

When told of the special attack, His Majesty said, "Was it necessary to go to this extreme? They certainly did a magnificent job." His Majesty's words suggest that His Majesty is greatly concerned. We must redouble our efforts to relieve His Majesty of this concern.

I have pledged our every effort toward that end.

That night I was told by my friend Captain Inoguchi, who had just arrived from Manila, "Admiral Ohnishi was completely upset when he heard the Imperial words at Manila. *I think that the Admiral interprets His Majesty's comment as criticism of the commander responsible for these tactics.*"

EXTENSION OF THE KAMIKAZE ORGANIZATION

BY INOGUCHI

ADMIRAL OHNISHI'S REASONING

Whatever feeling of self-recrimination Admiral Ohnishi might have had as the organizer of the Kamikaze Corps must inevitably have been wiped away by the results of the Battle of Leyte Gulf. For what had happened to Admiral Kurita's force on 24 October was but a portent of the catastrophe that was to befall the entire Japanese naval forces engaged. The very next morning, in the early hours before dawn, the force under Admiral Nishimura, attempting to slip through Surigao Strait to the south, had run into a waiting force of American battleships, cruisers, destroyers, and PT boats, and within brief minutes had been all but wiped out—the battleships *Yamashiro* and *Fuso* sunk, plus three destroyers, and the cruiser *Mogami* disabled. Admiral Shima's force, following closely, had suffered damages that forced it to turn back. And after daybreak the enemy's pursuing planes had caught up with and finished off the cruisers *Mogami* and *Abukuma*.

The carriers of Admiral Ozawa's decoy force to the north had run into the enemy's mighty task forces, and at the end of the action off Cape Engaño had lost all four carriers—the *Zuikaku, Chitose, Chiyoda,* and *Zuiho*—in addition to the cruiser *Tama* and several destroyers.

73

Ironically enough, the decoy strategem in itself was successful, in that it drew the enemy's fast carrier task forces to the north, leaving their transports and amphibious screens at Leyte completely exposed. Admiral Kurita, reversing his course during the night, had fallen upon the enemy's outer screen of destroyers and escort carriers shortly after dawn on 25 October. But confused by the recurring rain squalls and lack of reliable information from any source, and conscious of his diminishing supply of fuel, Admiral Kurita had turned around after sinking one enemy escort carrier and three destroyers,* and had retired westward through San Bernardino Strait again. Unfortunately the cruisers *Chikuma* and *Chokai* had been so badly damaged that they had to be sunk, and the pursuing enemy planes caught up with and sank the cruisers *Suzuya* and *Noshiro*. Within the space of three days the Japanese Navy had lost 3 battleships, 4 carriers, 10 cruisers, and 9 destroyers—over half its vessels engaged.

In all these widespread actions, the inability of our Second Air Fleet, despite its hundreds of planes, to achieve any worthwhile results by conventional methods was evident. As early as the middle of the *Sho* Operation, Admiral Ohnishi had become convinced of this—and he was further convinced that in the use of kamikaze tactics lay the only hope of checking the overpowering forces of the enemy. Immediately upon the arrival of the Second Air Fleet at Clark Field on 23 October, Admiral Ohnishi had conferred with its commander, Vice Admiral Fukudome. Admiral Ohnishi laid all his cards on the table.

"The First Air Fleet has been terribly shot up during the past month. It has fewer than 50 planes actually available for combat. There are about 30 fighters, and only a few bombers ('Betty'), *Tenzan* tor-

---

*The U. S. warships sunk by Japanese naval gunfire in this action to the east of Leyte Gulf were the escort carrier *Gambier Bay*, the destroyers *Hoel* and *Johnston*, and the destroyer escort *Samuel B. Roberts*.

pedo bombers ('Jill'), and *Suisei* carrier bombers ('Judy').

"With so few planes it is impossible for us to continue fighting by conventional tactics. To do so would just wipe out our remaining strength. In view of this situation, and after a full examination and investigation of the various possibilities, First Air Fleet has decided upon special attacks as offering the only chance of success. It is my hope that Second Air Fleet will join us in these attacks."

When Admiral Fukudome did not go along with this idea immediately, Ohnishi spoke to him again that evening. "I am not in a position to deny the value of mass-formation attacks such as you have trained for, but their effectiveness in this situation is very doubtful. We firmly believe that the First Air Fleet's special attacks will bring about the desired results, but we need more planes. We wish you to share some of your fighters with us."

But this was still not agreeable to Admiral Fukudome, who insisted that he would rely on the effectiveness of conventional mass-formation attacks: He was concerned that the adoption of suicide attacks might destroy pilot morale. Accordingly, the Second Air Fleet had made conventional attacks with 250 planes on both the 24th and 25th, the most important days of the operation, but they had succeeded only to the extent of damaging two cruisers and three destroyers.* Yet on the 25th alone, only five kamikazes of the First Air Fleet's *Shikishima* Unit had sunk one enemy carrier and damaged another two or three.

That night the admirals conferred a third time, and Admiral Ohnishi said, "The evidence is quite con-

---

*On 24 October the U.S.S. *Princeton* (CVL-23) was damaged by a dive bomber at lat. 15°12′ N, long. 123°36′ E, and had to be sunk by friendly ships; *Leutze* (DD-481) was damaged at lat. 10°50′ N, long. 125°25′ E, and *LST-552* at lat. 11°11′ N, long. 125°05′ E, by horizontal bombers; and the *Ashtabula* (AO-51) was damaged by aerial torpedo at lat. 11°03′ N, long. 125°22′ E. The only damage on the 25th attributable to Second Air Fleet was strafing of the *Richard M. Rowell* (DE-403) in lat. 10°05′ N, long. 127°10′ E.

clusive that special attacks are our only chance. In this critical situation we must not lose precious time. It is imperative that the Second Air Fleet agree to special attacks."

Admiral Fukudome was now convinced of the effectiveness of suicide attacks, but he was still uneasy about the possible effects on the morale of his men. Admiral Ohnishi reassured him on that point, and after a discussion with his staff officers which lasted until 0200 hours on the 26th, Admiral Fukudome finally agreed to adopt suicide tactics.

With both air fleets in agreement on the tactical concept, it was decided that they should have a unified command under Admiral Fukudome, with Ohnishi as his chief of staff. Captain Shibata of the Second Air Fleet was named operations officer and I was to be responsible for carrying out the special attacks. When these arrangements had been settled, Southwest Area Fleet issued a formal order setting up the "Combined Land-based Air Force."

It was Admiral Fukudome's intention to use only the former Twelfth Air Fleet fighters (which had come to him from the northern Kuriles) as kamikazes, leaving the rest of his Second Air Fleet planes for conventional attacks. But so ardent was the spirit of the Second Air Fleet in volunteering for special attacks that by 27 October the 701st Air Group alone had formed four kamikaze units under Captain Tasuhiko Kida.

The fighting spirit among the fliers from the Twelfth Air Fleet was also very high. They were assigned to a special attack corps immediately upon their arrival at Clark Field on the 26th. Next day 17 planes led by Lieutenant Kanno (including 13 just arrived from the north) left Mabalacat for Cebu, the forwardmost kamikaze base. On the way this group encountered and engaged 16 enemy carrier-based Grumman fighters over Marinduque.

Shortly after leaving for Cebu one pilot discovered that his landing gear would not retract. But he would not turn back. Instead, he followed closely behind

Lieutenant Kanno, who later complained of the tough time he had protecting that plane during the air battle with the American carrier planes.

With the adoption of kamikaze tactics by the Second Air Fleet and the additional planes from the north, our situation in the Philippines seemed greatly improved as far as special attacks were concerned.

AN UNORTHODOX COMMAND

During the entire three-day battle around Leyte, and to the north, off Luzon, I had remained at Mabalacat. On 26 October I returned to headquarters with my report concerning the special attack organizations. Upon entering Manila I was struck with the impression that the city was dirty. People in the street appeared haunted and nervous; many were evacuating the city, carrying huge bundles on their shoulders. Heavy smoke from enemy air raids hung over the harbor. At antiaircraft positions along the beach soldiers were busy clearing away shell cases and debris from the last raid. The whole Manila Bay area showed signs of the heavy enemy air attacks it had endured. I was particularly shocked to see the number of sunken vessels, evidenced now only by tips of masts piercing the surface of the water. I wondered how we could keep on bringing in military supplies under such terrific raids.

Upon my arrival at headquarters I found the staffs of First and Second Air Fleets working together, and learned of my new assignment and responsibilities.

Early next morning about 40 enemy carrier-based planes struck Manila. The attack concentrated on anchored ships, harbor facilities, and antiaircraft positions. Wave after wave of fighters, bombers, and dive bombers hit Nichols Field, and our headquarters was machine-gunned.

Admiral Ohnishi and I shared one of the small air raid shelters in the garden. Between noises of the attack the Admiral said, "Inoguchi, were you aware that

Captain Eiichiro Jyo had repeatedly asked to be named commander of a suicide attack unit? I think it was after returning from Rabaul that he first proposed such tactics, stating very positively that there was no other way out of our situation. At that time I did not see what he meant, nor could I accept his idea. Now, here, I have come to exactly the same solution and am putting it into practice."

He stared fixedly at the wall during bursts of machine-gun fire and then continued, "The fact that we have to resort to a thing like this shows how poor our strategy has been." After a long pause he concluded, "This is certainly an unorthodox command."

I was reminded at the moment of something that had happened two and a half years before. In those days, Admiral Isoroku Yamamoto, Commander in Chief of the Combined Fleet, was seeking opportunity for a great victory. I headed the Lieutenants and Lieutenant Commanders Division of the Personnel Bureau of the Navy Ministry in Tokyo at that time. One day in March 1942 Admiral Yamamoto's torpedo officer, Commander Arima, came to my office and said, "I must have some exceptionally able men."

"What are you going to do with them?" I had asked.

"They are needed to man midget submarines in attacks on the harbors at Sydney and Diego Suarez."

Surprised at this, I had expressed my view frankly. "Is it good to repeat time and again the midget submarine attack that was used at Pearl Harbor? It was acceptable then because so much seemed to depend upon that attack. But it is almost certain suicide; it is outrageous from the standpoint of command leadership. No matter how great and worthy Admiral Yamamoto is, if he resorts to suicide tactics, historians will condemn him for it a hundred years hence."

Arima had replied, "I believe that Admiral Yamamoto is thinking beyond you."

"Maybe so," I had said, "but the idea seems terrible. Such an inhuman thing will have to be answered for in heaven."

Yet now I, who had once called such a thing outrageous, was agreeing with Admiral Ohnishi, was assisting him in this very same sort of operation. It was ironical—yet there was a difference. Had not Admiral Ohnishi just remarked that kamikaze tactics were unorthodox? The Japanese Navy was staking everything on the successful defense of the Philippines. There was no way for our land-based planes to cooperate effectively with the surface fleet except by kamikaze attacks. Under these circumstances I thought they might now be allowable.

There in the little air raid shelter at Manila, between enemy raids, Admiral Ohnishi spoke again. "When I returned here on 20 October, after completing organization of the special attack unit at Mabalacat, I went directly to Southwest Area Fleet Headquarters to ask that Admiral Kurita's sortie be delayed until after kamikaze planes had a chance to strike. I arrived at headquarters to find that the sortie order had been issued two hours before. To recall the order would have thrown everything into confusion, so I gave up the idea and withdrew."

Admiral Ohnishi spoke without emotion. Yet I could imagine his feeling as he considered the terrible losses Japan was suffering around Leyte at this moment.

As the enemy air raid ended, we stepped out of the shelter. The attack was finished. Enemy planes were flying east in perfect formation, uninterrupted, undisturbed, unopposed. Another cloud of heavy black smoke was forming over the harbor.

ONLY A MATTER OF TIME

That evening I was relaxing in the lobby of headquarters when a young officer in flight gear entered the dark narrow doorway, came up to me, and said, "I am Tada, sir. Is Admiral Ohnishi here?"

It was Lieutenant (jg) Keita Tada, a member of the 71st graduating class of the Naval Academy, and now about 20 years of age. I always felt very close to young

Academy men because of my having taught there before the war.

"I am glad to see you, Lieutenant Tada," I said. "And what are you doing around here at this hour?"

"I wish to see Admiral Ohnishi."

"Very well, he is upstairs. I'll show you to his room."

Tada walked rapidly toward the door I indicated. At the threshold he called, "Hello, Uncle!" and walked in. There was a warming tone of homeyness in his voice.

I went downstairs again and looked at this young man's record. His father, Vice Admiral Takeo Tada, was Chief of the Naval Affairs Bureau.* Vice Admiral Tada and Ohnishi had been Academy classmates and were personal friends of long standing. Their families were very close, and having no children of his own, Ohnishi loved young Tada like a son.

From Lieutenant Tada's orders I found that he belonged to the 252nd Air Group of the Second Air Fleet. He had arrived at Nichols Field on 23 October and was assigned to command a special attack unit. Now he had come to say goodbye.

It was after 2200 and the headquarters was very dark when the two men came downstairs. In the garden the Admiral wished the young man good luck. Tada bowed, put on his cap, and departed.

The older man stood silently looking into the darkness for a long time and then returned slowly to his room. As he climbed the stairs I could appreciate how somber his thoughts must be, realizing that this particular young pilot would go soon to his death.

As it turned out, Lieutenant Tada was transferred to another kamikaze unit the following day. It was not until 19 November that he finally sortied for Leyte Gulf and was never heard of again.

A short time later I flew in a fighter plane to Cebu. This place, only 60 miles from Leyte, had a battle-like

---

*Vice Admiral Tada later became Navy Vice Minister.

tenseness. The landing strips were busy with the arrival and departure of scout planes, escort planes, and kamikazes. In this great movement of fliers I found a number of familiar faces from my teaching days at the Academy. Among these was Lieutenant Kenzo Nakagawa, who led the 165th Fighter Unit.

The enemy had landed at Tacloban a few days before and was now pouring in fighting men and materiel to occupy all of Leyte. Our army forces were in hill positions, doing their best to resist the invasion. I was in the Cebu command post one evening as a unit of six fighter planes arrived. The leader of this unit escaped my notice when he reported to the field commander. He was my nephew, Lieutenant (jg) Satoshi Inoguchi. He must have seen me at the post, for he later came to my quarters. He had just arrived from Clark Field, where he had landed that morning from the homeland. His departure from Japan had been delayed owing to the difficulty of collecting the six planes required for his unit.

My nephew had been a classmate of Lieutenant Tada at the Academy. Their class had graduated on 15 September 1943, and most of the men had gone directly to the Naval Air Force training center. He had been promoted to Lieutenant (jg) only in October. The six planes which he had brought to Cebu were part of Lieutenant Nakagawa's 165th Fighter Unit.

I had not seen this boy for several years and was happy to hear of his service career since graduation. When these explanations were over, he said, "What do you know about my father?"

His father—my brother, Captain Toshihira Inoguchi —had been given command of the battleship *Musashi* in August 1944 and had been on the bridge of his ship on 24 October. On that day the Kurita force, heading east in the Sibuyan Sea, was attacked by enemy planes from dawn to dusk. They had concentrated bombs and torpedoes on the "unsinkable" *Musashi*. She did not sink easily, but nothing afloat could have withstood that battering. I had already learned that the captain had stayed with her after ordering the crew to abandon ship.

Now all that I could say to his son was, "I understand that he went down with his ship."

The young man sighed helplessly and echoed, "Down with his ship." He had that very day flown over the Sibuyan Sea to reach Cebu. He was lost in thought, and I had the impression that he was now anxious to fly a kamikaze mission. I wondered if it was my place to offer any advice, but decided that this was a problem he would have to work out for himself. It was getting late, and knowing that my nephew must be tired, I urged him to get some rest. We retired to our billets.

A reconnaissance plane reported sighting more than 80 enemy planes at a Tacloban airfield in the afternoon of 2 November. An attack was quickly organized to strike this tempting target the next morning. The blue exhaust of idling engines spurted through the predawn darkness as 12 fighter planes led by Lieutenant Nakagawa were preparing to leave. My nephew, who had been standing in the operations room in ordinary uniform, was gone for no more than a minute when he suddenly reappeared in full flight gear. He ran out the door and toward the planes, some of which had already started down the runway. As the rising silhouettes and roar announced that the first planes were taking the air, a bewildered warrant officer pilot came to me and explained, "Lieutenant Inoguchi said, 'I am to go instead of you,' and he took my plane."

With the first light of day faint flashes of antiaircraft fire could be seen in the direction of Tacloban. Our planes had arrived over the enemy airfield. I prayed for their success.

Some 30 minutes later, one—and it was the only one —of our planes returned. The pilot's face was bloodstained as he climbed from the cockpit. "Fierce antiaircraft fire destroyed our formation as we passed over the mountains," he reported. "Enemy radar must have detected our planes, for his antiaircraft batteries were alerted. Needless to say, the surprise attack failed."

"Lieutenant Ino—?" I started to say, and then broke off. The expression on the pilot's face had already answered my question.

It was just ten days since his father had gone down with the *Musashi*—and now the son had found a last resting place not far away.

LIFE AT A KAMIKAZE BASE

BY NAKAJIMA

LIEUTENANT FUKABORI OF
THE 701ST AIR GROUP

On 27 October, the day after Admiral Fukudome consented to kamikaze tactics, my friend Inoguchi had assumed his new staff duties in connection with the special attack force. I was sitting in the operations room at Cebu after supper and was startled to hear the sound of a plane buzzing our field. I went outside to investigate. Wing lights identified it as friendly. I drove quickly to the field and found preparations being made to mark the darkened field for a night landing.

The field lighting arrangements at this frontline base were quite primitive. Battery-powered lights were used only for giving hand signals to planes landing at night. To outline the strip, men were stationed around its perimeter at regular intervals, each tending a kerosene lamp to be lighted with a match upon signal from the command post. This operation had to be well timed so that the lamps were lit just before the plane was set down on the field and extinguished as soon as the landing was completed. Any prolonged illumination would attract enemy night raiders, which came over almost every evening.

Two enemy raiders did come over, in fact, just as we were ready to light the field on this occasion. Our plane, unaware of the nearby prowlers, signaled repeatedly, "Prepare for landing!" The two enemy raiders, in turn, seemed equally unaware of our plane and its frantic efforts to land. When the enemy had moved away from the immediate vicinity of the field, lamps were promptly lit for our plane. But this illumination drew the two enemy planes right back, and we had to douse the lights and run for safety. The enemy finally dropped their bombs some distance from the field, and flew away. I then signalled from the command post that all was clear for landing. The lamps were lit and, after his long circling overhead, the perplexed pilot came safely in.

Lieutenant Naoji Fukabori, for that was the pilot's name, was soon reporting to me at the command post. He was from the 701st Air Group of the Second Air Fleet and had that morning been chosen as a unit commander of the Second Kamikaze Special Attack Corps. His unit had left Nichols Field to search for enemy warships around Leyte. On the way, he had discovered that his bomb fuse was defective, and had landed at Legaspi to fix it. That done, he had taken off again, but the sun had set by the time he had reached Leyte Gulf and so, unable to locate any targets in the darkness, he had flown on to Cebu.

This report was made in a most casual manner and Fukabori concluded by saying that he wished to leave early in the morning to complete the task he had started. He did not look like a man just come from an abortive suicide mission and eager for another chance to end his life.

After hearing his remarks I said, "It's all right for you to crash-dive into an enemy target alone tomorrow, but would it not be better if you returned to your base and waited for a chance to make your attack in concert with other kamikaze planes?"

I wished to remind him that a kamikaze plane stood less chance of reaching a target alone than it did when flying in a small group with escorts. He sat quietly while I spoke. We both knew that it was the duty of every special attack pilot to make the utmost use of his ability. He was giving deep consideration to the matter.

When he spoke his response was soft but firm: "What you say is true, but my comrades have already made their attack. I will go tomorrow."

We said goodnight with no further attempt on my part to influence him. He must have slept soundly, for he looked rested and fresh very early next morning at the command post. I asked if he had eaten breakfast. He nodded and said, "And they have already given me a lunch. Have you had breakfast?" The casualness of his manner gave impact to these simple words. I shall never forget them.

He expressed appreciation for the hospitality of Cebu and handed me his last report for delivery to Mabalacat and Nichols Field. It was still dark when he took off in his *Suisei*, accompanied by four fighter planes.

When the fighters returned they brought only an inconclusive report. They had become separated from Fukabori's plane just before reaching Leyte Gulf and had not observed his final plunge. At about the time that his plane should have arrived over the gulf, however, they did see the sky filled with puffs of enemy ack-ack fire.

I like to think that he was successful.*

His final report was a classic of selflessness:

27 October 1944

To: (1) Commander, 701st Air Group, Nichols Field
    (2) Lieutenant Commander Ema, Mabalacat Eastern Field

Today I made an emergency landing at Legaspi, because of trouble with my bomb fuse. After it was fixed I joined my unit and proceeded to Leyte, arriving there at 1850. We circled over the gulf at 1,000 meters but the sun had set and enemy ships were not distinguishable. Heavy ack-ack fire indicated their presence. The two planes with me appeared to have plunged into enemy ships, but there was insufficient light for me to identify a worthwhile target. I therefore

---

*On 28 October 1944, the light cruiser *Denver* (CL-58) was damaged by a suicide plane in the Leyte area in position lat. 10°57′ N, long. 125°02′ E.

abandoned the attack and headed for the airfield at Cebu.

Landed safely at Cebu about 2030. It is my intention to fly from here early tomorrow morning and find a suitable target for attack. The following observations are made in the hope that they will prove of value to those who come after me.

1. The bomb fuse lock should be checked carefully before departure.

2. Loaded with one 250-kilogram bomb and four 60-kilogram bombs, a plane can cruise at 125 knots. Bearing this in mind it is essential to calculate a proper time of departure. Ship types cannot be recognized readily unless the target area is reached by 1820 at the latest. From the air it is difficult to find a target at sea, even in the brightest moonlight.

3. In a properly timed dusk attack I believe that even a Type-99 carrier dive bomber can succeed in making a special attack.

4. I recommend consideration of dawn attacks, using Cebu as a stopover base. In a dawn attack there is less chance of being caught by enemy fighters, and additional fuel in the plane will add to the destructiveness of the blow.

5. Above all, do not lose patience. Wait until conditions for attack are satisfactory. If a pilot loses patience he is apt to plunge into an unworthy target.

Naoji Fukabori

Postscript: The good faith of our pilots makes me confident that the Imperial prestige will last forever. Our pilots are young but their behavior is brilliant. There is no need to worry about selecting kamikaze pilots. I wish you the best of luck and good health. Goodbye.

PILOTS' PARTY

In such a desperate flight, with such grim tactics, what was the atmosphere at bases where the kamikaze pilots waited their turn? As a flight commander at Mabalacat and Cebu I came in contact with most of these pilots and can truthfully say that I have no recollection of gloom or depression on their part. For instance, the *sake* party episode seems typical of their attitude.

Sometime in mid-November the garrison units at Cebu made a present of a dozen bottles of *sake* to the special attack pilots. Kamikaze fliers abstained from drinking when there was any possibility of their having to sortie, but no enemy task forces had been reported in the area at that time so I ordered the gift delivered to their billet.

A messenger came to the operations room after supper with an invitation for me to attend their party. Lieutenant Kanno, who was recovering from a leg injury, was also invited and he was carried in on the shoulders of several happy pilots. The party table was laden with a variety of delicacies, and *sake* flowed freely. For a forward combat area, it was a gala affair and everyone was having a fine time.

One pilot, who was getting his share of the drinks, surprised me when he walked up and said, "When can I make a special attack? Why don't you let me go soon?"

This inspired another to join in, "I've been a member of the special attack corps from the very first, and yet later volunteers have already gone. How long must I wait?"

Momentarily I was at a loss to answer these sudden questions, until an idea suddenly came to me. "Do you recall how Japan's most loyal of all her great warriors, Masashige Kusunoki, on the eve of his last battle summoned his warrior son and told him to go home to his mother?* Sooner or later the time comes for each of us. Special attacks of one kind or another will continue until peace comes to the whole world. You fellows should think of yourselves as being among the first of many, and not complain that you are a couple of days later than someone else."

They nodded, and the first man spoke again. "Yes,

---

*This story of the 14th century warrior hero is known to every Japanese schoolboy. Therein the value of loyalty is tempered and enhanced by the virtue of patience.

I understand what you mean, but I think it would be better to be the *elder* Kusunoki."

The line of conversation changed at this point when another man asked, "Is there discrimination according to rank at Yasukuni Shrine?"*

"There is no discrimination in Yasukuni Shrine," I replied. "Precedence is determined entirely by time of arrival."

"I will outrank you then, Commander, because you will have to send out many more pilots before you can go yourself."

"Say, what shall we do with the Commander when he reports in at Yasukuni?" said another.

"Let's make him the mess sergeant!" This was greeted with roars of approving laughter.

"Can't you do better by me than that?" I pleaded.

"Well, then, perhaps mess officer," the last speaker conceded, and they all roared again.

As the evening progressed I started to leave the party. Two or three pilots followed me to the door and even outside, pleading to be chosen soon for a special attack. Some of their colleagues who heard these entreaties shouted, "Unfair! Unfair! No special favors!" And these strange words mingled with and were lost in the sounds of general good cheer that finally faded from my hearing as I walked thoughtfully to my quarters.

The new pilots who reported in as replacements for those who had successfully sortied were equally eager. There was no need to lecture them on morale. However, whether at Mabalacat or Cebu or elsewhere, newly reported kamikaze pilots would not only be given refresher talks on the important points of making an attack, but would also be briefed on the location and condition of our Philippine air bases. I would usually give these talks among the high bushes at one end of the airfield where a blackboard had been set

*Yasukuni Shrine, near the Imperial Palace, is dedicated to the heroic dead who have given their lives for the country. It is the Shinto concept that the spirits of the dead return directly to the Shrine, where they consort in eternal fellowship.

up. At times, however, the lectures would be given in a dimly lit room of the barracks. They were almost always accompanied by the roar of enemy planes overhead.

Many special attack fliers sortied on their mission the very day after joining the corps; none ever knew more than a day in advance when his time would come. Yet they studied, asked questions, and displayed intense eagerness to learn. Their whole attitude belied any aspect of solemnity or gloom. They were cheerful and pleasant in company, but matter-of-fact, sincere, and industrious about their work. They were men with a job to be done.

There were new faces and missing faces at every lecture. The instructor and the subject remained the same, but the audience constantly changed. So it was that I took notice of one listener who came time and again to the refresher talk. This was Ensign Yonosuke Iguchi, who had been transferred from the *Jimmu* Unit of the second special attack corps to the 201st Air Group. He had been navigator of a *Suisei* carrier bomber ("Judy") and was now a member of the First Kamikaze Corps.

Each time he attended my lecture he would sit at the rear of the group taking notes on all that was said. When the talk was over and the others had asked their questions, he would invariably rise with questions of his own. His numerous visits were clearly to settle points of doubt in his mind and make sure he did not miss any new things that might be brought up.

In the evening of 13 December a powerful enemy surface force was reported moving westward in Surigao Strait. It was clear that the enemy, having secured a firm footing at Tacloban, on Leyte, was ready for a new landing operation. At this sighting report the command at Mabalacat, where I was again stationed, went into action. Seven *Gekko* ("Irving") and four float bombers were in the air at dawn next morning to search for the enemy along the southern shores of Negros Island. Although all results were negative, it was decided to launch an offensive strike at the yet-unlocated enemy. Accordingly, the largest air armada since the formation of the special attack corps took off this day. It consisted of 2 *Saiun* ("Myrt") reconnaissance planes for pre-attack search, 13 Zero fighters and 23 *Shiden* ("George") for air cover, the first special at-

Kawanishi N1K1-J, <u>Shiden</u> ("George")

tack unit of 17 Zero fighters, the second unit of 3 *Suisei* ("Judy"), and a third of 6 *Ginga* ("Frances"). Two Zeros were also sent along to confirm results. Ensign Iguchi took part in this attack as commander of the second kamikaze unit of 3 *Suisei*, flying in a plane piloted by Second Class Petty Officer Takeji Takebe.

The order to take off was received simultaneously by the Zero fighter unit at the western Mabalacat field and the *Suisei* unit at the eastern field, which was 2,000 meters away from the billet and command post. A fast take-off was imperative. I recall vividly how quickly Iguchi gathered his men, boarded an automobile, and sped off toward the eastern field. The Zeros were still taking off from the nearer field when his *Suisei* unit came over in tight formation, and they all joined in heading toward the target at 0730.

The plan of the day was to search for the enemy

along Negros Island and in the Mindanao Sea, starting at Dumaguete on the southeastern end of Negros, and to attack him the moment he was found. The group had to scatter, however, when they encountered a batch of enemy fighters around Batangas, 50 miles south of Manila. Efforts to reassemble were hampered by bad weather in the target area, and the planes were unable to locate the enemy ships. They had to land at fields of opportunity that evening, and about half of them returned to base next day.

But these unfavorable circumstances had not discouraged Iguchi. Continuing to fly the scheduled course despite the weather that had thwarted the others, he radioed to base, "No enemy around Dumaguete, 1150." Thereafter it was presumed that he would put about and return, so his next report came as a shock to everyone at the base, "Bomb won't release!"

It was evident that Iguchi had pushed persistently on through the unfavorable weather in search of the enemy, without success. Having already removed the safety pin from his bomb in anticipation of making an attack, he was now trying to release the armed bomb before landing at Cebu.

Iguchi and his pilot must have struggled in every way to clear their plane of the menacing bomb. Their next message, "We will execute attack on enemy in Leyte Gulf," made it clear that the effort had failed. Another radio message, "We are over Leyte Gulf, 1225," left all of us at headquarters in prayer that they might find a good target. Iguchi's next words, "No enemy fighters in the air at 1230," were startling because we were convinced that he had already made his plunge.

His voice was amazingly calm and composed. Even without enemy fighters in the air, the opposition from antiaircraft fire must have been severe. We held our breath as the speaker intoned, "We are now diving. It is 1237. Long live the Emperor!"

As evidenced by the messages, his attitude was magnificent. More important, however, is the fact that Ensign Iguchi and pilot Takebe acted properly every step of the way. Separated from their comrades during the air battle, faced with inclement weather, unable to find the reported enemy target, and, worst of all, unable to release a live bomb, they showed no confusion. Iguchi must have made very careful studies of bad-weather flying. He knew how long his fuel would last and where to find a target. The thoroughness of his studies had paid off, and one can well believe that the achievement fulfilled all his earthly desires.

MEN AND MORALE

In analyzing the attitude of these men it must be remembered that they considered kamikaze attacks merely a part of their duty. On many occasions, I heard them express this sentiment in words such as these, "When we became soldiers we offered our lives to the Emperor. When we sortie, it is with the firm conviction that we will fulfill this offer to help defeat the enemy. We would be remiss in thinking otherwise. Therefore, 'special attack' is just a name. The tactic, while unusual in form, is just another way of performing our military obligation."

This opinion prevailed generally and it was certainly true of the 201st Air Group pilots in the Philippines. Their sorties were a routine matter. There were no theatrics or hysterics. It was all in the line of duty.

In the ordinary pattern of events a kamikaze sortie would follow soon after the sighting of an enemy task force. Let us say that a reconnaissance detects such a target at 0800. The sighting would be radioed to headquarters in Manila, where it would be relayed to an appropriate special attack base. This procedure usually took about two hours. By the time the pilots were alerted and briefed, planes readied and taking off, another two hours would have elapsed. Thus it had to be estimated that four hours would pass between the time an enemy task force was observed and a special attack was on its way to strike.

In this time situation the pilots would usually be given a box luncheon while they waited. On receipt at our base of a sighting, my own work was completely frenzied until the planes actually took off. There was no time for anything but essential work. When I would finally rush to brief the pilots before their departure, some one or another of them, seeing how busy I was, would usually offer his lunch to me.

As they awaited my briefing I would frequently hear snatches of the pilots' conversation, such as, "How about aiming for the stack of a carrier? It would probably be very effective, since a stack is lightly armored."

"Yes, but stacks are usually curved, so it is hard to hit into them."

Such talk always seemed more like a discussion of a good fishing place than an analysis of a rendezvous with death. Observing the pilots of the 201st Air Group, I was convinced that their spirit and morale epitomized all that was desirable for the task at hand.

As the special attack program got under way, everyone concerned did his utmost to insure its success. Plane mechanics were especially zealous in their devotion to duty, and they worried constantly about the mechanical condition of their charges. A poorly maintained plane was likely to fail in its mission. If it returned to base because of mechanical trouble, the pilot's discouragement was pitiful to behold. Knowing how mortified a pilot would feel in such a case, the men of the ground crews took special care to keep planes in the best possible condition. On occasion a pilot would come running to me at sortie time and implore, "Commander, engine trouble! Give me another plane!"

In such a predicament it would do no good to order another plane brought up, because the rest of the flight could not wait. I would rack my brain for a satisfactory way of telling the dispirited pilot that he must abandon thoughts of making his flight that day. "The others have already gone. It would have been impossible for you to catch them. This is sad for you for it can't be helped. Go and rest. This was an act of Divine Providence. You will have a better chance next time."

It was always pathetic to see a pilot fail to make his sortie. He would walk away and sit alone to watch his comrades fly high into the sky. No words could console him. A news correspondent told me that there is no more miserable sight on earth than such a pilot, and it was equally pitiful to see the maintenance crew of his malfunctioning plane.

The work of the maintenance men continued day and night. On one occasion I called them together to express my gratitude for the splendid work they had been doing, and advised that they relax occasionally. I reminded them that the war would continue for many months to come and that it was important for them to have rest and recreation. They replied that I need not worry about them. "We can nap in the shade of our planes' wings whenever there is nothing to do during the day," said one.

Not only did the maintenance crews work almost constantly on plane repairs and upkeep, but they also had to clear the runways of bomb and shell fragments after each enemy attack. Such fragments, if left on the runways, punctured plane tires. Since the enemy raided every day, the clean-up job was both difficult and frequent.

There was one maintenance man who made a point of meticulously scouring and polishing the cockpit of each kamikaze plane he tended. It was his theory that the cockpit was the pilot's coffin and as such it should be spotless. One recipient of this service was so pleasantly surprised that he summoned and thanked his benefactor, saying that the neatness of the plane meant a great deal to him. The maintenance man's eyes dimmed with tears, and, unable to speak, he ran along with one hand on the wing tip of the plane as it taxied for its final take-off.

When planes returned to our airfield after a mission —those that did return—they were promptly met by ground crews, who, as soon as the pilot climbed from his plane, would push and tow it to a camouflaged hiding place safe from enemy air raids. Sometimes the patching and repair work was underway before the pilot had begun to make his report at the command post. I was always amazed at the speed and enthusiasm of these men. And their eagerness to cooperate was shared by everyone at the base, including men of the supply and medical corps, who normally were not directly involved in operational activities. All pitched in to help and did their very best, just as though each were a kamikaze pilot.

One day I was invited to see a decoy plane the carpenters had built in their shop. Painted dark green, with crimson discs on the wings and on either side of the fuselage, it looked almost exactly like a Zero fighter. I dubbed this first model "Cebu Contribution No. 1," and asked the chief carpenter, "How fast can these be turned out?"

"We can make two a day," he answered.

"The Cebu branch of the Imperial Naval Airplane Factory has a monthly production capacity of 60 fighters," I announced, to the amusement of the hard-working carpenters.

Several of these dummy planes were put out on an old airstrip and partially covered with bits of leaves and grass. Enough of each was left exposed to give the impression that an effort had been made to camouflage them completely. I studied the completed work through binoculars from the veranda of the operations room, and it did look most realistic.

Meanwhile, our real planes, fully camouflaged, were hidden deep in the woods and forests, near the foot of the mountains. Even the tips of the propellers were completely concealed. The paths leading to the real hiding places were also carefully covered over so they could not be detected from the sky.

Once all these preparations had been made, everyone suddenly seemed eager for the enemy to attack. It was strange, since always before this time enemy attacks on the field had been hated and feared. The men who had built the dummy planes were especially anxious, and waited expectantly.

When an air raid warning finally sounded, I wondered briefly what part of the field the enemy would strike. Then U. S. Navy Grummans appeared over the mountains west of Cebu and there was no doubt that they would concentrate on the prepared lure. Furious strafing attacks came in time and again through our heavy antiaircraft fire. I watched from the safety of an air raid shelter and smiled at the obvious success of the decoys, feeling a detached pity for the futile risks that the enemy pilots were taking to hit these unprofitable targets.

Cans of gasoline had been placed in some of the decoys, but none of these burst into flames. Strafing was followed by bombing, and then the raid was over. Half of the dummy planes had been damaged by machine-gun fire and one was completely demolished. They had achieved their purpose.

Production of mock-ups continued, and they continued to fool the enemy. But this was no way to win a war.

FINAL OPERATIONS IN THE PHILIPPINES

BY INOGUCHI

FORMATION OF THE SECOND KAMIKAZE CORPS

With the failure of the *Sho* Operation and the loss of half of Admiral Kurita's fleet, the original purpose and goal of the special attack corps—to make possible Kurita's breakthrough into Leyte Gulf by knocking out enemy flight decks—was gone. Yet the corps and its attack method continued.

Its new objective was to cooperate with the Army in the general destruction of enemy forces, now that the chance was past for eliminating the enemy's first beachhead at Leyte. Accepting this situation, the high command decided that the enemy forces on Leyte could be opposed effectively if the defending Japanese 16th Army Division were provided with sufficient reinforcements. Accordingly, starting in November, Japanese air activities were directed toward the support of attempts to reinforce the Leyte garrison. Toward this end, Japanese planes concentrated their attacks on disrupting enemy transportation. At first, kamikaze efforts had been directed solely against aircraft carriers; it was now settled that enemy transports were also targets worthy of these attacks.

So it was that naval planes were used in support of Army efforts at reinforcement.

However, the First Air Fleet, which had no more than 50 planes even before special attacks were started, soon exhausted its strength, as did also the Second Air Fleet. Yet, despite the continuing dauntless attacks by kamikazes, enemy task forces still cruised in the waters east of the Philippines and supported the consolidation of Tacloban and the development of its air bases. It became obvious that a new enemy landing could be expected at any time.

With the heavy attrition of land-based Japanese planes in late October and early November, it was evident that further reinforcements were necessary. Every effort was expended to send south from the homeland as many planes as possible in mid-November to supplement our land-based efforts in the Philippines. However, Vice Admiral Ohnishi, as Chief of Staff of the Combined Land-based Air Force, had already been convinced that any defense based on conventional air attacks was hopeless. He made a hurried flight to Tokyo in early November to inform Imperial General Headquarters and Combined Fleet of the critical Philippines situation and to demand 300 planes as reinforcements for the special attack corps. With 300 planes he believed that the enemy's anticipated move against Luzon could be met successfully.

As a member of the Admiral's staff I accompanied him on the trip to Japan. It saddened me to note at this time what a deep toll the daily strain of war had taken of him. His health was so poor, in fact, that on his return trip he had to be carried on board the Type-1 bomber ("Betty") on a cot.

Convinced finally by the crucial war situation as much as by Admiral Ohnishi's urging, Imperial Headquarters concurred in his views, but nowhere were 300 planes available for the Philippines. Desperate efforts finally squeezed a meager 150 planes from the training centers at Ohmura, Genzan, Tsukuba, and Koh-no-Ike. These planes were manned primarily by reserve ensigns (none of whom had more than 100 hours of flight training), plus a few student trainees and instructors. They were all incorporated into the First Air Fleet, organized as a new special attack corps, and transferred to Formosa for special training.

Thus, when Admiral Ohnishi returned to the Philippines, I rode back with him only as far as Formosa, where it was my duty to arrange for the special training of the new pilots. In the organization of the Combined Land-based Air Force the supervision of special kamikaze flight training had become one of my principal duties. By the time the first units arrived in Formosa my instruction program was ready to begin at Taichu and Tainan, the designated training bases.

INDOCTRINATION AND TACTICS

The indoctrination for the new Kamikaze Corps pilots lasted seven days. The first two days were spent exclusively in take-off practice. This covered the time from the moment the order to sortie was given until the planes of a unit were airborne and assembled. During the next two days, lessons were devoted to formation flying, with a continuation of interest in take-off practice. The last three days were given primarily to the study and practice of approaching and attacking the target. But here, again, take-off and formation practice were included. Had time permitted, this whole schedule would have been run through a second time.

Two months of experience in kamikaze operations had shown that certain methods were more effective than others in achieving successful hits against the enemy. Special emphasis was placed on instruction which pointed out all possible advantages to the pilots. Some of the more important points for consideration were as follows:

Approaching the Target

For such light and speedy planes as the Zero fighter ("Zeke") and the *Suisei* carrier bomber ("Judy"), two methods of approaching for a special attack were found most effective. The approach should be made either at extremely high or extremely low altitude. Although from the standpoint of navigational accuracy and range of visibility a medium altitude was most suitable, this was ruled out by other considerations.

Yokosuka D4Y2, Suisei ("Judy")

A high altitude of 6,000 to 7,000 meters was the best for avoiding enemy fighter planes. Planes at that height are not easily visible from sea level and, although enemy radar could detect such an approach well in advance, it took time for enemy fighters to climb up within attack range. Also, the higher the altitude, the greater the difficulties of interception. Above 4,000 meters the air is rarefied, and pilots must use oxygen. At 7,000 meters a pilot's ability to fight is impaired, as vision and accuracy of judgment decrease. At this altitude any trouble with oxygen equipment may result in the pilot's blacking out and losing control of his plane. These factors made a high-altitude approach most desirable from the standpoint of evading enemy fighters.

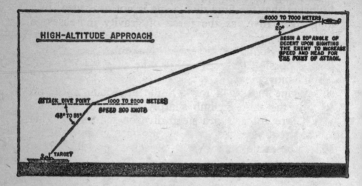

In an extremely low-altitude approach, our planes would fly close to the surface of the sea to prevent early detection by enemy radar. In late 1944, enemy radar was believed to have an effective range of about 100 miles at high altitude and less than 10 at medium or low altitude. Visual detection of our planes skimming low over the water was also difficult for the enemy's combat air patrol, so that the danger of their being intercepted was further reduced.

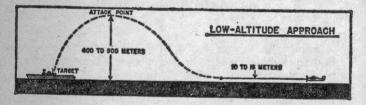

Both these methods had been used to advantage in the Philippines during October and November. When several attack units were available, both high and low approach methods were used in conjunction with varying approach courses. When the enemy target was sighted, planes of all units would converge toward the point of attack for the final run in.

Angle of Attack

In a high-altitude approach, caution must be taken to insure that the final dive angle is not too steep. In a long steep dive, as the force of gravity increases, a plane is more difficult to pilot and may go out of control. It is essential, therefore, to make the dive as shallow as possible, taking careful note of wind direction and the movement of the target.

A plane making a low-altitude approach must, on sighting the target, climb sharply to 400 or 500 meters before going into a steep dive on the target. This method requires skill on the pilot's part because the hit should be made down onto the deck of the target ship for greatest effectiveness.

As an example, one day a flight of several Zero fighters took off from Cebu, and, flying low, took a circuitous route through Surigao Strait toward Tacloban. They suddenly discovered an enemy cruiser near Dulag. One of the planes made an abrupt steep climb and an almost perpendicular plunge for a direct hit on the target's deck. The ship split in two and sank. Since this action was reported by a high-flying fighter plane, the ship attacked may have been a destroyer instead of a cruiser; but the prompt sinking proved the effectiveness of hitting the deck at a steep angle.

Point of Aim

Against carriers the best point of aim is the central elevator—or about one-third the length of the ship from the bow. Next best is either the fore or aft elevator —both being vulnerable locations—since the destruction of these sections destroys the operational effectiveness of the ship. Against other types of ships the base of the bridge, where the ship's nerve center is located, is the most desirable target. A direct hit there is almost certain to render the ship inoperational. Against destroyers, other small warships, and transports, a hit any place between the bridge and the center of the ship is usually fatal. Small warships and transports, having no deck protection, are extremely vulnerable to aerial attack. A single kamikaze plane could sink such vessels with a direct hit.

Target Selection

Had there been no shortage of planes, it would have been desirable to send four kamikazes against a large carrier, two to strike the central elevator, and one each the fore and aft elevators. In theory, two or three attackers were considered ideal against an escort carrier. In practice, however, there were too many enemy carriers, and we had too few planes available to set any such standard. Accordingly, in the hope of a telling direct hit, a single plane was usually sent against each carrier.

Emphasis was also placed on the importance of the type of target to be selected. When targets were plentiful, it was especially important that efforts be concentrated on the most valuable ones. For example, on 30 October a kamikaze unit left Cebu at 1330 to attack an enemy task force at a point distant 40 miles, bearing 150° from Suluan Island. At 1430 these planes discovered three American carriers and a battleship south-southeast of Suluan Island. Of the first group of three attacking planes, two scored direct hits on a large carrier and one hit a medium-sized carrier. After observing these hits the second group of three kamikazes plunged in. One of them hit the big carrier again, and the others hit a small carrier and the battleship. The big and medium carriers stopped dead in the water, gushing huge clouds of smoke, while the small carrier and the battleship were heavily damaged.*

This was a fine example of appropriate target selection. Every effort was made in training to achieve this kind of judgment and ability.

Take-off

In carrying out special attacks it is very important that a pilot board his plane, take off, get into formation,

---

*The *Franklin* (CV-13) and the *Belleau Wood* (CVL-24) were damaged by suicide attack this date in position lat. 10°20′ N, long. 126°40′ E.

and move toward the target with all possible speed. A properly camouflaged plane parked away from the airstrip is seldom damaged by enemy plane attacks. But once the camouflage is withdrawn and the plane is moved to take-off position, it is in clear view and as vulnerable as a sitting duck on a pond. Even after a kamikaze plane has gained the air, it is still very vulnerable to attack because its 250-kilogram bomb load prohibits radical offensive or evasive tactics. Consequently, special attack pilots were given intensive take-off training to develop speed and agility so that they could avoid interception at the critical start of their sortie.

The morale of kamikaze pilots was so high that they sometimes sortied even if the planes' engines were not functioning properly. Foolhardiness in this regard often resulted in failure to carry out the mission, or even forced landings and damage to the plane. To forestall such mischance, it was strongly impressed on the pilots that they must check and promptly report any malfunction of their craft.

In a heavily loaded take-off it is important to keep the nose of the plane from rising too soon, to manipulate the controls slowly, and to hold an altitude of 50 meters until good flying speed is achieved. Pilots were also cautioned to concentrate all their energies and attention on getting off the ground, and not to be distracted by their comrades at the time of take-off.

A final important element at the beginning of a mission is the matter of joining and keeping formation with a minimum of time and effort. To attain formation without circling, planes should be airborne at 100-meter intervals after the leader and then gradually close ranks. It was repeatedly stressed that individual planes should keep formation no matter what weather was encountered.

Navigation

Navigational training is of utmost importance if a pilot is to locate assigned destinations. Accordingly, kamikaze trainees were firmly impressed with the need for checking reference points, holding to course, and keeping track of time and distance flown in search of the enemy. But so hastily were the units of the special attack corps thrown together that much basic training had to be taken for granted.

In mid-November, for example, an enemy task force was reported to the east of Lamon Bay, and three kamikaze planes were dispatched to attack it. The following day the No. 2 plane returned to base. The pilot reported that they had arrived at the location given only to find bad weather and no enemy task force. While searching the area the planes became separated. When this particular pilot lost his mates, and was still unable to find the enemy, he flew westward in search of Luzon Island and his base. He finally sighted land and put down in the first open space he saw. It was Echague, nearly 150 miles north of Manila! The next day he flew southward, following the canyons, until he reached an air base and landed at Clark Field.

In checking this unbelievable tale it was found that the pilot had no map or chart—and no timepiece other than the rumblings of his empty stomach! Without a leader he was practically flying blind. And this was not an isolated case!

It was constantly urged that every pilot should have, in addition to an air chart, an outline map of the Philippines drawn by himself, so that he would be familiar with the general area. In the urgency and anxiety of the period such basic precautions as this were relegated to a mere hope that each pilot would take it upon himself to exercise essential care and caution. The error of such wishful thinking should have been learned and remembered from the Battle of Midway.

Bomb Safety Release

Escorting planes would sometimes report direct kamikaze hits, but no explosion on the enemy ship. This was a result of the pilot's failure to release the bomb safety before making his final plunge. Such cases were most regrettable because they meant the loss to us of an irreplaceable pilot and plane, with only negligible damage to the enemy. The individual reasons for such improvidence—thoughts of god status, concern at self-immolation, fatigue, excessive excitement, or emotionalism—we shall never know. It is likely that the pilot's very concentration on scoring a telling hit made him forget that one vital step toward his goal.

The first kamikaze pilots were instructed to release the bomb safety as soon as they were clear of land and flying over the sea. But then, if they were unable to find a target, the bomb would have to be jettisoned before they could make a safe landing back at the base. To correct this wastefulness pilots were ordered to release the bomb safety only upon sighting the enemy. Still, some pilots would forget. This practice of pulling the release upon sighting the enemy was maintained, however, and provision was made that the leader of the fighter escorts would fly close to the special attackers on nearing the target and check to see that the safety had been released in each plane. Frequently he would have to signal a reminder to a forgetful pilot.

Such was the substance of instructions given to kamikaze trainees in Formosa, in the new course that I set up. The students took to their lessons with great enthusiasm. There was no actual practice given in low-altitude approaches because the steep climb and sudden dive involved were too dangerous. But there was practice in 45- to 55-degree angle dives, using the airfield command post as a target. The pilots would come diving in at such a rate that we felt sure they would crash. It was frightening to see how close they would come, so great was their zeal in learning. Despite the short period of their indoctrination, the training was effective, and many of these Formosa-trained pilots achieved brilliant results.

MORALE IN THE NEW CORPS

There is seldom a morale problem with frontline troops who are in daily contact with the enemy. Men who have faced the chilling whine of air attack, the bomb blasts, the booming of heavy bombardments, or a machine-gun's staccato; men who have seen companions become the dead and dying victims of war; such men can readily develop the desire and maintain the will to fight and risk death. But to develop, let alone maintain, the same spirit in rear-area troops is a difficult task. It was no problem to find the spirit required for kamikaze operations among the pilots in the Philippines, who had suffered relentless enemy attacks and had seen the futility of conventional bombing efforts against the enemy. But after the failure of the *Sho* Operation new pilots as well as planes were needed in the battle theater if special attacks were to continue. The greatest problem for everyone concerned was how to instill the required aggressiveness and morale for special attacks into men fresh from flight training in the homeland.

Imperial Headquarters ordered the organization of the new special attack corps with great misgiving. Its personnel were inexperienced and its equipment was in poor condition. Of the first 150 homeland planes assigned, not more than half were actually expected to reach the Philippines. Even with skilled pilots and good equipment, in other ferrying flights from Japan an average of only 70 per cent arrived in the Philippines. On one occasion, for example, 15 fighters were promised to reinforce the Philippines sector. Their arrival was looked for daily, but no word came even of their departure from the homeland. Finally it was reported that they had taken off from Kanoya, but only 12 planes. The next information was that they were delayed in leaving Oroku in Okinawa. Ten were eventually able to continue from there. On the next hop one was forced to land at Miyako Jima and another at Ishigaki Jima, so eight reached Formosa. Though there was nothing difficult about the last leg—crossing Bashi Channel to Luzon—only five of the eight made it to Manila and landed at Nichols Field. Of these, one broke his landing gear and another damaged his tail wheel. Thus, three planes actually arrived in flyable condition. Tragic, indeed. In the light of such experience, what could be hoped for from untrained kamikaze newcomers?

Various delays were expected in obtaining the new volunteers and making necessary preparations for their transfer. The first group of 150 planes, from Genzan in Korea and from Tsukuba and Koh-no-Ike in Japan, came in short hops by way of Omura, Kanoya, and Oroku. To the surprise of all, they arrived in Formosa within seven days after being ordered. Even more surprising, of the 150 that set out, 140 planes and 148 airmen actually reached Tainan for training. Only ten planes were damaged in getting to Formosa, and only two pilots dropped out because of illness. The eight extra men had squeezed in with friends, determined to come along even though no substitute planes were then available for them.

Training of the new kamikaze candidates was completed as rapidly as possible, and each unit was rushed to the Philippines just as soon as it had finished its instruction. By early December the enemy had begun heavy bombardments of our ground positions on Ormoc Bay, on the western side of Leyte Island, and followed these shortly by landings along the bay. The focal point of our attacks was thereupon shifted from Leyte Gulf to the vicinity of Ormoc and the Camotes Sea. Despite all our efforts, however, we were unable to repel these enemy landings. And on 14 December the Americans pushed northward through the Mindanao Sea and landed on Mindoro Island, evidently in preparation for an assault on Luzon itself.

By that time my intensive training program was almost completed. I found, however, that while I had 28 pilots, there were only 13 Zero fighters left.

I gathered the pilots together and said, "Since there are just 13 planes available, only that many of you will go. We will send for the rest of you when circumstances permit."

This raised a great problem. The pilots who were scheduled to remain behind searched through all the hangars and revetments, and in the far corners of the field. They begged mechanics to put the best parts of condemned planes together into something that would fly. Many of these remnants had been sitting around for a long time. The mechanics caught the pilots' mood, and went feverishly to work, urged and inspired by the eager young men. By departure time, 12 additional planes had been thrown together, bringing the total to 25. The three extra pilots figured that they could ride along in the radio equipment spaces of three planes, and begged to be taken to the Philippines. But the clear light of day showed that the 12 jury-rigged planes would never pass a test flight, and despite the willingness of every pilot to risk flying these mended crates, only the 13 scheduled planes took off.

That these fledgling pilots managed to deliver more planes than could have been expected of more experienced men gave assurance of the high morale of the kamikaze recruits, and showed how keenly they felt their responsibility. Such spirit would seek to make possible the impossible.

With my duties on Formosa completed, now that the last planes were going south, I flew to the Philippines with the group of 13 Zeros and landed at Clark Field on the evening of 23 December. There I found that First Air Fleet headquarters had already been moved out of Manila and was located on a small hill near Bamban Air Base, at the northernmost end of Clark Field.

WITHDRAWAL TO FORMOSA

The reason for moving from Manila was that the enemy already was pushing beyond Mindoro. Enemy traffic through Surigao Strait was endless and undisturbed except for our conventional aerial attacks against warships and shipping, which were repeated almost nightly. These were largely ineffectual against the vast might of the enemy, but kamikaze planes were not substituted because they were being saved for the decisive battle which appeared inevitable and imminent at Luzon Island.

With conservation of aerial suicide forces in mind, the Japanese strategy was to move the greater part of its land forces to the north, around Baguio, leaving a few Army and Navy troops to defend Manila to the death. The northward movement had already begun.

Agreements were drawn up between the Naval Air Force and Army units at Clark Field for defense preparations. In negotiations with the Army, Rear Admiral Ushie Sugimoto, of the 26th Air Flotilla, and Captain Toshihiko Odawara, chief of staff of the First Air Fleet, represented the Navy. The latter was a famous aviation expert, a writer, and a man of high character and ability. It illustrates the extent to which the situation on Luzon had deteriorated that these two naval air authorities had to attend to matters pertaining to land warfare.

The site chosen for the defense of Clark Field was a mountain three kilometers to the west of Bamban. Positions were to be constructed in depth, starting at an elevation of about 300 meters. Admiral Ohnishi left the direction of all air operations to Admiral Fukudome, and devoted his own energies to preparing land defenses. Traveling the hazardous mountain paths, he made several trips to give personal attention and detailed orders concerning the building of the defense works. He appeared to have made up his mind to fight to the last at this place where so many young men, using the tactics he had sponsored, had flown off never to return.

At Bamban on New Year's Day 1945, everyone assembled in an open space near the air raid shelters. Standing in ranks, we bowed in the direction of the homeland and prayed reverently for the health of the Emperor. Our traditional broth with rice cakes was served to celebrate the arrival of the New Year. This was really a treat, considering our sparse food rations which had been stretched by a monotonous diet of watery soup.

That evening a festive air pervaded the operations room, where boiled sweet potatoes and yokan (sweet bean jelly) from the homeland were being served as refreshments. The yokan had been passed around and there was just one portion remaining when a message was brought in from the radio room. Admiral Ohnishi stopped the young messenger as he was about to leave and gave him the remaining bit of jelly.

When Misaka, the code chief, was making his nightly inspection, shortly afterward, he noticed a hum of excitement in the radio room. On closer look he found all ten of the young radiomen jabbering gaily as they witnessed the cutting of a small portion of sweet bean jelly into ten equal bits—one for each of them.

These young men had arrived in the last ship to reach the Philippines. They worked, half naked, for long hours each day in the radio room, which was located in a hot, unventilated air raid shelter. They were undernourished and so thin that their ribs stood out like a skeleton's.

When Misaka told of their delight with the small gift of *yokan,* our hearts went out to these boys. Facing hunger and hardship, they stood stoically by the radio equipment at all hours of the day and night. When later it came time to retreat, they marched deep into the mountains with all their heavy gear and kept on working without complaint. They were, in their own way, the equal of the men who met death by plunging into enemy warships.

That New Year's celebration was the last festive occasion we were destined to know at Bamban—or anywhere else in the Philippines. Exactly a week later the full force of the United States Navy descended on Lingayen Gulf, 100 miles to the north of Manila. For two days the guns of the most powerful navy in the world hammered the western shore of Luzon, and the planes of the innumerable U. S. carriers swept the skies overhead. On 9 January the enemy began landing operations from a force of more than 1,000 ships.

Throughout these enemy advances, from Leyte on, the planes of our special attack force continued to operate whenever possible. By the time of the Lingayen landings, however, the total Japanese air strength in the Philippines was reduced to fewer than 100 planes—a force utterly inadequate to check the progress of the enemy.

Well before the Lingayen landings, however, the ultimate outcome was plain to the Japanese high command. Decision had already been made to establish the main defense in the mountains to the north of Manila. The bulk of the troops were being moved northward, leaving only a last-ditch detail of picked men to fight to the death from street to street and house to house. Now, with our air force almost bereft of planes, decision had to be made as to the disposition of our remaining air force officers and men.

Shortly after noon on 4 January, Admiral Ohnishi summoned me to his office. Also present was Rear Admiral Tomozo Kikuchi, Chief of Staff of the Second Air Fleet.

Admiral Ohnishi came immediately to the point. "Now that there are no planes left, I am of the opinion that personnel of the Second Air Fleet should withdraw to the north and leave us of the First Air Fleet here to fight on to the last. How do you feel about that, Inoguchi?"

I considered the question, with full realization of the Admiral's responsibilities, and replied, "This area is under First Air Fleet jurisdiction, and since we are no longer capable of conducting air operations here, I believe that the First Air Fleet too should move to the north while there is still a chance."

Admiral Kikuchi had also been giving the matter deep thought. After a little hesitation, he spoke up, "I would not like to think of leaving the First Air Fleet behind. After all, our organization is still intact."

Admiral Ohnishi looked from one to the other of us. "Thank you, gentlemen. I will pass this on to Admiral Fukudome."

It was two days later before we learned the result of that interview. In the meantime the First Air Fleet was making rapid progress taking up its mountain positions for the final battles on land. The pilots, who now had little else to do, were the first to move. They marched to the mountains carrying what they could of weapons, food, and camping equipment.

On 6 January Admiral Ohnishi summoned us back to headquarters. Present this time also was First Air Fleet Chief of Staff Odawara. Admiral Ohnishi began by handing us a Combined Fleet order which had come in by way of the Southwest Area Fleet headquarters at Baguio. The substance of this order was as follows:

1. Second Air Fleet will be disbanded and its air units placed under command of First Air Fleet.
2. First Air Fleet jurisdiction will be extended to include Formosa.
3. First Air Fleet headquarters will withdraw to Formosa.
4. Pilots and superior radio technicians will be withdrawn to Formosa.
5. This order is effective 8 January 1945.

Admiral Ohnishi explained that succeeding messages had already advanced the effective date so that the order now stood for immediate execution, and he asked for our comments. When Captain Odawara seemed reluctant to speak, I said, "Admiral Ohnishi, please take your adjutant and leave at once. Captain Odawara and I can take care of things here and assist the commander of the 26th Air Flotilla."

I firmly believed that Admiral Ohnishi was the only man capable of leading the way out of the miserable situation that confronted us. When I had accompanied him to Tokyo in late November, I had recommended to friends of mine in the Personnel Bureau and the Naval General Staff that he be called to Japan at once to direct the war effort. Aerial aspects of the war were becoming increasingly dominant, and he was an air admiral to the core. At this critical juncture of the struggle he was the very man to take charge. I had said this in Tokyo and felt it even more strongly at this time. That is why I now urged him to return to the homeland and direct operations from Tokyo, where his ability could have full opportunity to be most effective.

He responded brusquely, "You know full well that I cannot act as headquarters by myself."

"Of course," I agreed, "but your staff will follow at first opportunity. Please go while you can. The fact that the execution date of this order has been steadily advanced makes it obvious that they are trying to keep you alive for further tasks."

"Victory is now impossible, even if I did return to the homeland."

"You may not win," I argued, "but you can still fight. Our forces are sadly weakened on the sea and in the air, but our submarines are still powerful."

"People would say that Ohnishi had made a hasty decision," he murmured. "Furthermore, I am not too hopeful about our preparations for land fighting, and I cannot leave someone else responsible for matters just because I do not feel confident about them."

"And how long will it take for you to get things in shape so that you will feel confident about them?" I begged.

"I need at least ten days more," he said.

"In ten days it will be impossible to get out," I protested. "And if you tried to leave ten days hence, the attempt would probably end in disgrace. You must make your decision to leave now."

"I cannot make any decision until I have talked to Rear Admiral Sugimoto and Vice Admiral Kondo.* They would be responsible for this area if I leave, so it is only fair to ask their opinion."

These talks were arranged, and at their conclusion the various units were immediately notified that all airmen who had evacuated to the mountains were to be mustered again.

The order was a difficult one to carry out. These fliers without wings had already dispersed and were scattered throughout the forest tangle over wide areas of the mountains. It amounted practically to going into the far reaches of the mountains to summon each man individually.

In addition, a serious problem of morale was involved. The number of fliers to be evacuated to Formosa was limited strictly by the number of transports available for this withdrawal effort. Accordingly, the

---

*Rear Admiral Ushie Sugimoto was commander of the 26th Air Flotilla and Vice Admiral Kazuma Kondo was chief of the Air Arsenal.

number of fliers notified had to be kept within this limit, since it was feared that general rumor of the withdrawal might cause the high spirit of the troops to break.

Despite the difficulties involved, however, the designated men were assembled at headquarters by the afternoon of the following day. I had made all arrangements for their departure to the north that evening, 7 January.

As a further result of Admiral Ohnishi's conference with Sugimoto and Kondo it was decided, at the request of these commanders, that Ohnishi and his staff would wait three days before their departure—leaving then only if the enemy had not invaded Luzon itself. Admiral Ohnishi had also agreed to leave behind two of his staff officers: Commander Miyamoto, in charge of land fighting, and Commander Yaguchi, of ordnance. When the Admiral informed me of this and ordered the necessary arrangements I objected, saying, "If we are going to leave behind two members of your staff, let us all remain. If the staff is going to leave, let us all go."

Admiral Ohnishi conferred again with Admiral Sugimoto on this last point and they reached an understanding that no members of the First Air Fleet staff would be left behind.

During the following three days, half of the pilots and staff officers started overland toward Tuguegarao, where they were to enplane for Formosa. This group, which had to fight it out with Filipino guerrilla forces on several occasions along the way, suffered great privation and hardship before reaching its destination.

It was midnight on 9 January when the rest of us bade farewell to Admiral Sugimoto on the hill at Bamban and proceeded to Clark Field, where our plane for Formosa was waiting.

We did not take off from Clark Field, however, until 0345 the next morning. Our departure was delayed for more than an hour because Admiral Ohnishi got involved in a discussion with the commander of an air group remaining at the base and was unwilling to leave until he had won his argument.

The sun was, therefore, bright in the sky by the time we reached Formosa. This was a matter of great concern, because the enemy now had complete daytime control of the air, even over Formosa, and we feared a fighter attack. To make matters worse, the island was blanketed with low-hanging clouds which made it impossible to land.

While flying back and forth in search of a break in the cloud layer, we were suddenly greeted by bursts of antiaircraft fire from the outskirts of Takao. To stay clear of this we circled wide toward the sea and tried another approach, this time very low. We were lucky to find a clearing in the clouds over Tainan and made a safe landing at Takao airfield. As we were rolling to a stop, an air raid alert was sounded, and, within five minutes after we drove away, enemy carrier planes made a heavy attack on the airfield. We had had a narrow escape.

Admiral Ohnishi later recalled this incident and remarked, "If we had been shot down at that time, we would have avoided many later difficulties."

He also thought many times of the men left behind in the Philippines, and while we were still in Formosa I once heard him say, "Some day I must parachute into the mountains around Clark Field and pay a visit to Sugimoto and his men."

PHILIPPINE EXODUS

BY NAKAJIMA

THE LAST SORTIE FROM MABALACAT

What was happening at headquarters was not always immediately known to the operating forces, but throughout November and December we at Mabalacat knew that the situation in the Philippines was rapidly deteriorating. On 23 December, when my friend Inoguchi finally flew in with a group of 13 Zeros, we knew by his presence that there would be no more reinforcements coming from Formosa.

Reinforcements to Mabalacat were always routed in just before dark, to minimize the chance of their running afoul of the enemy. Commander Tamai and I would usually be at the field to greet the new arrivals, and also to observe their landing with a critical eye.

We watched the landings of a new group from Formosa one evening and Tamai nodded approvingly.

"Such smooth landings, Nakajima! It is amazing—considering their youth and inexperience."

The ground crews were ready and waiting. They took charge just as soon as each plane stopped rolling, and stowed them in safe hiding places. The pilots themselves were brought to the command post by automobile. The leader lined his men up in front of Commander Tamai and spoke in a loud voice, full of self-assurance.

"Lieutenant Kanaya of the 201st Air Group, report-

ing in with 12 men." Then, indicating one pilot who
stood slightly apart, he concluded haughtily, "This man
is not a member of my group."

Kanaya's words and tone showed that he considered
this man an interloper. I had to smile, for the man he
mentioned was a veteran pilot of the 201st Air Group
who had just completed a special mission of bringing a
plane back to the Philippines from Formosa. I could
not help thinking how wrong Kanaya was with all his
assertiveness, but at the same time I thought that this
new "Lieutenant of Kamikazes" was a young man of
promise.

Heeding our advice about the importance of speedy
takeoffs, Kanaya spent most of each day in practice. He
would lead his men on the run from the command post
to the planes and through all the preparations for take-
off, in an effort to minimize their time in this routine.
Despite the warm weather, these exercises were conducted in full flight gear.

One day I was watching Kanaya's men at their drill,
when the air raid warning suddenly sounded, and I
saw a large formation of enemy B-24s approaching
from the east. It was too late to reach air raid shelters,
so I ordered everyone to cover. There were no foxholes
or ditches, and the bamboo groves where our planes
were hidden seemed the best place for safety.

For myself, I found a small depression about five
inches deep and lay there on my back, watching the
huge bombers come over. They approached in line
with our position, flying at about 3,000 meters. I
thought how terrible it would be if they made an accurate run on our location. Then, as all the enemy planes
released their bombs simultaneously, I realized happily
that the fall would be "over."

The veritable cloud of bombs whistling earthward
sounded like an approaching typhoon, for they were
not very far off target. There were moments of uncanny
silence until thunderous explosions from the direction
of Clark Field verified that we were safe. The enemy
planes were gone.

We crawled out of our various niches and were able

to laugh now that the tension was released. Without saying it, each pilot seemed to be thinking, "We are lucky. Until we hit the enemy, our lives are very dear. We can't afford to squander them by getting killed carelessly."

Kanaya's men continued to practice, and their timing improved. But mere improvement did not satisfy their leader, and each day the rehearsals went on.

In organizing a special attack I would ask the leader of each group to present an availability and preparedness list. From these I would make out an organization schedule for the commander. Every list submitted by Lieutenant Kanaya had his own name in top position. I explained, after making up the first list without choosing him, that if he went there would be no one to take care of the others in his group. Nevertheless, the very next time there was a call for candidates from his unit, Kanaya's name again headed the list. His every act demonstrated the true spirit of a special attacker. He was a model member of the corps.

Having consolidated his grip on Leyte and pushed a spearhead to Mindoro, the enemy moved in for the final landing assault on Luzon in early January 1945. This action called for the employment of our entire air strength, including the carefully husbanded special attack forces. But the might of the enemy was staggering. A reconnaissance plane reported, "Group of 300 enemy vessels west of Mindoro Island, course north, speed 14 knots." And this was followed by, "A second group of 700 enemy vessels sighted to the south of first group, course north, speed 12 knots."

At these reports we were amazed, shocked! Never before had we encountered such a concentration of strength. What we did not know was that *yet another group of three or four hundred enemy vessels followed after the second group that had been reported*. The waters from Mindoro to Leyte were swarming with enemy ships, and these included many heavily armed warships which bristled with antiaircraft guns to cope with our special attacks.

The alerts and advance warnings from our reconnaissance planes were valuable, of course, but they gave no indication of the enemy's actual destination. Was he planning to land at Manila, or in Lingayen Gulf? Perhaps it was Aparri in northern Luzon, whence he might hope to cut off our withdrawal from the Philippines. With all these imponderables, there was one unfortunate thing of which we were sure: our 201st Air Group had available *only 40 operational planes* to counter the operations of the overwhelming enemy.

Headquarters ordered all available planes to make an attack, stating further that any planes not operational at this time should be destroyed by fire. Thereafter, the personnel of all forces were to be considered as ground fighting troops. In compliance with this order, our 40 planes were mustered for one final attack against the enormously superior enemy.

At 1557 on 5 January 1945, Kanaya led two escort planes and 15 bomb-laden kamikazes from Mabalacat in suicide attacks on north-bound enemy ships to the west of Lubang Island. We now know that these ships were headed for Lingayen Gulf. It was reported that Kanaya's plane made a direct hit on one of them.* That was the last day of planned operations by the First Air Fleet in the Philippines. Kanaya had looked after his men well and carried out his duties to the end. His mission in life was accomplished.

So it was that the 5th of January came and passed. All operational planes had been launched. All unnecessary and unusable gear had been ordered burned. Combat infantry shoes were issued to all flight personnel. The time had arrived for us to become ground troops.

On the morning of the 6th, however, I awoke to a most surprising situation. There were five Zero planes

---

*It is impossible to determine which ship Kanaya hit, but seven U. S. Naval vessels were damaged by suicide attacks on 5 January 1945, in the Luzon area between Lubang Island and Lingayen Gulf: *Manila Bay* (CVE-61), *Savo Island* (CVE-78), *Louisville* (CA-28), *Helm* (DD-388), *Stafford* (DE-411), *Orca* (AVP-49), and *Apache* (ATF-67). None of these, however, was sunk.

on the field, ready and in flying condition! In the long months of their association the Zero had become a part of the lives of the maintenance men, and to them the order to burn the inoperable planes had been unthinkable. They had worked the whole night through, scavenging bits and parts from the various damaged hulks around the field. By dint of these arduous efforts five miraculously rejuvenated planes now stood ready to take off!

Commander Tamai reported this development to headquarters and obtained permission to send these planes on a mission. This, in fact, proved to be the last attack by the naval air arm in the Philippines. When these five planes departed, the difference between pilots and mechanics would cease to exist, as all became land fighting troops ordered to carry on the battle in the mountains. Such was the miserable strait to which our once-victorious air fleets had been brought.

Here on the field at Mabalacat, though, there was still the problem of choosing pilots for the five salvaged planes. Of the 30-odd fliers available, only five could still be special attackers. Those not chosen were doomed to miss the kamikaze opportunity for which they had volunteered.

Five planes would amount to little against the countless strength of the enemy. But these men had all earnestly sought their destinies as special attackers, and it was only fair to provide this opportunity for fulfillment. Yet because of the present alternative of land fighting in the mountains, assuring at least a slight prolongation of life, some of the men might wish to change their minds.

I was often asked by visitors to the base if it was not difficult to order the sortie of special attack pilots. Such a question was as hard to answer as the subject was hard to explain. There were many ramifications. The order to sortie, for kamikazes, was tantamount to saying, "Go out and die in battle!" If the order had been contrary to the will of the pilots, it would have been cruel beyond description, and I could no more have given it than I could have expected the men to carry it out.

In the course of the kamikaze effort there were dozens, scores—indeed hundreds—of special attack sorties launched upon my order. Neither my conscience nor the souls of those pilots could rest easy if their deed had been the product merely of command decision. In these crucial moments of the Empire, however, dire circumstances called for extreme measures, and the young pilots rose to the situation. My ordering the sorties was but a function within the system, and my presence in the system was almost as defiant of rationality as the system itself.

In view of the special circumstances now that the 201st Air Group was practically disbanding, however, instead of simply designating the day's fliers, this one time I decided to call for volunteers.

I ordered all of the pilots to assemble in front of the shelter. When they had gathered I addressed the group, reviewing our situation and explaining how the splendid work of the maintenance men had provided an additional five planes.

"These are not in first-class condition," I pointed out. "In fact, two of them cannot carry a 250-kilogram bomb, so they have each been loaded with two 30-kilogram bombs. When these planes have been dispatched, our air battle will have ended and the rest of us will join in the fight as land troops. In making plans for this last special attack I want to know your wishes."

With this I paused to give them a chance for reflection. When it was clear that they had understood my message, I continued, "Anyone who wishes to volunteer for today's sortie will raise his hand."

The words were scarcely uttered before every man had raised his arm high in the air and shouted, "Here!" as they edged forward with great eagerness. I was startled, almost overwhelmed, by this demonstration. My heart beat faster and my chest swelled with pride at the dedicated spirit of these young men. I breathed deeply and tensed my facial muscles into a scowl to keep from betraying the emotion that flooded over me.

"Since you all want so much to go, we will follow the usual procedure of selection. You are dismissed."

As I turned to enter the shelter, several of the pilots reached out to grab at my arms and sleeves saying, "Send me! Please send me! Send me!"

I wheeled about and shouted, "Everyone wants to go. Don't be so selfish!"

That silenced them, and I entered the shelter to confer with the air group commander about the composition of the final list.

We were in complete agreement as to who should lead this unit. Lieutenant Nakano had recently been hospitalized with tuberculosis in Manila. Upon his release he had said to me, "I am now recovered, but there is no telling when I may have a relapse. If this recovery were complete I could wait my turn for duty at the regular time. But if the illness returns there would be no chance for me to serve. Therefore, please send me on a mission at the earliest opportunity."

Remembering his plea, I had kept him in mind for some short-range mission that would not tax his strength. This flight would not be long, and this was the last chance. Considering all the factors, Nakano was the ideal man for leading the mission.

The four other pilots were selected purely on a basis of ability. They were Warrant Officers Goto and Taniuchi for the first unit, and Lieutenant (jg) Nakao and Warrant Officer Chihara for the second.

Enemy air raids continued all this while, so that we hardly dared risk showing our heads. Enemy ships were swarming at Lingayen Gulf, and a landing there was imminent.

In preparation for a 1645 take-off, the five planes, hidden at various points around the Mabalacat airfield, had their camouflage removed and engines warmed up. Now the training which had been practiced so enthusiastically proved valuable. The pilots moved swiftly. As the first plane started to roll, the others followed in close order.

The field was pock-marked with bomb holes, but following my hand signals, the planes were skillfully taxied to their starting places without mishap. As I waved my right hand in the signal for taking off, Lieutenant Nakano raised himself in the cockpit and shouted, "Commander Nakajima! Commander Nakajima!"

Fearing that something had gone wrong, I ran to the side of his plane to learn what troubled him. His face was wreathed in smiles as he called, "Thank you, Commander. Thank you very much!"

The simplicity of the words, the spirit of supreme dedication, robbed me of speech. I wished that I could find words appropriate to the exaltation of the moment, but no words would come. So, realizing that enemy raiders might appear at any moment and there was not an instant to lose, I wordlessly gave the signal for taking off.

Nakano's plane started forward with a roar. As the second plane passed in front of me the engine was revved down momentarily as the pilot screamed, "Commander! Commander!" I flagged him on with a vigorous wave of my arm, but through the din came back his shrieked farewell: "Thank you for choosing me!" I pretended not to hear these messages, but they tore at my heart. The scene repeated itself as each smiling pilot passed my position and I waved on the next: No. 3 . . . No. 4 . . . No. 5—each did the same as he flew off to his destiny, leaving me behind in a cloud of earthly dust.

Assembling in formation, the five circled the field and then flew to the north with the evening sun of the Philippines glistening brightly on their wings. They must have felt the fervent blessings of their earthbound comrades who stood and watched as they disappeared into the afternoon sky. . . .

These five planes broke through enemy interceptors and plunged into targets at Lingayen Gulf. An accompanying observation plane reported that one hit a battleship, another a cruiser, and the other three each struck large transports. All these direct hits were followed by terrific explosions.* The scout plane took photographs of these hits, but in the ground fighting that followed, these photographs were lost, leaving us no tangible evidence of what this valiant flight achieved.

So ended the work of the special attack corps at Mabalacat—and very shortly from all Philippine airfields. The corps had been in existence only since 20 October. Yet in that time, up until disbanding or withdrawal of the Japanese air forces from the Philippines, a total of 424 planes had sortied from Philippine bases for kamikaze attacks, and according to the best reports obtainable, they had scored the following successes:†

Type of Enemy Ship	Sunk	Damaged
Carriers	5	13
Battleships	1	3
Cruisers	5	8
Destroyers	3	1
Transports	23	34
Total	37	59

FOOT SOLDIER FOR A DAY

The reports on the last kamikazes from Mabalacat did not reach me immediately, for I had been sum-

---

*In the vicinity of Lingayen Gulf this date the U. S. minesweeper *Long* (DMS-12) was sunk; the battleships *New Mexico* (BB-40) and *California* (BB-44) were damaged, as were the cruisers *Louisville* (CA-28), *Minneapolis* (CA-36), and *Columbia* (CL-56), the destroyers *Allen M. Sumner* (DD-692), *Walke* (DD-723), and *O'Brien* (DD-725), as well as the minesweeper *Southard* (DMS-10) and the transport *Brooks* (APD-10)—all by suicide planes. There is no telling who hit what, but some of these hits must have been made by Nakano and his followers.

†Actual successes by kamikaze attacks against U. S. ships from October 1944 through January 1945 are as follows:

Type of Ship	Sunk	Damaged
Carriers (CV, CVL, CVE)	2	23
Battleships	0	5
Cruisers (CA, CL)	0	9
Destroyers	3	23
Destroyer Escorts (DE)	0	5
Transports (AP, APA, APD, LST)	5	12
Others	6	10
Total	16	87

moned to a headquarters conference at Bamban just after they had taken off. At Bamban I found that the conference was concerned with two related but independent projects. One was the study of how best to convert units of the First Air Fleet into effective land combat troops. The other was the organization of a farewell party for the Second Air Fleet upon the occasion of its withdrawal to Formosa.

As a member of the First Air Fleet I was in attendance with the leader of my group. Since my flight training at Kasumigaura air station I had spent 12 years as an aviator. Yet, with the sortie of the five planes led by Lieutenant Nakano that afternoon, my flying career had come to an end and I was to become an infantryman.

The day's discussions, which actually generated more heat than light, centered about problems quite alien to anything for which we naval aviators had either training or experience. Our concern from now on, it appeared, was to be with building defensive positions, finding out where to assign our various units, and learning how to secure weapons, ammunition, and food.

The only issue of infantry equipment that had been made was a half dozen carbines allocated for the use of sentries. In addition, a few light (7-mm.) machineguns had been dismounted from damaged planes, but the 20-mm. machineguns of the Zeros were too heavy and cumbersome to be carried away for use in our mountain positions. I was apprehensive about fighting on land, and tried hard to recall some of the basic elements we had studied at the Naval Academy 20 years before.

When the land-warfare meeting ended I went with my commanding officer to join in discussion of the other subject of the moment. Since its arrival in the Philippines a short two months before, the Second Air Fleet had tasted with us all the bitterness of war. Now we were gathered together in a small shelter cave to bid them farewell. Dishes of dried cuttlefish and cups of *sake* were arranged on long tables. The festivities got under way when Admiral Fukudome and his Second Air Fleet staff arrived.

With the food and drink went the usual exchanges of the commonplace: "Pleasant trip," "May you have success," "Good luck," "See you soon," and so on; but in our hearts we knew that this was a permanent leavetaking.

Two bombers were coming from Formosa that evening to pick up the Second Air Fleet staff officers. At the conclusion of the party there were cars waiting to take them from our mountain position to the waiting planes at Clark Field.

Word came, before our farewell party had ended, that a large convoy was west of Iba and moving northward. There was now no doubt that its destination was Lingayen Gulf.

REMOVING THE RECORDS TO FORMOSA

Commander Tamai and I were on the point of returning to our quarters shortly before midnight that evening of 6 January when a messenger brought word that Admiral Ohnishi wanted to see us. Tamai led the way through the meandering cave to the commander in chief's living space. Although I had frequently been to his office headquarters, this was my first visit to his personal rooms. The area was small but arranged in very neat order. The furnishings, consisting of a table, bed, and several chairs, were simple and plain.

When we had exchanged greetings Ohnishi asked us to be seated and began speaking in a slow, deliberate voice. "The decision has been made for our First Air Fleet to make its stand in these mountains, so that matter is settled. Yet I feel it is important that someone convey the true spirit of the special attack corps and its meaning to our people. I believe that you two men are the best qualified for this task. Since the 201st Air Group is staying in the mountains and Tamai is its commander, it would seem improper for him to do other than remain with his organization. Accordingly, I feel that you, Nakajima, should be the one to go."

This turn of events took me completely by surprise.

Until now the 201st and its men had been my whole life and I had felt that my place was with them to the end. Thus, to be suddenly confronted with the thought of parting from their company gave me many things to consider. Ohnishi peered intently at me, but I was unable to speak.

Silence seemed to compress the air of the small room as I groped for words to express my feelings. The Admiral spoke again, and his words showed that he had understood my thoughts. "I know it is difficult, Nakajima, for you to think of leaving your men. But this is no time for personal feelings. The people at home have no real idea of what the special attack corps is and what has been done. Someone must get out to tell them the truth. If you choose not to go, I will order you."

This statement left no room for equivocation, but it did not resolve my inner conflict. Still, it would be disgraceful to have to be ordered; I could do nothing but accept. The words almost choked me as they came out, "I will go and carry the message."

Admiral Ohnishi smiled. He got up from his chair, and came over and shook my hand warmly as he said, "That is fine. I will leave everything to you."

We had already evacuated the town of Mabalacat and were occupying an air raid shelter beside the airfield. I left Admiral Ohnishi and rode back to my quarters by automobile, reflecting on the importance of my mission. It was startling and no little bit frightening to think that I had been selected as the one to represent my valiant colleagues to the people at home. I alone of the First Air Fleet was chosen to escape death in the mountains of the Philippines.

It took a full day and night of steady work for me to collect all the documents and records of the special attack corps, its organization and achievements. Two complete sets of the records were prepared. One set was for me and the other would be carried out separately by Lieutenant (jg) Takeshi Shimizu, who had been picked from the remaining kamikaze pilots, to increase the chances of getting a copy of the records to safety. Two reconnaissance planes had been prepared; their revolving turrets had been removed to make space for us and the documents.

We took off from Mabalacat at dawn on 8 January amid the cheers and good wishes of our comrades. The two planes flew very low—eastward at first to avoid enemy planes presumed to be swarming in the vicinity of Lingayen Gulf, then northward along the coast and toward Formosa. The landing gear of my plane got stuck and could not be retracted, cutting down our speed greatly, and the other plane soon left us far behind.

It had been planned for each of us to follow a separate course so that one might reach the destination if the other were intercepted. But fate is a queer thing. The other plane reached Formosa far earlier than ours and was confronted by a heavy fog which covered the island. While circling and waiting for the fog to lift, the aircraft hit the side of a mountain near Takao. The pilot was killed and Shimizu was seriously injured. But by the time my plane reached Tainan the fog had lifted and we landed safely.

My own welcome, however, was as nothing compared to that which greeted the safe arrival of Admiral Ohnishi two days later. Combined Fleet headquarters indeed was as delighted as anyone, for Admiral Ohnishi was everywhere recognized as one of Japan's most capable air admirals. Personally I was overjoyed, knowing the constant danger of interception by enemy planes in every mile of the skies between Luzon and Formosa.

Upon hearing that Admiral Ohnishi's plane had landed, I rushed by car to his hillside headquarters east of Takao. Deep in his office bunker I found him already at work with his First Air Fleet staff. My friend Inoguchi greeted me with a broad grin. Even the Admiral's face lighted for a moment in a grim smile as he saw me and said, "Well, we meet once again."

I was too overcome with emotion to say anything, but I did manage to salute. The burden of the important task which had been assigned me at Bamban four days earlier—to preserve the records of the Kamikaze Corps and carry them to safety—was now lifted from my shoulders.

PART THREE

SPECIAL ATTACK UNITS IN FORMOSA

"Forward, even with only a spear"
—SAMURAI PROVERB

THE DIVINE WIND
IN FORMOSA

BY NAKAJIMA

FIRST AIR FLEET REORGANIZATION

There was plenty of work for all of us in Formosa. The initial task of the First Air Fleet after its withdrawal from the Philippines was to organize new fighting groups in the kamikaze effort.

For planes it had to draw mainly on the training aircraft which were already in Formosa; there were also a few of various types which had been successfully withdrawn from the Philippines. And that was all.

The supply of pilots was similarly limited to the ones who had been evacuated from Tuguegarao and Aparri, and those who might yet be expected to escape from the Philippines. The organizing of kamikaze groups under these circumstances was not easy, as we all soon learned. And there was no time to spare.

The war situation for Japan deteriorated as rapidly as the tempo of attacks by enemy task forces was accelerated. Imperial General Headquarters and Combined Fleet, anticipating that the next invasion attempt would be at Okinawa, deployed their main air strength in Kyushu, the southernmost of the Japanese home islands, leaving no more than 100 planes as replenishments for Formosa. Encouraging as this seemed in its small way, such replenishments would have to

135

come by way of the Ryukyu Island chain, and our hopeful prospects were dimmed by continuing and increasing enemy attacks on these islands.

Planes carrying pilots from the Philippines had to make their landings in Formosa during the sparse intervals between enemy attacks. Most of the evacuated pilots were assembled at Taichu and Tainan fields, where they trained and waited to be incorporated into the new air fleet organization.

There was a serious shortage of ground crews in Formosa but, although thought was given to the idea, it was impossible to bring out any of the skilled men we had left in the Philippines. There they remained, part of the 26th Air Flotilla, to fight as ground troops and, later, as guerrillas.

By 5 February the reorganization of the First Air Fleet was complete and all successful evacuees to Formosa were ordered into four new air groups designated as the 132nd, 133rd, 205th, and 765th. As subsequent air activity came to be centered in the vicinity of Okinawa, most of the First Air Fleet moved toward the northern part of Formosa. Some detachments were even moved to Ishigaki Jima and Miyako Jima, between Okinawa and Formosa. Beginning in April, all of them cooperated in the Okinawa campaign.

FORMATION OF THE NIITAKA UNIT

As the ferocity and intensity of enemy air attacks increased, not only from carrier task forces but now through B-29 raids from the mainland of China, the need was manifest for greater effort on our part. Reflecting the adverse war situation, a new special attack corps was organized in Formosa. In it were Zeros ("Zeke") and *Suisei* carrier bombers ("Judy") drawn from the Tainan Air Group.

The christening ceremonies of this corps took place at Tainan at 1700 on 18 January, and Admiral Ohnishi was personally in attendance. This was the first special attack corps to be formed in Formosa, and it was designated the *"Niitaka* Unit," after the Formosan mountain of that name. Admiral Ohnishi delivered a speech on this occasion, the gist of which was the same as that of the speech he had delivered almost three months before at Mabalacat. But this time he made a special point of adding, "Even if we are defeated, the noble spirit of this kamikaze attack corps will keep our homeland from ruin. Without this spirit, ruin would certainly follow defeat."

The words, "Even if we are defeated," sounded strange to us who had hitherto been thinking only in terms of winning the war. In retrospect it appears that Admiral Ohnishi's determination in continuing these superhuman tactics was directed not solely toward victory in the war, but also toward the far greater goal of perpetuating Japan, even in defeat.

After the christening ceremony, there was a small celebration. Corned beef, dried cuttlefish, and other such dishes were a rare treat for those of us who had just returned from frontline duty. There were even small portions of *sake* for all hands. It was a most pleasant party, in which the Admiral and his staff officers joined. Admiral Ohnishi poured *sake* for the newly appointed kamikaze pilots.

Following the party, I was scheduled to give the new kamikaze fliers a lecture on attack methods and various other points, but learning that movies were being shown, I announced that the lecture would be postponed. A movie was a special treat for the men, and it would do them good to relax. Shortly after returning to my room, however, I was surprised by a visit from the senior officer of the newly organized group, who asked me to please come and give the lecture as planned. My suggestion that the men would enjoy the movie and could hear the lecture at some later time fell quite flat when he responded, "We have been assigned to the special attack corps with the important mission of destroying enemy ships. Should the enemy appear tomorrow morning our sortie would have to be made without the benefit of your lecture, and we would lack confidence. All of the men are assembled in the hall and have asked to hear your lecture rather than see the movie. Will you please come and talk to us?"

Such conscientious men could not be refused, and it was with great pride in them that I consented.

I have never had such an interested and eager audience. They absorbed my every word and, at the end of the talk, had questions which went on until almost midnight. Even after I had retired the men continued to study their notes and discuss various problems among themselves until early in the morning. Their enthusiasm persisted to the very day they sortied.

THE NIITAKA UNIT SORTIES

The decision to launch an attack with the *Niitaka* Unit was made on 21 January when the First Air Fleet received a report that an enemy task force had been sighted east-southeast of southern Formosa. The unit was divided into three attack sections of the following composition:

No. 1 (from Shinko)
    Attackers: 2 *Suisei* ("Judy")
                       2 Zero ("Zeke")
    Escort: 2 Zero

No. 2 (from Taitung)
    Attackers: 2 *Suisei*
                       2 Zero
    Escort: 3 Zero

No. 3 (from Taibu)
    Attackers: 2 *Suisei*
    Escort: 2 Zero

I had placed special emphasis on two points about the sortie. One was that the assembly point after take-off should be to the north of the field, the other that flight to the assembly point should be at minimum altitude. These measures were necessary as precautions against the constant threat of enemy raids. It was essential to get the planes away from the field as quickly as possible, and by flying low they would run the least risk of being observed by the enemy. Every second would count.

Having ordered the planes to be readied, I climbed to the top of a sandbag shelter and looked about in all directions. The weather was beautiful. Scattered white clouds at 1,000 meters covered about 30 per cent of the sky. In the direction of Takao all was quiet. There was no enemy plane in sight. I gave the order for take-off.

The ground crews, who had been standing by in almost complete silence, now began scurrying over the field like so many mice, and the sudden roar of engines was intense. Everyone knew the importance of acting quickly, and despite the excitement and the anxiety at the possibility of a sudden enemy raid, each man carried out his job efficiently in bringing the planes to starting positions. Here again, practice and training were paying off.

From the top of the shelter I watched the preparation of the carrier bombers and their Zero escorts. There was no question about the fighter planes' capability for speedily gaining the air, but there was some doubt in my mind about how the *Suisei* would do. This was the first sortie of its kind for these heavier planes, and although drills and practice had been successful, I had fears that they might not measure up when the time came for an operational sortie.

Events proved my fears to be unjustified. Within three minutes after the engines were started, the first *Suisei* was lumbering toward the runway, followed promptly by a second and then a third. My surprise at this performance was accompanied by a sudden thought that the *fighters* might prove to be a delaying factor. But I was relieved to see them follow immediately. The first Zero paused for a moment at the south end of the strip, gunned its engine, and moved forward, rapidly gathering speed. The rest followed in rapid succession, disappearing to the north in a straight line, flying very low, according to plan. The take-off of the first section was perfect.

The two other sections were ready and standing by

I again scanned the horizon. No enemy planes were in sight, and our search radar still reported no contacts. I ordered both of the remaining sections to take off. When the first of these planes appeared on the runway to take to the air, I was disturbed to find it was the third section and not the second. Its planes got off nicely, however, but I was concerned about that damned second section. After an interminable delay, during which I expected enemy planes to appear at any second, the planes of the last section rolled over the field toward the runway. My relief in seeing them accelerate and get into the air at last was short-lived, for they proceeded to assemble by circling directly over the field. I was just thinking how terribly inferior this second section was, when they capped all earlier errors by flying off to the south!

But even this was a relief, for at least they were in the air and away from the field. Then the air raid alarm sounded. It is a sound that one never hears without anxiety. To the south over Takao the approaching enemy planes were tiny spots. There was a distant rattle of gunfire. I thought despairingly of the course being followed by the second section of the *Niitaka* Unit. Flying southward to skirt the mountains before heading to the east, they were almost certain to encounter the enemy. Their delayed take-off increased the hazard. There was nothing to do now but hope against hope for their safety.

Minutes after the enemy planes appeared above Takao they were swarming over the field from the south. Thundering antiaircraft fire was joined by the staccato of the enemy's machineguns. With all our planes at last safely airborne, however, the enemy attack on the field was but a brief irritation. We rested secure in the knowledge that, no matter how heavily the enemy bombed and strafed, the airfields of Formosa were unsinkable. Our prayers were all for the success of the day's attack unit.

It was a great relief to have just sent the planes off safely from the base. I sat down in the command post to have a quieting smoke while my thoughts followed the course of our kamikazes. As the minutes passed and the time approached for them to be nearing the target, my worries began anew. Concern was mingled with wishful thinking as my mind alternately created worries and then banished them. . . .

Will they locate the target? Of course! They cannot miss! Will enemy fighters intercept the attack? No, no, our planes will get through all right.

About now the attack is being completed. The escorts are on their way back. Did the attackers find their targets? Did they make hits? If they failed to find the targets, will our planes make it safely back to base?

This was a period of endless waiting. The attack objectives were some 200 miles away. The return flight alone would take an hour and a half. But time was meaningless and endless in the anxiety of waiting.

We on the ground could only wait quietly—hope—wait—pray—and wait. It was unbearable. And then in an instant endless time had passed and a lookout post reported, "Two Zeros, so and so degrees, altitude so and so meters." All that remained was to await reports that had assumed a familiar pattern.

This day, unfortunately, the report was not routine. The second section, delayed in its departure, had met enemy Grummans west of the mountains. Flying low, its planes had been greatly handicapped in the fight that followed, but the escorts had engaged the enemy while the *Suisei* flew on. As a result of the dogfight the three escorts had lost contact with the kamikaze planes and could do nothing but return to base. One plane had been so damaged in the fight that it could not land and the pilot had to parachute to safety. The pilots of the escorts were filled with remorse that they had failed to accompany the *Suisei* to the target area. There was, accordingly, no report on the results achieved by the second section of the *Niitaka* Unit.

Escort planes of the first and third sections returned shortly to base, however, with reports that direct hits had been scored on enemy carriers. One of the targets successfully attacked was identified as the American aircraft carrier *Ticonderoga*.*

A MOTHER'S REQUEST

One day early that spring a lady paid a call on the 765th Air Group, based at Kijin, in Formosa. She was met by the group commander, Captain Shogo Masuda, who learned that she was Mrs. Misao Kusanagi, the wife of a judge in the Taihoku Higher Court. She handed a muffler and a lock of hair to Captain Masuda, asking that one of the special attack pilots might carry these into battle. Her son, a student pilot, had died of illness before completing his flight training. She felt that her son's desire would be fulfilled if these mementoes of him could go into battle. A message was written on the muffler and signed with the mother's name. It read:

> *I pray for a direct hit.*
> MISAO

Captain Masuda accepted these tokens and when the special attack unit of his air group moved from Kijin to a forward base, he presented them to the leader. This group leader himself carried the mementoes when he later dived into an enemy ship.

---

*The *Ticonderoga* (CV-14) was damaged this date by suicide plane in position lat. 22°40′ N, long. 122°57′ E. Also damaged by suicide planes this date were the light carrier *Langley* (CVL-27) at lat. 22°40′ N, long. 122°51′ E, and the destroyer *Maddox* (DD-731) at lat. 23°06′ N, long. 122°43′ E.

THE TAN OPERATION

BY INOGUCHI

KAMIKAZES AT IWO JIMA

In order to gain time for the replenishment and training of our land-based air forces, it was important to delay the enemy's next advance as much as possible. Toward this end the Fifth Air Fleet, which was organized in early February, had promoted the idea of attacking the enemy's forward base at Ulithi.

Before this could be accomplished, however, the enemy moved surprisingly fast to attack the Tokyo-Yokohama area (Kanto plain). This strike strengthened our conviction that the next enemy invasion effort would be against Iwo Jima.

The Third Air Fleet, which was deployed in the Kanto area, tried to counter the enemy attack but failed to achieve any marked results with its conventional tactics. It was again painfully clear that ordinary methods of attack could not impede the enemy's advance. Third Air Fleet pilots themselves were so vociferous in their desire for a special attack corps that on 16 February Vice Admiral Kimpei Teraoka ordered the 601st Air Group commander, Captain Riichi Sugiyama, to arrange for its organization.

The 601st Air Group had been trained and scheduled to operate from carriers. The morale of its members was even better than that of ordinary groups, despite their having been under the steady strain of

143

combat. Captain Sugiyama purposely delayed his request for volunteers to allow the spirit of his pilots to react to the Kanto failure. He finally made the announcement on 18 February, and the rolls were filled immediately with eager aspirants.

The flight officer, Lieutenant Commander Shintaro Takeda, was in charge of making the selections; but when he had completed the task, a conflict arose. The men who had not been selected raised a vigorous protest and, feeling that Takeda was no one to settle their grievance, proceeded directly to Captain Sugiyama. Unselected volunteers came to him singly and in groups throughout most of the ensuing night to press their claims for consideration.

The vexation of having to soothe these pilots merely added to Captain Sugiyama's other worries. He had reserved to himself the choice of a leader for this special attack unit, and there were complications enough in that. The choice came to be between Lieutenant Murakawa, who commanded the carrier bombers, and Lieutenant Hida. The former claimed priority because his bombers comprised the largest group of available planes, and Hida's claim to preference was based on his seniority. Neither would give way. The selection was finally made in favor of Murakawa, and Hida was disconsolate until Captain Sugiyama calmed him with the promise, "In the present situation you will certainly have another opportunity to go."

Mitate Unit No. 2 was christened on 19 February by Almiral Teraoka. It consisted of 32 planes organized into five groups:

> No. 1: 4 fighters, 4 carrier bombers
> No. 2: 4 fighters, 4 carrier bombers
> No. 3: 4 fighters, 4 carrier bombers
> No. 4: 4 carrier torpedo-bombers
> No. 5: 4 torpedo-bombers

Early in the morning of 21 February these groups took off from their base at Katori, refueled at Hachijo Jima and then launched attacks on enemy vessels around Iwo Jima and in the waters east of Chichi Jima. Reports received that evening indicated that one United States carrier and four transports had been sunk, and another carrier and four other warships damaged. After the war it was learned from an announcement by the United States Navy that the escort carrier *Bismarck Sea* had been sunk that date by kamikaze attack.*

It was a notable feature of these actions that several of the escorting fighters themselves tried to make ramming attacks after they had completed their escort mission. It is also notable that the leader of Group No. 2, Lieutenant (jg) Iijima, and the leader of Group No. 5, Lieutenant (jg) Sakuraba, both found at Hachijo Jima that their planes had developed engine trouble. Undaunted, they transferred to other planes and went on to fulfill their mission, Iijima was reported to have crashed into a transport, and Sakuraba to have plunged into a *Saratoga*-class carrier. There was no question about the morale of the 601st Air Group.

THE AZUSA UNIT ATTACKS ULITHI

The over-all picture of the war, however, was darkening relentlessly for Japan. The land battle at Iwo Jima was unfavorable to us from the very beginning. After prolonged off-shore bombardment by the United States Navy and days of fierce bombing and strafing by enemy planes, the island was invaded on 19 February. The Japanese garrison force put up a furious and desperate resistance but, overwhelmed by superior numbers and weapons, they were finally annihilated, and the island was secured by the enemy on 16 March. As early as 6 March the enemy had occupied and was using the Iwo airfields.

When enemy task forces had completed their support of the action at Iwo, they moved off to the south,

---

*The *Bismarck Sea* (CVE-95) sank in lat. 24°36′ N, long. 141°48′ E. Also damaged in the vicinity of Iwo Jima this date by suicide attack were the carrier *Saratoga* (CV-3), the escort carrier *Lunga Point* (CVE-94), the net cargo ship *Keokuk* (AKN-4), *LST-477*, and *LST-809*.

and subsequent radio intelligence seemed to indicate that they had retired to Ulithi. A *Saiun* plane ("Myrt")

Nakajima C6N1, Saiun ("Myrt")

of the Fourth Fleet, flying a reconnaissance mission from Truk, confirmed on 9 March that enemy task forces actually were anchored at Ulithi. Upon receipt of this information it was decided to launch our long-planned *Tan* Operation. The objective of this effort was to destroy enemy warships at their base. An order was issued directing the attack for 10 March and outlining the following procedure:

1. One flying boat will leave Kagoshima Bay at 0300 for weather reconnaissance along a course from Cape Sata, via Okinotori Shima, to Ulithi.
2. Four land-based bombers will leave Kanoya at 0430 and patrol in advance of the main force.
3. Four flying boats will leave Kagoshima by 0730 to guide the main force to Ulithi.
4. The main force of 24 *Ginga* bombers ("Frances") will join the guide planes over Cape Sata and proceed to Ulithi to carry out special attacks against enemy surface craft. Each plane will carry one 800-kilogram bomb.

The *Azusa* Special Attack Unit, as the new organization was christened, sortied on 10 March according to plan, but was recalled to the base because of a sudden message from Truk. This message purported to give the results of a photo-reconnaissance made the previous day, showing that only one enemy carrier was then present at Ulithi.

Only after the *Azusa* Unit had returned to base was an amplifying message received which showed that the U. S. Navy actually had *eight* carriers and *seven* escort carriers at Ulithi. It was then too late to resume the operation that day. On the 11th, however, the unit rendezvoused with the guide planes over Cape Sata at 0920 and again proceeded to the attack.

The early morning of 11 March was clear, but rain squalls developed in the vicinity of Okinotori Shima, and our attack planes had to climb above the weather. They descended through the clouds in the estimated vicinity of their target, but failed even to sight the atoll. The *Gingas* separated from the guide planes around 1830, shortly after which they sighted Yap, some 20 miles to the east, and thus were able to set a proper course for their goal.

The sun had set at 1852 and Ulithi was already dark when the kamikaze planes drew near. Their delay in reaching the atoll was caused not only by the navigational error, but also by a head wind which greatly reduced the planes' speed. Of the 24 *Gingas* which had sortied that morning, 13 developed engine trouble on the way and had to drop out. Most of these cripples were fortunate enough to make safe landings on islands along the way, but two had to be ditched in the sea. The remaining 11 now made an undetected approach on targets that were not blacked out until our first plane went into its final plunge at 1905. By 1930 all 11 planes had dived at enemy targets. Because there were no escort planes to observe the results, it was not known whether any hits were made.

Next day, 12 March, a *Saiun* reconnaissance plane from Truk confirmed that there were no damaged carriers in the anchorage at Ulithi. It was evident that this attack had failed.*

---

*Not entirely. The U. S. carrier *Randolph* (CV-15) was hit and damaged by kamikaze at Ulithi on 11 March 1945.

PART FOUR

THE ISLANDS
OF JAPAN

"Speak of next year and the devil laughs"
—JAPANESE PROVERB

來年の事を言へば鬼が笑ふ

THE WAR NEARS JAPAN

BY NAKAJIMA

LAST-DITCH PREPARATIONS

By early 1945 Japan's military leaders were faced with the fateful problem of how to check the enemy's relentless advance toward the homeland. With the fall of Iwo Jima and the seizure of the Philippines, the main islands of Japan were cut off from the resources of the southern regions—Malaya, Borneo, Sumatra— and the way was open for the enemy to select his next point of invasion. Where would he strike? Would it be Formosa? Okinawa? The south coast of China? Imperial General Headquarters and Combined Fleet were in general agreement that the next enemy attack would probably be aimed at Okinawa, in the Ryukyu Islands, where vigorous defensive preparations had been underway since early January.

Because Japan's navy had lost much of its surface strength in June at the Marianas sea battle and most of the remainder in October at Leyte, it was no longer possible to challenge the enemy in an ordinary naval engagement. Our only hope was to defend the homeland, and our only chance of doing this lay with land-based air forces.

On 11 February 1945 all of the Navy's air fleets were reorganized with a view toward increasing the strength of the air arm. From Third Air Fleet came the 25th Air Flotilla and other units, which were merged with Combined Fleet's 12th Air Flotilla. These were formed into the Fifth Air Fleet and disposed in Kyushu to cope with prospective enemy landings at Okinawa.

Another grouping, the Tenth Air Fleet, was made on 1 March out of the 11th, 12th, and 13th Combined Air Groups, which were all training in the homeland. This new organization was established as a reserve component of the Fifth Air Fleet. The remainder of the Third Air Fleet was deployed for the most part in the Kanto plain to guard the eastern approaches to central Japan.

By early March 1945, Japan's naval air strength and dispositions were as follows:

Air Fleet	No. of Planes	Deployment
First	300	Formosa
Third	800	Tokyo area
Fifth	600	Kyushu
Tenth	400	Honshu
	2,100	

These 2,100 planes presented an impressive total—but such pilots and crews as were available to man them were sadly lacking in training and experience. They were not really ready for battle; in fact, the Tenth Air Fleet was still undergoing basic training. With the enemy's next major offensive expected in early April, it was clearly evident that there was little chance for orthodox aerial tactics to be successful.

The First Air Fleet in Formosa had been concentrating on special attack methods ever since its withdrawal from the Philippines. Imperial General Headquarters in Tokyo now sent word to the Fifth and Tenth Air Fleets that there was no longer any alternative to general use of special attacks, in which even inexperienced pilots could score a hit. It was decided to employ the better-trained Fifth Air Fleet against enemy task forces, and the Tenth against transports and smaller vessels.

OHKA ("BAKA") BOMBS

In addition to the kind of special attacks begun in the Philippines in October 1944, there was ready for Okinawa another sort of kamikaze whose origin lay in events of the preceding summer.

On 19 June 1944 Vice Admiral Shigeru Fukudome, Commander of the Second Air Fleet, had been inspecting the airfield of the 341st Air Group at Tateyama, southeast of Tokyo. Captain Motoharu Okamura, commander of the 341st, took this opportunity to urge some of his views upon the Admiral. "In our present situation I firmly believe that the only way to swing the war in our favor is to resort to crash-dive attacks with our planes. There is no other way. There will be more than enough volunteers for this chance to save our country, and I would like to command such an operation. Provide me with 300 planes and I will turn the tide of war."

Captain Okamura had been closely connected with naval aviation ever since completing his flight training in 1925. It was natural in these critical circumstances for him to think that only fliers could save the country, and he was convinced that there was no alternative to this last desperate tactic.

Four days earlier the enemy had invaded Saipan, in the Marianas, where at that very moment there was fierce land fighting, while our carrier forces were about to be engaged in the waters to the west. This string of islands constituted the key position in Japan's shrinking ring of outer defenses in the western Pacific, and it appeared that they could not hold out long.

To Okamura's fervent recommendation Admiral Fukudome had replied, "I can do nothing with your suggestion but convey it to headquarters when I return to Tokyo."

A few days later Fukudome had met with Vice Admiral Seiichi Ito, Vice Chief of the Naval General Staff in Tokyo, and told him of Okamura's views. He added that since this idea was being widely and seriously discussed by air units at the front, it would be well for the high command to give it earnest consideration.

"I will relate Okamura's view to the Chief of the Naval General Staff," Ito responded, "but I personally think that the time is not yet right for such extreme tactics."

The Marianas Islands fell, one after the other, and Japan's situation had become increasingly worse. Each defeat and setback strengthened Okamura's determination that crash attacks by our planes were the only solution. He had continued to push his recommendations to that effect, directly and indirectly, through channels and out of channels, until a study of his proposal was finally undertaken in August of 1944.

During that same summer Ensign Ohta, an aviator who was engaged in flying transport missions to Rabaul, invented a piloted rocket-driven projectile which could be loaded beneath a Type-1 land bomber ("Betty"). The aviation research department of Tokyo Imperial University helped him in drawing the plans, which were submitted to the Naval Aeronautical Depot at Yokosuka. So it was that both the tactical concept of special attacks and a new type of ordnance designed specifically for such peculiar missions had been thought of and submitted for consideration at about the same time.

As a result of official studies the Navy High Command and the Aeronautical Department decided to adopt Ohta's design. Experiments were conducted with all possible speed, and this projectile, afterward named *Ohka* ("cherry blossom"), had been put into production in late 1944. It was kept secret from everyone, however, even within high naval circles, except for the limited few who were directly concerned with the project. I first heard of this craft only on my return to Japan after being transferred from Formosa, and did not actually see one until April 1945, upon my transfer to the 721st Air Group.

Captain Okamura had been given command of this unit in September 1944. It was his mission to establish a special attack unit at Koh-no-Ike air base, northeast of Tokyo. He had set immediately to work, and pilot training was started at once. Practice and training continued even though the 721st was transferred to Kanoya when the air fleets were reorganized.

The *Ohka,* a small single-seated wooden craft, contained 1,800 kilograms of explosives. Carried to within 20,000 meters of the target by a twin-engined bomber, it would then be released to plummet toward its goal, accelerated by blasts of its five rockets. From 6,000 meters' altitude it had a range of 30,000 meters. The *Ohka* pilot would ride in the mother bomber until the action area was approached. He would then climb through the bomb bay of the mother plane into the narrow cockpit of the bomb. When enemy targets had been verified and their position made known to the pilot, he would signal his readiness to the crew in the bomber; he would pull the release handle and would be on his way in this missile of destruction, only minutes from the target. Once the release handle was pulled it became a one-way ride for the *Ohka* pilot. When this weapon became known to the Americans, they gave it the derisive name of *"Baka"* ("foolish") bomb.

In a moment of sudden emergency it is not so difficult to make up one's mind to die. But it must have been agony for the young men who were chosen to train and study for *Ohka* special attacks, because it was more than six months after the training started before even the first of them got a chance to die in battle. They were carefully selected from throughout the air force, and all were well qualified. These men were especially well prepared during their long training period. They proved to be just as dependable and capable about their duty as the kamikaze pilots who gave their lives in the Philippines.

THE OPENING SORTIES

The Allied invasion of Okinawa was heralded by American task force assaults against Shikoku, Kyushu, and western Honshu on 19 and 20 March. About 50 special attack planes rose to meet this challenge on the first day and damaged four enemy carriers (the *Enter-*

prise, Yorktown, Intrepid, and *Franklin**). Our interceptors also claimed to have shot down several dozens of enemy planes. Our own losses at Kanoya and other air and naval bases were heavy.

On 20 March a special attack unit of 20 *Suisei* bombers ("Judy") struck at the enemy and was reported to have damaged an *Essex*-class carrier and set fire to one of the *Saratoga* class.† At dawn of 21 March a reconnaissance plane spotted three enemy carriers southeast of Kyushu. They were reported to be off the southeastern tip of Kyushu, in position 320 miles, bearing 145° from Toizaki, with no protective planes overhead. This last made it seem that these were warships damaged by our fierce attacks of the preceding two days.

Vice Admiral Matome Ugaki, Fifth Air Fleet commander, took this sighting as a welcome opportunity for using *Ohka* in special attacks. All available fighter planes were accordingly ordered up immediately to escort the attack force. In spite of all his eagerness and conviction that *Ohka* could do the job, however, Captain Okamura had always been apprehensive about an insufficiency of fighter escorts. He realized that the bombers, slow enough at best, would be slower than usual when loaded with the heavy *Ohka* and would need a powerful escort in order to reach the target area.

When the order was issued calling for the *Ohka* planes to sortie, Captain Okamura ran to the headquarters operations room, highly troubled, and said, "Can't we have more fighter escorts?"

Ugaki's Chief of Staff, Rear Admiral Toshiyuki Yokoi, explained, "All fighters of the 201st Air

---

*The U. S. carriers *Essex* (CV-9), *Franklin* (CV-13), and *Wasp* (CV-18) were all damaged on 19 March off Shikoku and Kyushu, but not by kamikazes. The *Essex* was accidentally hit by friendly naval gunfire, the other two by conventional aerial attacks.

†The *Enterprise* (CV-6) was the only U. S. carrier damaged this date, and that damage was caused by friendly naval gunfire. But suicide planes did damage the destroyer *Halsey Powell* (DD-686) at lat. 30°27′ N, long. 134°28′ E, and the submarine *Devilfish* (SS-292) at lat. 25°36′ N, long. 137°30′ E.

Group* have been ordered to cover the attack force. As it turns out, that group has been hit hard lately, but it can muster 55 planes."

"Can't you send more?" inquired Okamura. "I do not think it is enough."

"There is no alternative then," said Yokoi, "but to cancel the attack." He turned to the air fleet commander and said, "Admiral Ugaki, you have heard the situation. Shall we call it off?"

Admiral Ugaki, who had been in the operations room constantly since the start of the enemy attacks on 18 March, rose from his chair and patted Okamura's shoulder as he replied, "If the *Ohka* cannot be used in the present situation, there will never be another chance for using it."

Captain Okamura winced perceptibly and a flash of bitter resignation crossed his face as he said, "We are ready to launch the attack, sir." With these words he excused himself and left the room.

The certain-death aspect of an *Ohka* mission was obvious, but it was heartbreaking for Okamura to think of sending his men on an assignment which he felt to be hopeless and useless, and thus have them killed for nothing. It was his desire that their death be not only heroic, but worthwhile as well, so that their deed would be remembered forever.

Veteran pilot that he was, Captain Okamura was fully aware of the remarkable capabilities of the enemy's Grumman fighter. He knew that 55 Japanese fighters of limited skill and ability would be no match for such interceptors. Upon leaving the operations room he resolved to lead the difficult mission himself.

The attack force consisted of 18 bombers, all but two of which were loaded with *Ohka*. The scheduled flight leader was Lieutenant Commander Goro Nonaka, a capable flier and a veteran leader of torpedo bombers. He was a hard-driving man who placed great

---

*This was a newly organized group, entirely different from the earlier 201st in the Philippines.

emphasis on the traditional samurai spirit. At the same time, he was always thoughtful of his men. They were a congenial group united and loyal, happy and proud to follow their leader even unto death.

Take-off preparations were already underway when Lieutenant Kai, one of the younger officers, confronted Nonaka with a request to take his place in leading the attack. Kai was well aware of the dangers involved in this day's work and wanted to sacrifice his own life in place of Nonaka's. The younger man's sentiment was appreciated, but Nonaka, completely dedicated to his task, brushed Kai aside and paid no more attention to his entreaties.

It was at this moment that Captain Okamura approached and said, "Nonaka, I am going to lead the attack today."

Nonaka saw immediately the intention of his senior officer, and forgetting his customary respect, he shouted angrily, "Is it, sir, that you lack confidence in me? This is one time I refuse to obey your order."

With these words Okamura felt something deep in his heart and knew that Nonaka could not be deprived of leading this mission.

The stirring sound of sortie preparations filled the air. Flight crews ran to assemble in front of the command post. Nonaka stood erect before the group as Lieutenant Iguchi, the senior *Ohka* pilot, approached him and reverently said, "Commander, I pray for your success this day."

Iguchi had not been chosen for the day's flight. Instead, Lieutenant Kentaro Mihashi had been selected as lead *Ohka* pilot, though he was actually junior to Iguchi.

The order was given to prepare for take-off, and all bomber crews hurried to their planes. Mihashi and Iguchi embraced and exchanged their last words, the latter saying, "Be sure to do a good job."

Mihashi laughed and replied, "Don't worry about this sortie. You take care of the next one!"

The *Ohka* pilots were all shouting their thanks and farewells and running toward the mother planes of their own craft. Nonaka smiled as he spoke his last words, "This is Minatogawa,"* and hurried to his plane. Admiral Ugaki stood beside the command post for the take-off. There were tears in his eyes as he watched the sortie of the *Ohkas*.

At 1135 the bombers began taking to the air in rapid succession, Nonaka's plane leading the way. The *hachimaki* (white cloth wrapping) around each pilot's helmet was conspicuous and impressive to the spectators, who waved sad farewells.

Fastening the hachimaki

Of the 55 escorting fighter planes assigned to this mission, only 30 fulfilled their duty. Some could not even take off, while others were forced to turn back along the way because of engine trouble. In the meantime, further sighting reports by reconnaissance planes revealed to Fifth Air Fleet headquarters that the enemy force was divided into groups containing three,

---

*This refers to the shrine of that name at Kobe, erected to Masashige Kusunoki, the 14th century patriot, who said before his death, *"Shichisei hokoku!"* "Would that I had seven lives to give for my country!"

two, and two carriers, respectively. The enemy force was headed to the southwest and was considerably more powerful than originally reported.

With such news as this, the chances for success in the day's mission became increasingly doubtful. There were suggestions that the whole flight should be called back, but Admiral Ugaki was firmly determined that it continue. The entire headquarters staff waited anxiously for a report that the enemy had been sighted, but there was no word from our planes, and officers and men grew restive. The time came and passed when the planes should have reached their targets. The silence at headquarters was broken only by the sound of the wall clock's effort to measure endless time. If our planes were not yet heading back to base, their fuel supply must now be dangerously low.

As anxiety and apprehension mounted, Captain Okamura was heard to say, "What has happened?"

The only answer was a troubled and painful silence.

A message was radioed to the attack force, and we all listened to the hopeful words, "If no enemy is sighted, proceed to Marcus Island." There was nothing to do but wait, and nerves wore thin in the suspense.

A small element of escorting fighters finally returned to base bringing the distressing story of what had befallen our force. It had been attacked at 1400 by about 50 Grumman fighters at a point estimated to be 50 to 60 miles short of the enemy warships. Our escorting fighters had tried desperately but vainly to drive off the interceptors, who concentrated their efforts on the *Ohka*-carrying bombers.

These heavy planes, powerless to evade or fight back effectively, had to jettison their *Ohka* burden (the pilot remaining in the mother craft) in order to lighten their load and to increase maneuverability. Enemy planes darted in and out of the formation, riddling it with a deadly hail of bullets, until the rear bomber spurted flames. The fire spread until the huge plane spun into the sea, trailing a thin finger of smoke to mark for the moment its final landing place.

In quick succession, then, 14 more of our bombers

were shot down as the escorts fought unsuccessfully to protect them. Pilots of the stricken planes in turn waved a final salute to Nonaka as they broke formation. When only Nonaka's and two other bombers remained, the three of them managed to dive into a cloud bank, but they were never heard of again.

Grumman F4F Wildcat

Thus, after six months of intensive training, did this effort come to nought but suicide and failure. The general grief at this failure and defeat was beyond expression. Lieutenant Commander Nonaka's farewell words were brought to mind at sight of his unit's *HI RI HO KEN TEN** pennant flown at the Kanoya base to memorialize this ill-fated mission.

OKINAWA LAND FIGHTING

On 25 March, American forces began landing on Kerama Retto, 15 miles west of Okinawa, and con-

---

*This is the *on* or Chinese reading of the five ideographs on the pennant. Their literal meanings are, respectively: Injustice, Principle, Law, Power, Heaven. They represent the syllogistic philosophy, and a favorite saying of Masashige Kusunoki.

HI wa RI ni katazu,	Injustice cannot conquer Principle,
RI wa HO ni katazu,	Principle cannot conquer Law,
HO wa KEN ni katazu,	Law cannot conquer Power,
KEN wa TEN ni katazu.	Power cannot conquer Heaven.

solidated their first foothold in this island chain. Accordingly, on the following day *Ten* Operation No. 1 (for the defense of Okinawa) was ordered with the hope that it would succeed in crushing the Allied invasion.

The Third and Tenth Air Fleets were placed under operational control of the Fifth Air Fleet in western Japan. With this move the commander of the Fifth Air Fleet could muster the entire air strength of the Japanese Navy against an enemy attempt to invade Okinawa.

The outlying island of Kamiyama was occupied by the enemy on the last day of March while his relentless naval bombardment and air attacks on the main island, which had started six days before, continued. This was followed by landings in Okinawa proper on 1 April, for which the enemy had amassed more than 1,400 surface vessels of all types, carrying four Army and two Marine divisions for the assault. These invasion troops numbered 100,000 men, backed up by powerful task forces and a floating reserve of another 50,000 troops.

The defending force consisted of two divisions and two mixed brigades of the 32nd Army, commanded by Lieutenant General Mitsuru Ushijima. There were, in addition, some naval garrison troops under Rear Admiral Minoru Ota, plus Captain Tanamachi's Nansei Shoto Air Group, which together numbered another 7,000 men. The defenders fought desperately and inflicted heavy damage on the invaders, but were gradually pushed back to the hills in the southern part of the island.

Admiral Ota's naval troops made a final charge on 13 June against the forces which had landed in the vicinity of Oroku. Nothing more is known of Ota and his men. The last message received from him had been sent on 6 June:

More than two months have passed since we engaged the invaders. In complete unity and harmony with the Army, we have made every effort to crush the enemy.

Despite our efforts the battle is going against us. My own troops are at a disadvantage since all available heavy guns and four crack battalions of naval landing forces were allocated to Army command. Also, enemy equipment is greatly superior to our own.

I tender herewith my deepest apology to the Emperor for my failure to better defend the Empire, the grave task with which I was entrusted.

The troops under my command have fought gallantly, in the finest tradition of the Japanese Navy. Fierce bombing and bombardments may deform the mountains of Okinawa but cannot alter the loyal spirit of our men. We hope and pray for the perpetuation of the Empire and gladly give our lives for that goal.

To the Navy Minister and all my superior officers I tender my sincerest appreciation and gratitude for their kindness of many years. At the same time, I earnestly beg you to give thoughtful consideration to the families of my men who fall at this outpost as soldiers of the Emperor.

With my officers and men I give three cheers for the Emperor and pray for the everlasting peace of the Empire.

Though my body decay in remote Okinawa,
My spirit will persist in defense of the homeland.

Minoru Ota
Naval Commander

The loyal determination of an isolated air unit, the 931st, was likewise voiced in the final message sent by its commanding officer on 10 June:

My men are in high spirits and fighting gallantly. We pray for the final victory of the motherland.

We will fight to the last man in defense of this outpost.

My contact ends with this message.

Captain Jiro Haneda
931st Air Group Detachment

Around 16 June the enemy succeeded in penetrating the main defense positions of the Army in the south. General Ushijima rallied all his forces for a last offensive, and finally broke off communications with the following message:

> With a burning desire to destroy the arrogant enemy, the men in my command have fought the invaders for almost three months. We have failed to crush the enemy, despite our death-defying resistance, and now we are doomed.
>
> Since taking over this island our forces have, with the devoted support of the local population, exerted every effort to build up defenses. Since the enemy landing, our air and land forces, working in concert, have done everything possible to defend the island.
>
> To my great regret we are no longer able to continue the fight. For this failure I tender deepest apologies to the Emperor and the people of the homeland. We will make one final charge to kill as many of the enemy as possible. I pray for the souls of men killed in battle and for the prosperity of the Imperial Family.
>
> Death will not quell the desire of my spirit to defend the homeland.
>
> With deepest appreciation of the kindness and cooperation of my superiors and my colleagues in arms, I bid farewell to all of you forever.
>
> Mitsuru Ushijima

There was a poetic postscript to his letter:

> *Green grass dies in the islands without waiting for fall,*
> *But it will be reborn verdant in the springtime of the homeland.*
> *Weapons exhausted, our blood will bathe the earth, but the spirit will survive;*
> *Our spirits will return to protect the motherland.*

HOMELAND
SPECIAL ATTACK UNITS

BY NAKAJIMA

KIKUSUI OPERATIONS AT OKINAWA

As we have seen, planned kamikaze tactics had their beginning in the Philippines in October 1944, and those efforts, while desultory, were so effective in damaging enemy surface forces that the Japanese high command became convinced that only kamikaze tactics could halt the enemy's advance. In the Okinawa operations, for the first time, the suicide efforts of the Navy's air fleets and of Army air forces were coordinated.

This coordination resulted in a series of attacks, designated "*Kikusui*," of which there were ten between 6 April and 22 June 1945. (See next page.)

These general air offensives were conducted with planes of all kinds. The flights were launched by day and by night, and this series accounted for the heaviest of all kamikaze-inflicted damage against the enemy.

LIEUTENANT DOHI'S SUCCESSFUL
OHKA ATTACK

The enemy had already landed at Okinawa when, in early April 1945, I was assigned to Captain Okamura's group near Kanoya, in southern Kyushu. After checking in with fleet headquarters, an air raid shelter in the suburbs, I went directly to Captain Okamura's camp. It was located on the western side of the airfield, and

I was struck by the terrible conditions that existed there.

Kikusui No.	Date	Planes Navy	Planes Army	Total*	Results in Enemy Ships Sunk	Results in Enemy Ships Damaged
1	6– 7 April	230	125	355	4	24
2	12–13 April	125	60	185	1	14
3	15–16 April	120	45	165	1	9
4	27–28 April	65	50	115	0	9
5	3– 4 May	75	50	125	3	14
6	10–11 May	70	80	150	0	5
7	24–25 May	65	100	165	1	9
8	27–28 May	60	50	110	1	6
9	3– 7 June	20	30	50	0	7
10	21–22 June	30	15	45	0	5
	Total	860	605	1,465	11	102

There had been little opportunity to prepare accommodations because of the great and sudden influx of troops to Kyushu as a result of the enemy's invasion of Okinawa. Here the fliers were billeted in a primary school building which must have been half a century old. The window panes had all been destroyed as a result of air attacks, and the sky showed through holes in the roof. The men had to sleep on a plain wooden floor, and the whole place was indescribably filthy.

I had experienced frontline conditions at Rabaul, New Guinea, and in the Philippines, but this homeland billet of the 721st Air Group was the worst I had ever seen. My first night there was sleepless and miserable. The one blanket provided gave no protection against the cold wind which scattered delicate cherry blossoms throughout the wretched building. It seemed to me that a billet for special attackers could be made more comfortable, no matter how humble it had to be.

---

*The United States Strategic Bombing Survey's Report, *The Campaigns of the Pacific War*, p. 328, mentions a report by the Commander in Chief, U. S. Pacific Fleet, that 26 ships were sunk and 164 damaged by suicide attacks during this period, but this count must include, in addition to *Kikusui* successes, the victims of sporadic, small-scale suicide efforts which occupied another 200 Army and Navy planes.

Next morning I called in Lieutenant (jg) Saburo Dohi and instructed him to organize a work detail for improving conditions in the living quarters. Dohi, a graduate of a normal school in Osaka, belonged to an *Ohka* special attack unit which was subject to sortie at any moment. He set promptly to work, getting from the supply and construction units what assistance they could give. Holes were patched, giving better protection from the weather, and straw mats were collected to provide a little sleeping comfort.

I was surprised one day to find that Dohi had rallied a group of junior officer pilots and had them hard at work mopping the floor. I stood watching them for a while, admiring their industry, and when I complimented them, one answered, "Well, it sure was dirty. The only way to get it clean is to clean it."

Dohi continued to acquire straw mats and he even got a few bamboo beds. These were narrow, but they were a great improvement over none at all, and everyone was grateful for Lieutenant Dohi's good work.

Meanwhile, the Okinawa battle intensified, and *Ohka* sorties were ordered for 12 April as a part of operation *Kikusui* No. 2. Dohi was one of the pilots named that morning. He came to me after eating his final meal and said, "I have ordered six beds and fifteen straw mats. They are supposed to arrive today. May I ask that you watch for them and make sure they go to the billet?"

With these words he climbed into the waiting mother bomber and was gone.

Eight *Ohkas* participated in this day's attacks, along with 80 kamikaze planes and more than 100 escort fighters. They headed for Okinawa by varying courses in order to approach their targets from numerous points, both east and west of the island, at the same time, and to take advantage of the concealment afforded by the high bluffs which surrounded the enemy anchorages.

Those of us who stayed behind could do nothing but see them off, pray for their success, and wait for results. In the sheltered radio room, men hunched over their receiving sets in tense concentration to catch every report from our planes. I put on a set of earphones as the first group of special attackers was approaching Okinawa. Attack reports were coming in continuously. My interest was centered on the progress of the *Ohka*-laden bombers.

The *Ohka* effort of 21 March had ended so ignominiously that this might be our last opportunity to prove the worth of the method. We all hoped fervently that this time the arduous efforts of our devoted pilots would be rewarded.

"Enemy fighters sighted!" I tensed at this first report from Lieutenant Dohi's plane. Would the *Ohka* attempt be thwarted again by interceptors? Time seemed to stop. How could those cumbersome bombers make their way through the screen of enemy interceptors?

The next report brought relief mingled with surprise. "We have avoided enemy fighters."

Mitsubishi G4M2 ("Betty") and Ohka Glide Bomb

How could this be? But there was no time now for conjecture. Messages came in rapid succession:

"Standing by to release *Ohka*."

"Targets are battleships."

In a matter of seconds the *Ohka* would be released from the mother plane. They were nearing the target.

Then, "Let go!"—and I visualized the scene as Dohi plummeted toward a great battleship, his speed boosted by rocket thrusts, and then the final successful direct hit.

Of the eight mother planes in this attack, six were shot down after making their release. Only one returned safely to base, and that was the one that had transported Lieutenant Dohi's *Ohka*. Its crew told how at take-off Dohi said he wished to nap and asked to be called 30 minutes before arrival in the target area. He had stretched out on a makeshift canvas cot and gone to sleep. Upon being awakened he had smiled and said, "Time passes quickly, doesn't it?"

He had then shaken hands with the plane commander and climbed through the bomb bay into his rocket craft. To the mother ship there was a voice tube connection through which he announced when all was ready. The *Ohka* carriers closed the island from the west and could see enemy ships in great numbers. They arrived at the extreme range of the *Ohka*, but it was still desirable to shorten the distance to the target as much as possible.

A battleship was selected as Dohi's objective. At 6,000 meters' altitude, and distant 18,000 meters from target, the optimum position was reached and Dohi's *Ohka* was released. The bomber crew watched anxiously as it plunged downward, wavering for an instant. Then, steadily, while gathering bulletlike speed, the missile quickly grew smaller. The mother plane had promptly withdrawn to the west at top speed for it could not stay to make observations in that enemy-infested sky.

The crew's last sight of their *Ohka* could prove only that it was gathering speed, was under control, and was on its way. They had, however, seen a column of heavy smoke belching 500 meters high from the general location of Dohi's target as the bombers withdrew.*

As the April days passed, the battle around Okinawa increased in ferocity. The earlier kamikaze pilots were replaced by new ones, who in turn were replaced by still newer ones. They slept on the straw mats and in the bamboo beds which Lieutenant Dohi had struggled to provide, and their noble spirits followed his as their turn came for the one-way mission. The cherry blossoms had fallen, but the trees were fresh and green.

KAMIKAZES VERSUS GRUMMANS

Our air raid shelter was located about 100 meters north of the schoolhouse billet of the 341st Air Group. Our communications center had been set up in the shelter from the very first so that radio work could continue without interruption by enemy air attacks. As daytime and even nighttime raids became more frequent, beds were brought to the shelter so that pilots could sleep undisturbed. It was a safe and quiet place, but because of poor ventilation the air was humid and sticky, and sleep was not easy.

Among the special attackers was a young officer who had graduated from a technical college in Muroran Hokkaido. He had stayed on at the college as an assistant professor, and he continued with advanced studies right up to the moment when his application for the naval air corps was accepted. He already had several patents to his credit, and despite his youth showed great promise as an inventor. Some of his inventions were already in production in Japan, and doing very well.

I summoned him to the shelter one evening for a chat, knowing that he had volunteered for special attack duty at the first opportunity. He responded amiably

---

*The only hits on 12 April by piloted (*Baka*) bombs were one which sank *Mannert L. Abele* (DD-733) at lat. 27°25′ N, long. 126°59′ E and one which damaged *Stanley* (DD-478) at lat. 27°12′ N, long. 128°17′ E.

to questions, but I found him to be less talkative than most of the kamikaze pilots.

"The special attack corps is not the only place to serve our country," I remarked to him. "Japan will have need in the future for a man with your skill. Have you considered that your technical ability might be more valuable to our country than anything you could do here?"

He gave careful consideration to my words before answering. "I have thought many times of the things you say, and cannot disagree with them. I realize that my technical training could prove of value to Japan, and that has made my decision more difficult. So I hope that you will understand and do nothing to interfere with my decision, because I do not wish to change my mind."

From the tone of his quiet reply our topic of conversation could have been nothing more serious than the weather. Never before had I in any way sought to influence a man's decision about volunteering for special attacks. Now I was suggesting the obvious fact that this man was of far greater value to his country alive than dead—and he responded with casual objectiveness that he wished to die for his country. There was no affectation in his attitude. It was not from fear that his statement omitted any mention of death, I am sure, but rather that death meant nothing to him in the consideration of performing his duty. I said no more and my professor friend left apologetically, as though in fear that he had offended me.

This seemingly unique case was really typical of all Japanese men devoted to their country. It demonstrated a spirit of loyalty derived from generations of loyal ancestors.

A few days later he sortied, leading four Zero fighters for a crash-dive attack on enemy vessels at Okinawa. Each plane carried a 500-kilogram bomb.

About 60 miles north of Amami-Oshima they sighted four Grumman fighters of the enemy. The Zeroes were flying south at this time, barely 20 meters above the surface of the water.

The American Grummans first appeared to starboard, flying a reciprocal course at about 1,000 meters. But they circled back and headed down for the heavily laden Zeros, which immediately jettisoned their bombs and turned about to engage their attackers.

Typical of most Japanese special attack pilots, these men had experienced no more than three gunnery practice sessions, and their ability in aerial combat was sadly limited. Accordingly, I had instructed them, like the others, to take no chance of trying to match skill with the well-trained enemy pilots, but rather to make the best of a hopeless situation by ramming their opponents.

Two Zeros were destroyed in the ensuing one-sided dog fight, while the flight leader actually succeeded in shooting down one of the Grummans. Before he had time even to take a deep breath, he saw another enemy plane approaching to attack from a favorable position, and he at once decided to ram. As the planes closed each other at blinding speed, the Grumman turned off at the last moment and fled. Its pilot must have been dumbfounded by this unexpected tactic of his opponent.

Having decided to collide, the Japanese pilot was equally surprised at his opponent's sudden flight and looked about for some other target. The remaining enemy plane, which seemed to be that of the flight leader, was banking as the Zero came at him. The American pilot must have sensed the determination of his adversary, for he took but one look and likewise flew away at top speed.

With the bomb gone and no enemy planes remaining, the Zero turned homeward and landed safely at the base, where its pilot reported the encounter.

EPISODES AT KANOYA

At Kanoya, a large open field ran along a stream south of the pilots' quarters. Though not actually a part of the base, this area was considered to be within bounds to the extent that fliers could stroll there without obtaining a pass. The stream, about five meters wide, wound leisurely through bamboo thickets and grain fields. White roses blooming wild along its banks were a great joy to behold.

One kamikaze pilot, enjoying the beauties of a stroll in these fields, stopped to watch the harvesting of wheat nearby. He observed that the work was being done entirely by young children and old men and women. Hurrying back to the billet, he asked my approval for him to help with the harvesting. Seeing no harm in the idea and realizing that it would be a worthy diversion, I readily consented. The word spread, and before the day was through some thirty pilots had gone to help in the fields. They returned at sunset, weary and sunburned but contented, wishing only that they had been able to do something more.

It did not take long for the people of nearby farms and villages to hear about the helpful pilots, and soon gifts were pouring in for these men. Such gifts were properly supposed to be distributed through the local headquarters, but it seemed that the people wanted to make sure of where their gifts went and they always found some pretext for leaving them directly at the kamikaze billet. The total extent of these gifts reached surprising proportions and, to my knowledge, the special attack corps pilots at Kanoya received thousands of fresh eggs, hundreds of chickens, three pigs, and even a cow.

A mother and her daughter from Tokyo came to the billet one day to see the young woman's fiancé. His last letter had said that he was moving to Kanoya. Having heard nothing more, they were worried and had come to pay him a visit. They did not know that he was a kamikaze pilot and had already flown his mission to Okinawa a few days before.

The pilot's close friend, who had received the two women, was lost for words of explanation, and sought my advice. It would have been cruel and heartless to tell the truth; so, at my suggestion, he told the two visitors that the officer in question had left a few days before to go to an advance island base. He then showed them around the billet and even took them to see the room that had recently been occupied by the young officer. They looked fondly around, and the girl touched the bamboo bed in which he had so recently slept.

No further questions were asked—but they seemed instinctively to understand what had happened.

NOT ALWAYS GODS

By the time of the enemy invasion of Okinawa there was a noticeable change in the attitude of special attack pilots. In the Philippines and in Formosa, corps membership had been made up entirely from volunteers, and there was a spontaneous enthusiasm that was inspiring and contagious. Also, in the early days, there had been an obvious purpose—and even some hope —that these extreme tactics might be successful in turning the tide of battle in favor of Japan. But now huge formations of enemy B-29s from the Marianas

B-29 Superfort

and the Chinese mainland were striking Tokyo, Osaka, and other important cities of Japan. These attacks exposed civilians as well as military forces to the desperate realities of war.

To cope with this critical situation there remained nothing to do but continue to increase the kamikaze attacks. In this circumstance the volunteer system of earlier days was plainly inadequate. So there developed a pressure, not entirely artificial, which encouraged "volunteering," and it is understandable that this change in circumstance would effect a change in the attitude of the men concerned.

Many of the new arrivals seemed at first not only to lack enthusiasm, but, indeed, to be disturbed by their situation. With some this condition lasted only a few hours, with others for several days. It was a period of melancholy that passed with time and eventually gave way to a spiritual awakening. Then, like an attainment of wisdom, care vanished and tranquillity of spirit appeared as life came to terms with death, mortality with immortality.

An example of the achievement of this spiritual calm was seen in the case of Lieutenant (jg) Kuno, who was extremely perturbed upon arrival at the base. Then suddenly, after several days of sulking about, he came with jaunty step and a spark in his eye, asking permission to divest his plane of all unneeded equipment, saying that it was being inconsiderate to homeland workers to take nonessentials along on a kamikaze mission.

Then there was Ensign Tatsuya Ikariyama, a reserve officer, who flew in from Kitaura to join the Takuma Air Group in Shikoku on 4 May 1945. He was to participate in a special attack at Okinawa. On arrival he learned that three friends who had joined the Navy with him were at this base, and he looked for them immediately. Shortly after dinner he stood at the door of their room and said, "I heard you fellows were here and wanted to see you."

It had been a long time since they had all been together, so this was a happy reunion. When his friends suggested that they have a drink to celebrate the occasion, Ikariyama said, "Sorry, but I am going on a suicide attack tomorrow and want to be in top condition, so I do not care to drink."

"How about some canned pineapple?"

"No, thanks, I've just had supper and don't want to take the risk of overeating."

Thus he refused food and drink out of concern that

it might spoil his chances of flying the next day. The reunited friends talked about their days together at Tsuchiura flying school, of their experiences since then, of absent friends, of vacations, and of home. When it got to be 2200, Ikariyama took leave of the others and retired.

He sortied on schedule the next day, and they never saw him again.

Such devotion to duty, however, was not always the rule at this critical stage of the war. The special attackers were neither saints nor devils. They were human beings, with all the emotions and feelings, faults and virtues, strengths and weaknesses of other human beings. So they sang songs, laughed, cried, and got drunk; did good things and bad.

In this respect kamikaze pilots based in the homeland were sometimes unfortunate. In an excess of veneration some people came to look upon them as gods and were disappointed when they did not act accordingly. It was even more regrettable when a few of these pilots, unduly influenced by a grateful and worshipping public, came to think of themselves actually as living gods and grew unbearably haughty. Then, as so often happens, the reputation created by a few came to be attributed to the many. I feel that any criticism against the special attackers in general was undeserved because, neither better nor worse than other men, they were after all just ordinary men.

But in the Okinawa battle these ordinary men had established some extraordinary records. Almost 1,700 Army and Navy planes made kamikaze sorties toward this area between 11 March and the end of June 1945. Yet even this great sacrifice was not enough to stem the inevitable tide of the war, and Okinawa was overrun by the enemy. With the end of fighting on that island, our air operations shifted to the next scene of activity—the homeland of Japan.

The total battle results claimed for the special attack corps in the Okinawa campaign are listed in the following table. These data, which begin with 11 March and go to the end of hostilities on Okinawa, are based on contemporaneous Japanese reports and may well be in excess of the actual results achieved.

Ships	Sunk*	Damaged*
Carriers (CV)	5 (0)	9 (4)
Carriers (CVE and CVL)	3 (0)	2 (3)
Battleships (BB)	12 (0)	18 (10)
Cruisers (CA and CL)	29 (0)	27 (5)
Destroyers (DD)	18 (11)	9 (61)
Minesweepers (AM and DMS)	3 (1)	2 (22)
Others (including unidentified types)	27 (4)	22 (80)
	97 (16)	89 (185)

*Data in parentheses in the Sunk and Damaged columns are based on official U. S. reports of individual losses, definitely attributable to kamikaze attack. These include one ship sunk (the destroyer *Mannert L. Abele*, on 12 April), four damaged by piloted (*Baka*) bombs, and four damaged by suicide boats.

THE END OF
THE IMPERIAL NAVY

BY NAKAJIMA

A SURFACE SUICIDE OPERATION

The Battle of Leyte Gulf, which had seen the beginning of the Kamikaze Corps, had also seen the end of the Japanese Navy as a practical fighting force. When the Second Fleet returned to the homeland after that disastrous encounter, the main strength of its cruiser squadrons had been wiped out, and its only remaining battleships were the *Yamato, Nagato,* and *Haruna.* Japan no longer had enough warships to form a single real fighting force. Furthermore, owing to the extreme shortage of fuel in the home islands, by January of 1945 the Japanese Navy had operational in the Island Sea anchorage of Hashirajima only the battleship *Yamato,* the light cruiser *Yahagi,* and five destroyers.

When the enemy began landing in the Ryukyu Islands on 26 March 1945, feeble remnants of the once-powerful Imperial Fleet rallied to offer what opposition they could. Destroyer Squadron 11 joined the Second Fleet at Kure. On 28 March these ships moved to Kabuto Jima. The Second Fleet was to exit from Bungo Strait, skirt the southern coast of Kyushu, and move up to Sasebo in an attempt to lure enemy warships within striking distance of land-based planes in Japan. Thus the Second Fleet had been relegated to the role of a decoy.

This role had been altered on 1 April, however, when the enemy landed on Okinawa, where he soon occupied and developed the airstrips and began to put them to use. This turn of events moved Japan's land-based air forces to cooperate at Okinawa on 6 April in the first coordinated, all-out suicide assault—*Kikusui* Operation No. 1. At the same time, the Second Fleet was reorganized and assigned the task of making a sortie against the enemy at Okinawa in coordination with the all-out air attack.

This surface force was commanded by Vice Admiral Seiichi Ito. It consisted of the battleship *Yamato,* the light cruiser *Yahagi,* and eight destroyers from Destroyer Divisions 17, 21, and 41. These ships departed Ube on 6 April at 0600 and stopped at Tokuyama, where they were fueled and nonessentials were unloaded. Vice Admiral Seiichi Ito, Commander in Chief 2nd Fleet, radioed his battle message to the crews:

> In coordination with the Army, the Imperial Navy is mobilizing all land, sea, and air forces against the enemy at Okinawa.
> The fate of the homeland rests on this operation. Our ships have been organized as a surface special attack corps. The force sortieing today will concentrate an all-out effort in the impending battle. Thereby we shall live up to the glorious traditions of the Imperial Navy and convey the glory of those traditions to posterity. Every unit participating in this operation, whether or not it has been assigned for a special attack, is expected to fight to the bitter end. Thereby the enemy will be annihilated and the eternal foundations of our motherland will be secured.

The operation plan called for the Second Fleet to beach itself in front of the enemy forces at Okinawa and fire every gun of every ship until the last shell had been expended or the last ship destroyed. From the very inception of the plan, there was no thought that any of these ships would return. It was truly a kamikaze mission.

The Second Fleet cleared Tokuyama by 1600 on 6 April. It was scheduled to reach the enemy landing beaches on the southwestern shore of Okinawa just before daybreak on the 8th. An antisubmarine formation was assumed after passing through Bungo Strait at 1930. Moving southward at 20 knots, the ships passed through Osumi Strait at about 0600 the following morning. An hour later they moved into a ring formation, and speed was upped to 24 knots as they swung toward the south. Twenty Zero fighters of the Fifth Air Fleet flew cover for about three hours, starting at 0800, during which time there was no sign of the enemy. At 1130, however, a shadowing enemy flying boat was sighted to the east. At the same time, a radio message was received from Amami-Oshima, "About 250 carrier-based planes flying northward." At noon the *Yamato's* radar detected a large formation of planes approaching from the south, distant 100 kilometers.

Action was but minutes away. The day was cloudy, with a heavy, low-hanging overcast which afforded perfect protection for the attackers. From start to finish the enemy planes would burst out of the cloud cover, make their strike, and dart back to the safety of clouds so quickly that ships' gunners had little chance to determine the range and to fire effectively. Although a number of enemy planes were shot down, the antiaircraft fire was relatively ineffective in protecting the surface force.

In all, about 300 U. S. carrier-based planes hit the ships with bombs and torpedoes. By 1500 the *Yamato,* the *Yahagi,* and the destroyers *Asashimo* and *Hamakaze* had all been sunk. Two other destroyers, the *Isokaze* and *Kasumi,* dead in the water, were sunk by companion ships after the crews had been rescued. The four remaining destroyers returned to Sasebo the following day. This greatest of suicide actions, which aborted at latitude 31° N, longitude 128° E, had cost Japan six out of ten ships and the lives of more than 2,500 men.

The last desperate fleet sortie of the Imperial Navy ended in miserable failure. The once-glorious Imperial Fleet, which had prided itself on commanding the waters of the entire western Pacific Ocean, was thus driven ignominiously from the seas of the homeland.

ADMIRAL UGAKI'S KAMIKAZE SORTIE

The air base at Kanoya in southern Kyushu had sent many kamikaze pilots against the enemy at Okinawa. But so rapidly were the Okinawa airfields occupied and put into operation by the invaders that the enemy's land-based planes were soon augmenting his carrier task force raids on the main islands of Japan. So severe were these attacks that our air bases had to be reestablished in central and northern Kyushu, Shikoku, and western Honshu. In the course of these moves Fifth Air Fleet headquarters was shifted from Kanoya to Oita, in northeastern Kyushu. There the command post was set in a bunker built into a hill on the southeast side of the field.

Before daybreak on 15 August the senior officer of the Fifth Air Fleet staff, Captain Takashi Miyazaki, was summoned to headquarters. He reported to the duty officer, Lieutenant Commander Takekatsu Tanaka, who told him with some concern that the fleet commander, Vice Admiral Matome Ugaki, had given orders for the preparation of bomber planes at Oita to sortie for Okinawa.

Miyazaki was disturbed by the thought that Ugaki might have decided to lead a final suicide attack in person. He went directly to Admiral Ugaki's quarters, where he was readily welcomed, to determine if this was so.

The headquarters was also located in the hillside cave. A partitioning screen set off a small part of this cave as Admiral Ugaki's personal quarters, which was furnished with only a crude desk and a couch. This was a far cry from what is generally considered appropriate for the commanding officer of an air fleet.

The Admiral was seated, grim-faced, on the couch when Miyazaki entered.

"The duty officer tells me that you have ordered preparations for a sortie of carrier bombers," he said. "May I ask your plans, sir?"

The Admiral's expression softened as he answered matter-of-factly, "I am going to accompany an attack. Go relay the order."

"I fully understand how you feel, but beg you to reconsider, sir," protested Miyazaki. "It is my own opinion that such an action is not now practical."

"You have my order," replied Admiral Ugaki, gently but firmly. "Please carry it out."

Miyazaki promptly withdrew and went to consult with Ugaki's chief of staff, Rear Admiral Toshiyuki Yokoi. He did so reluctantly, because Admiral Yokoi was in ill health and had been confined to his bed for several days; but Miyazaki felt need of his counsel.

When told of the situation Admiral Yokoi got out of bed, sick as he was, and went directly to Admiral Ugaki's barren quarters to speak his mind. "I can fully appreciate your decision to die," he said. "But after a surrender there are important affairs, such as deactivation of your command, which you must feel obligated to perform. I beg you to withdraw your decision."

Ugaki silenced further entreaties by his chief of staff when he smiled calmly and replied, "Please allow me the right to choose my own death."

This left Yokoi nothing to say. He went to consult with Rear Admiral Chikao Yamamoto. They decided that Ugaki's intimate friend, Rear Admiral Takatsugu Jojima, was the only man who might now dissuade him from making the sortie.

Like the others, Jojima was greatly disturbed by the news. He went immediately to talk his friend out of his determined plan. As a close personal friend, Jojima could speak more bluntly to Admiral Ugaki than the others could. "I know that, as commanding officer, you accept full responsibility for the Fifth Air Fleet," he began. "But, in addition to what is past, you must consider the future. There, too, you have duties and responsibilities. I have been told of your present intention and am in complete sympathy with your feelings. Nevertheless, for the good of everyone concerned, I urge you to call off this sortie."

Ugaki listened patiently to his friend's words. Then he answered with disarming directness and simplicity, "This is my chance to die like a warrior. I must be permitted this chance. My successor has already been chosen and he can take care of things after I am gone."*

Jojima saw that Ugaki was unshakable. Perhaps, too, he shared the sentiments of his friend. Nothing remained but for the orders to be carried out, and notice was sent to Lieutenant Tatsuo Nakatsuru, dive-bomber commander of the 701st Air Group, to prepare planes for sortie. A formal written order followed: "Oita Detachment of 701st Air Group will attack the enemy fleet at Okinawa with three dive bombers. This attack will be led by the commanding admiral."

That morning Japanese forces everywhere had been alerted for a noon broadcast from the Emperor. It had been sadly rumored that the subject would be a rescript of surrender. With heavy hearts the Fifth Air Fleet staff assembled at headquarters to hear the announcement. Reception was very poor and many parts of what was said were not clear. Enough came through, however, to make it plain that we had been told to surrender. This was verified soon afterward when local newspapers provided a full transcript of the Imperial

---

*One of the great mysteries growing out of the entire kamikaze effort is the matter of how Admiral Ugaki could have resolved to make his suicide sortie in view of the Emperor's direct order to lay down arms and surrender. As a military man and loyal subject, Admiral Ugaki owed unquestioning allegiance to the Emperor and was bound to do his bidding. How then, even though determined to end his own life, could he have so violated an Imperial command? Furthermore, as he must have realized, if his attack had succeeded in sinking any Allied ships, it might have led to a continuation of hostilities that would have been disastrous.

announcement. Until that moment Admiral Ugaki seemed to have entertained hope that the Emperor would call for a fight to the finish. There now remained no room for such hope.

There was a small farewell party for Admiral Ugaki. He spoke to the group, expressing regret that his efforts had failed to achieve the desired results. His voice was soft and impassive, and he smiled gently as he explained that we should all cooperate in the work remaining after his departure. His words, simple and direct, gripped everyone present.

When this session ended, Admiral Ugaki went out to the airfield. His uniform was stripped of all insignia of rank. The only things he carried were a short samurai sword and binoculars. The sword had been presented to him by the late Admiral Isoroku Yamamoto, Combined Fleet Commander in Chief during the first two years of the war.

Captain Miyazaki had been standing by quietly and solemnly, but finally, unable to restrain himself any longer, he stepped forward and said, "Please take me with you, Admiral."

Ugaki answered him sternly, "You have more than enough to attend to here. You will remain."

This refusal was too much for Miyazaki. He stopped in his tracks and burst into tears, crying openly and unashamedly as the others walked past.

On the airstrip eleven planes were lined up with their engines roaring, and 22 airmen stood ready beside them. Chief of staff Yokoi's surprise at this array was unconcealed. In amazement he addressed the leader, Lieutenant Nakatsuru, saying, "Did not the order call for only three planes?"

The younger man's answer was excited and spirited, almost to the point of brusqueness. "Who could stand to see the attack limited to only three planes when our commander himself is going to lead in crash dives against the enemy? Every plane of my command will follow him."

Admiral Ugaki, after listening to this exchange,

stepped up on a small platform and spoke to his men for the last time. "This is, indeed, a touching thing. Are you all so willing to die with me?"

The hand of every flier flashed upward as they shouted a unanimous response. There was not the slightest doubt of this group's sincerity. Admiral Ugaki gave the order to prepare for take-off and went directly to Nakatsuru's plane, where he climbed into the rear seat. Nakatsuru's observer, Warrant Officer Akiyoshi Endo, was plainly discomfited at this and ran to the Admiral saying, "It is my seat, sir! You have taken *my* seat!"

Admiral Ugaki smiled understandingly and said, "I have relieved you. You will stay."

This was more than Endo could bear. To the surprise of everyone, he clambered up the side of the plane and squeezed into the same seat with the Admiral. Ugaki accepted this display of determination with a good-natured shake of his head and moved over to make room for the enthusiastic young man. Everything was ready. The eleven bombers moved in turn down the runway and were airborne, as spectators on the field waved last farewells.

Four of these planes were forced down because of engine trouble. The others made their way to Okinawa. Endo maintained radio communication with the base and gave occasional reports on their progress. The last report contained a final message from Admiral Ugaki:

I alone am to blame for our failure to defend the homeland and destroy the arrogant enemy. The valiant efforts of all officers and men of my command during the past six months have been greatly appreciated.

I am going to make an attack at Okinawa where my men have fallen like cherry blossoms. There I will crash into and destroy the conceited enemy in the true spirit of *Bushido*, with firm conviction and faith in the eternity of Imperial Japan.

I trust that the members of all units under my command will understand my motives, will overcome all hardships of the future, and will strive for the reconstruction of our great homeland that it may survive forever.

Long live His Imperial Majesty the Emperor!

This transmission concluded at 1924 with a static-riddled statement that the Commander's plane was crashing into a target. Each of the other six bombers also sent messages that they were making their final plunge at about this same time.*

From the moment of taking command of the Fifth Air Fleet, Admiral Ugaki seemed to have decided to take part in a suicide attack. He had frequently been heard to remark that one and all would get a chance to make a suicide sortie. His every act reflected the firmness of this determination.

---

*There is, however, no U. S. warship record of kamikaze attacks on this date, 15 August 1945.

LAST DAYS
OF ADMIRAL OHNISHI

BY INOGUCHI

JAPAN

With the enemy's assault on Iwo Jima and the inevitable threat to Okinawa and the homeland, Admiral Ohnishi had been proved completely right. There could be no doubt now that conventional air attacks against the vastly superior American forces would be useless. Adoption of kamikaze attacks as the primary tactic for all the armed forces was an inevitable result, with the consequent sorties of the special attack corps from Formosa and, later, Kyushu.

In early March, I was ordered to Japan to join the staff of the Tenth Air Fleet, the reserve component of the Fifth Air Fleet. I took advantage of my return to the homeland to visit various high-ranking naval officers of my personal acquaintance in order to press my plea that Admiral Ohnishi be called back to Tokyo to take command of naval operations. I was more than ever convinced that he was the one man for the job.

My pleas were in vain, however. All of the high command in Tokyo were of the opinion that Admiral Ohnishi was most sorely needed in his present job— so much so that he could not be spared from it. Disappointed, I took up my new duties, which consisted mostly of visiting all the bases of the Tenth Air Fleet to lecture on the operations of the kamikaze units in the Philippines. The idea was to inspire the young men training for special attacks and to bolster their morale. I completed the tour in June and was then given command of the Suzuka Air Group.

Soon afterward I was overjoyed to hear that Admiral Ohnishi had been appointed Vice Chief of the Naval General Staff. I still hoped he might be able to work some miracle to turn the war in our favor.

Miracle it would have to be, for not only did the enemy invade Okinawa on 1 April, but within two months he had annihilated its defenders. Throughout the whole sixty days of that campaign, his mighty armada remained in constant support despite countless attacks by our kamikaze fliers.

The capture of Okinawa was clearly a prelude to operations against the home islands themselves. In July and early August huge enemy air raids struck Japan in increasing fury.

Suddenly, on 3 August, I was ordered to Tokyo as a staff officer in Imperial Naval Headquarters and the Naval General Staff. I was delighted with this assignment because it meant that I would once again be close to Admiral Ohnishi. It was on 9 August, while I was riding from Suzuka to Tokyo, that I learned that the entire city of Hiroshima had been wiped out in a single enemy air attack. It was incredible news—and then came rumors that the agent of destruction had been an atomic bomb.

My first awkward reaction was a hope that our own scientists might also have developed this same kind of weapon, and that it might be available for use by our special attackers. If such were the case, Japan would still have a chance of surmounting the overwhelming odds against her.

These fond hopes were dashed upon my arrival in Tokyo, however, for I learned there that Japan had no such weapon. Our scientists had been making studies for an atomic bomb, but they knew that no less an industrial capacity than that of the United

States was necessary actually to produce it. I was thereupon forced to the grim acknowledgment that Japan no longer had any chance whatsoever of winning the war. Some military leaders were sparking and fanning the idea of turning the whole nation into a force of special attackers, but I could only muse gloomily that such an effort would be meaningless against the devastating power of atomic bombs.

Admiral Soemu Toyoda, Chief of Naval General Staff, to whom I reported, was the only unruffled person I encountered in all of official Tokyo. His staff, however, like the Navy Ministry, was in utter chaos. There was no opportunity to see Admiral Ohnishi and hear his views, but I learned that the final decision on the war had already been reached by the Supreme War Council. In a meeting which started during the evening of 9 August and continued until 0230 next morning, the decision had been made for surrender. The Emperor was present and had himself made the determination. The Navy Minister, Admiral Mitsumasa Yonai, had insisted from the beginning of the meeting on the absolute necessity of terminating the war.

There were still, however, many naval strategists who were not reconciled to immediate surrender. They urged a delay, arguing that one more all-out offensive effort might enable Japan to obtain better terms of surrender than could be realized by immediate capitulation.

Such was the agitation upon my arrival in Tokyo. Sides were drawn, opinions set, and there were heated arguments on every hand. I felt like, and was, a stranger to the scene. Reporting my arrival to Prince Takamatsu, a younger brother of the Emperor, then working in the Military Affairs Bureau, I spoke to him of the kamikaze effort and Admiral Ohnishi's inspired leadership. In talking with the Prince and other officers about Ohnishi, I observed that they did not always concur in my high opinion of him. In fact, the general attitude in Tokyo toward Admiral Ohnishi and his policies had recently turned very cool.

I learned that this attitude had had its beginning several days before at an operations conference where Admiral Ohnishi had announced his determination to fight to the bitter end, no matter what happened, and had asked to hear the opinions of other staff members on this point. I knew Admiral Ohnishi well and could understand his making such a startling statement. He had made equally alarming remarks in the Philippines and in Formosa—with the specific intention of shocking his listeners and thus finding out what they really thought. Being familiar with this device I could also understand that the present staff members, not accustomed to such shock treatment, were greatly disturbed by it.

At another recent conference Admiral Ohnishi had spoken in sharp rebuke of Rear Admiral Sadatoshi Tomioka, First Bureau Chief of the Naval General Staff. Tomioka, a man of great integrity and extremely personable, was very popular with the high command in Tokyo. Ohnishi's words to him were so harsh that, to the others present, they seemed openly insulting. This kind of behavior was unprecedented in the Imperial Navy, and it was especially resented when directed against a high-ranking officer whose brilliance was respected by all of his colleagues.

These two incidents were more than enough to place Ohnishi in a bad light with his Tokyo associates. But, knowing him so well, I could understand and make allowances for—if not justify—these actions. He was a virile and robust man, confident of and faithful to his conviction of what was right. In addition to considering his basic personality, it must be realized that he had already decided to commit hara-kiri if Japan should surrender. Knowing that his own time was running out, and that he was dealing with men who were not planning to die, he must have been infuriated at the idea of their accepting the humiliation of defeat. Their complacence must have been galling to this man who was so firm in his resolution not to survive the defeat of Japan.

Admiral Ohnishi was desperate. He tried in every way possible to learn the feelings of the man in the street in regard to continuation of the war. At the same time he sought by every means to persuade his colleagues to continue fighting. It is reported that in his last meeting with Navy Minister Yonai he wept openly in a fervent plea to keep on fighting.

In the evening of 13 August the chiefs of the Operations Section of the Army and Navy General Staffs met with the chief of the Military Affairs Section of the War Ministry. They agreed to delay the calling of an Imperial Conference as long as possible while they attempted to win over the state leaders, who were favoring surrender, to a last-ditch battle. It was decided that Admiral Ohnishi should ask Prince Takamatsu to put pressure on Navy Minister Yonai and Admiral of the Fleet Osami Nagano, leaders of the pro-surrender group. Toward the same end, Commander Dohi was chosen to see Admiral Nagano, Rear Admiral Tomioka to see Admiral Koshiro Oikawa, and Captain Toshikazu Ohmae was selected to influence Admirals Naokuni Nomura and Nobutake Kondo.

Admiral Ohnishi was thus on his way to see Prince Takamatsu the first time I saw him after my arrival in Tokyo. He greeted me warmly, but his stern countenance gave evidence that he was very preoccupied. Recalling the unfortunate effects of his recent provocative remarks, and hopeful that he would avoid making any shocking statements to the Prince, I said, "I saw His Highness three days ago and told him what a fine job you have done. I also assured him that you always carry out orders meticulously, and that you would certainly abide by whatever the Emperor said."

"And am I supposed to go right on carrying out orders even while our nation perishes?" asked the Admiral brusquely.

"Who knows whether or not our nation will perish?" I protested. "Is not your idea of its perishing purely a product of your own thinking? Ought you not now do as Dai Nanko* did after his interview with Bomon, and accept the word of the Emperor?"

Admiral Ohnishi weighed these words, paused for a moment, and then went on his way without answering my question.

As the day passed I was naturally anxious about the outcome of Admiral Ohnishi's meeting with the Prince, and I decided to wait in his office at headquarters until he returned.

The night was dark and cloudy. A light drizzle around midnight was the only sound to break the hushed and gloomy silence. Time wore slowly on. At 0200 a car pulled up to the portico. The Admiral climbed the stairs slowly, gave a deep sigh as he entered the room and muttered, "All is over."

"The Prince," he continued, "will not try to influence the admirals unless there is a concrete and realistic plan to strike the enemy a telling blow. Knowing the Navy view, I went to see the Army chief of staff. He offered no encouragement because the Army had no plan either. All is certainly over."

I shared his despair and answered, "How tragic!" Then a sudden thought occurred to me, and I added, "Is there a chance that *this* might work? Stall for time, asking for a delay while the Emperor's representative reports the decision to the Grand Shrine?† The request is not unreasonable, since the Emperor normally re-

---

*Dai Nanko is an allegorical name applied to Masashige Kusunoki, who, in his last battle defending the Emperor at Kyoto, planned for withdrawal of the Imperial forces from that 14th century capital to Mt. Hiei. Then, when the rebel forces had moved into Kyoto, it was Kusunoki's idea to move in and capture the enemy. Kiyotada Bomon, the Emperor's chief adviser, reminded him that the Emperor's forces had never in history been defeated, even when outnumbered, and that Divine Providence had always protected him. He added that to desert the capital would appear to the people as a sign of weakness. Thereupon, Kusunoki harkened to the word of the courtier Bomon, as being the representation of the Emperor's wish.

†The Grand Shrine at Ise is dedicated to Amaterasu Omikami, the Sun Goddess, founder of Japan; it contains the Mirror, one of the three Great Treasures. All important affairs of state are reported here to the Imperial Ancestors, either by the Emperor or by his designated representative.

ports such important decisions to the shrine, as he did at the outset of war. Such a concession would allow us further time to organize a plan. Couldn't we ask the Prince to make such a request?"

"It's worth a try," said Ohnishi. "See the Prince, and ask him to make the request."

But the day that followed was hectic. I could not get in to see the Prince. The decision for Japan's unconditional surrender had already been made, and it would stand.

HARA-KIRI

Japan's decision to surrender was publicly announced on 15 August. That evening Admiral Ohnishi invited several staff officers to his official residence. They talked until around midnight, and then the guests departed.

Sometime before daybreak Admiral Ohnishi's aide was notified that the Admiral had committed hara-kiri. Rushing to the Admiral's residence, the aide found Admiral Ohnishi in the second-floor study where he had disemboweled himself in the traditional manner with a Japanese sword. The abdominal cut was cleanly done, but the following attempt by the Admiral to slit his throat was not so successful. When the aide arrived the Admiral was still conscious and said, "Do not try to help me." Thus, refusing both medical aid and a *coup de grâce,* he lingered in agony until six o'clock that evening. His desire to endure this prolonged suffering seemed to be an act of expiation. Alone, after the departure of his staff officers the evening before, Admiral Ohnishi had penned a note which read:

I wish to express my deep appreciation to the souls of the brave special attackers. They fought and died valiantly with faith in our ultimate victory. In death I wish to atone for my part in the failure to achieve that victory and I apologize to the souls of these dead fliers and their bereaved families.

I wish the young people of Japan to find a moral in

my death. To be reckless is only to aid the enemy. You must abide by the spirit of the Emperor's decision with utmost perseverance. Do not forget your rightful pride in being Japanese.

You are the treasure of the nation. With all the fervor of spirit of the special attackers, strive for the welfare of Japan and for peace throughout the world.

PART FIVE

THE DIVINE WIND

"Consider the other side
before making a decision"
—JAPANESE PROVERB

Mitsubishi J2M2, Raiden ("Jack")

ADMIRAL OHNISHI'S CREDO

BY INOGUCHI

THE MAN AND THE HOUR

From the very beginning of his career Admiral
Ohnishi had been a flier. I had heard of him long before my assignment to his First Air Fleet at Manila.
Though not myself an aviator, I worked very closely
with him and had a unique opportunity to study and
appreciate his personality.

From his earliest Navy days he had been a contro-
versial figure. There were many who considered him
impulsive, straight-forward, and simple-hearted; a man
who followed his convictions regardless of circumstances. Others saw in him a hard worker and a man of
action, but one who carefully mapped out his plans before trying to put them into effect. Everyone agreed
that he was a man of unusual ability and common
sense.

As a young officer he had often spoken and acted
without too much consideration for protocol or the social amenities, which some considered affectations on his
part. However right or wrong his decisions might be,
he never shirked responsibility for their consequences.
He was fearless and undaunted, aggressive and full of
fighting spirit. These were the opinions of his fellow
naval officers, and they were borne out by all my observations of him.

He had a sincere affection for his subordinates, and

this was in turn reflected in their devotion to him. He captivated his followers, for he led by example as well as by command.

Admiral Ohnishi placed tremendous confidence in young men. I shall never forget his words on 20 October 1944 to that first group of kamikaze pilots led by Lieutenant Seki. He recognized the spirit of sacrifice in those young men and wasted no time in idle flattery or empty compliments. Yet he left no doubt about the importance of their work and of his high opinion of the men. He was an instinctive leader.

On 23 October the Second Air Fleet had moved to the Philippines to join with the First Air Fleet in operations against the enemy. Three days later, when he had arrived at Clark Field from Manila, Admiral Ohnishi summoned all officers of flight leader rank and above. The assembly was delayed, because many officers were slow in returning from afternoon sorties. It was late that evening before they had all gathered in the temporary officers' quarters of the 763rd Air Group.

Kerosene lamps, hung from the overhead, provided the only illumination in the shabby billet. Admiral Ohnishi's voice was solemn as he addressed the group in this somber setting. "The First and Second Air Fleets have been joined to conduct operations. Admiral Fukudome of the Second Air Fleet is in command; I will assist as his chief of staff. We will tolerate no criticism of any kind of the operations that are about to be undertaken. We know that younger men do not complain or gripe, but old-timers are frequently given to criticizing the decisions of their superiors. Stern discipline will be meted out to anyone who criticizes orders or neglects to carry them out. In flagrant cases there will be no hesitancy about exacting the extreme penalty."

The silence of his listeners deepened and the atmosphere became increasingly tense. I was surprised to find how outspoken the Admiral could be.

Once again, when First Air Fleet was later transferred to Formosa for reorganization, Admiral Ohnishi had spoken to an assembly of his men and said,

"If Japan is to be saved, it is up to the young men to do it—men of 30 and younger. It is these young men with their self-sacrificing spirits and deeds who may be able to save our country. The entire effort of field operations, as well as high-level strategy and politics, should therefore be placed in full support of these young men. It must be so."

His final testament addressed young people as "the treasure of the nation," and he had expressed this feeling elsewhere in many ways. For example, the Admiral was an excellent calligrapher, and people had frequently requested a specimen of his work. One of his favorite inscriptions on such occasions was, "The purity of youth will usher in the Divine Wind."

Throughout his career Admiral Ohnishi had sought flight training of every sort. He had flown all kinds of aircraft—planes and dirigibles—and had even taken the course of training for paratroopers. He personally had led many sorties during the fighting in China, where he commanded the Second Combined Air Group. Whenever it was reported that the morale of a certain group was sagging, Ohnishi could be counted on to take command of the outfit and invariably bring it out of the doldrums.

He had occupied practically every important aviation post in the Navy, and always discharged his duties in exemplary fashion. At the outbreak of the Pacific War he was, without question, the Navy's Number 2 exponent of aviation—second only to Admiral Isoroku Yamamoto himself. In fact, there had been many traits in common between the two men. Both were intelligent and brave leaders. Each liked the other. It may well be that Yamamoto was the only Navy man who ever commanded Ohnishi's full respect. And while Yamamoto had mapped out and sponsored the attack on Pearl Harbor, it was Ohnishi who had conducted the extensive studies and research which showed the attack to be practical.

When I had come to Manila in October 1944 and had first begun serving under Ohnishi, it was without personal prejudice for or against him, one way or the other. On the subject of Ohnishi's personality I seemed to be one of the few indifferent members of his staff.

It must be remembered that Ohnishi was not altogether popular throughout the Navy. His very character, dynamic and aggressive as it was, led many non-aviators to the impression that he was a dangerous man. And there were some aviators who felt that he was overbearing and difficult to please. By the same token, Ohnishi did not wholeheartedly approve of everyone with whom he himself had to deal.

In his judgment of people the Admiral did not simply follow his first personal impression and thereafter like or dislike accordingly. He favored men of action —men who could be counted on to put words into deeds. He was opposed to men who merely talked and argued on paper without accomplishing anything. In talking with him one always had the feeling that his penetrating gaze was fathoming one's innermost thoughts.

At the outbreak of the Pacific War, Admiral Ohnishi was serving at Takao (Kaoshiung), Formosa, as Chief of Staff in the Eleventh Air Fleet. During the momentous hours when Admiral Nagumo's task force was making a success of its attack on Pearl Harbor, all of Formosa was weathered in. In Takao the staff argued about waiting for the weather to clear completely before striking the Philippines, which was the next step after the Pearl Harbor attack. Admiral Ohnishi made the resolute decision to go ahead with attacks on Luzon. These proved successful, and all the Philippines were soon under Japanese control.

However, upon Ohnishi's return to the Philippines in October 1944, the situation had changed considerably. Even his arrival at Manila had been delayed by enemy air attacks on bases in Formosa, where Ohnishi was forced to wait in mounting fury. When he finally did reach the Philippines, the situation was almost hopeless, and he had found Japanese air strength at its lowest ebb. It was impossible even to raise an effective force to defend against daily air raids by the enemy. One can imagine Ohnishi's bitterness at this situation when he recalled the glorious days of Japan's early successes in the war.

Until transferred to command of the First Air Fleet, he had been working with the Munitions Ministry and knew better than anyone else the supply situation in the homeland, especially in regard to planes. He was well aware that no substantial air reinforcements could be expected, either then or later. Perhaps it was this knowledge which had firmed his determination and decision to exploit the scant supplies on hand to the very limit.

Some of Admiral Ohnishi's critics professed to find him willful and arrogant. Such was not my experience. I found him meticulous in following all orders from higher authority. On several occasions I had tried to interpret orders we received in headquarters, so as to make them easier to carry out in the field. Ohnishi had frequently rejected my "easy" interpretation and carried out the orders to the letter, and he expected his own orders to be carried out in the same manner.

As Japan's plight went from bad to worse, Ohnishi's fastidiousness for procedural matters increased. He redoubled his efforts to make the fullest use of available men and planes. This may seem an entirely ordinary and expected thing, but under the desperate circumstances of the time it required extraordinary valor and fortitude. I think that Ohnishi was chosen to fill the Philippine post because he could be counted on to act with composure even in such hopeless circumstances.

Ohnishi's determination to carry out crash attacks had been an ultimate extremity, arrived at and carried out with utmost exactitude. Any hitch in planning or execution would cause such an operation to fail completely. Lacking the proper commander, no satisfactory results could be expected. If no satisfactory results were obtained, not merely would the tactics end in failure, but the morale of the entire Navy would be wrecked, and despair would follow. How important, then, was the choice of leader for these suicide tactics, and further, how important that his decisions be right.

With Ohnishi's assumption of command of the naval

air forces in the Philippines in the dying months of 1944, there had come an obvious rise in morale. He had arrived in Manila at the very moment when our surface forces had also decided on a death-defying attack against the enemy. It appears that the right man had arrived at the right time for the formation of Kamikaze Special Attack Corps in the Philippines.

OHNISHI'S VIEWPOINT ON KAMIKAZE ATTACKS

It was to be expected that opponents of the Kamikaze Corps would criticize the tactics and the sponsors. It was natural, too, that Ohnishi, as the man who had ordered these operations, would be the target of criticism and abuse. He was.

From the very start there were some naval aviators who opposed the kamikaze. For example, Lieutenant Commander Tadashi Minobe, flight leader of a group of night fighters in the Philippines, was openly skeptical of the suicide operations. But in spite of his blunt remark about not tolerating any criticism, Admiral Ohnishi never forced Minobe to take special attack orders. Minobe was, however, transferred to the homeland, where he satisfactorily fulfilled duties as flight leader of the 131st Air Group until the time of surrender, and thus lived up to his own convictions.

Admiral Ohnishi once said to his aide, "A man's value can never be determined at his death. In my case there will probably not be anyone, even in a hundred years, to justify what I have done."

His every action and decision had been premised on the idea that Japan would never surrender. His position becomes more understandable and open to sympathy, when one considers that he had been told to turn the tide of war at any cost. In creating the Kamikaze Corps under these circumstances, he could not have dreamed that Japan would be surrendering in less than a year.

This creation of Admiral Ohnishi's was not without precedent. In the Russo-Japanese War of 1904–05, Admiral Heihachiro Togo had organized a "death-defying unit" to blockade Port Arthur. Admiral Yamamoto had sent midget submarines into Pearl Harbor —to almost inevitable doom*—at the start of the Pacific War. But neither of these was a suicide action in basic concept, because both Togo and Yamamoto had at least attempted to provide all possible means for survival of the death-defying warriors.

Ohnishi's kamikaze operations, on the other hand, called for certain suicide, and he knowingly originated the fatal concept. Therein lies the difference between the tactics employed by Togo and Yamamoto and those of Ohnishi and Ugaki. The doctrines of the latter two seem completely unforgivable. (Are they less so, however, when one considers that these sponsors of the kamikaze had the end of their own lives in mind too?)

Also, one cannot but wonder why these inhuman tactics were continued so long. The fact is that when Ohnishi decided to institute the kamikaze he intended that the four original units, 13 planes in all, would be the only ones devoted to this kind of operation. When the suicide corps was first organized on 19 October, I had suggested to Admiral Ohnishi that it be named *"Shimpu"* (kamikaze). He readily accepted this idea and just as readily turned to his aide and dictated, "The *Shimpu* Special Attack Corps will be made up of the *Shikishima, Yamato, Asahi,* and *Yamazaqura* Units."

His readiness in producing these names convinced me that he had had them fully prepared in advance. He must have considered the whole matter on his way from Manila to Mabalacat, including even names for the units needed to do the job. It must be remembered that the tactical mission of the first kamikaze units was merely to put enemy carrier decks out of operation for about a week.

That Admiral Ohnishi was not inconsiderate of the lives of these volunteers was made plain to me on the very day the new special attack corps had been or-

---

*Four out of the five Japanese midget submarines which tried to penetrate Pearl Harbor were sunk with their two-man crews.

ganized. At about 1500 a report was received of the first sighting of an enemy force thought worthy of attack by the new corps. I had immediately charted the reported position and showed it to the Admiral, who had deliberately remained over at Mabalacat for the day on the chance that he might be on hand to see the first results.

Upon presenting the report and chart to him, I had said, "These targets are near the maximum flying range of our planes. Do you advise that an attack be ordered?"

Admiral Ohnishi, after carefully considering the situation, had answered, "Suicide tactics are so final. I would advise using them only if there is a full chance that the goal may be achieved."

Nevertheless, when the first units were not successful in checking the enemy carriers at Leyte, additional units had been organized, and these too took off on their one-way missions. When we had returned to Manila I had reminded Admiral Ohnishi of this, saying, "Since the enemy has already landed at Leyte should not the crash-dive tactics be stopped?"

The reply was surprisingly blunt and undoubtedly sincere. "These young men with their limited training, outdated equipment, and numerical inferiority are doomed even by conventional fighting methods. It is important to a commander, as it is to his men, that death be not in vain. I believe therefore that a broad perspective indicates the wisdom of crash-diving tactics. To think otherwise would be taking a narrow view of the situation. I honestly think that it is better for all concerned to continue the suicide operations."

It is significant that Ohnishi had conceded, soon after its formation, that the need for the Kamikaze Corps was regrettable; and yet he had rapidly changed to the view that it was "better for all concerned." This transition in his attitude must be borne in mind when evaluating the kamikaze development.

There are many, even among the Japanese, who criticize the crash-diving tactics, but even these critics join with everyone else in agreement that the effort and the spirit of the young pilots deserve a "well done." It is likely that Ohnishi and Ugaki, accepting the vituperation that was heaped upon them personally, would be gratified by this accolade for the men who had faithfully carried out their plans.

It must be said that both the suicide pilots and the men who guided them were moved by more than merely destructive aims. They realized that the fight had to be carried out regardless of personal chances of survival. They fought for an ideal. Their road toward that ideal was *Bushido,* but their goal was the "world-peace" enunciated by Ohnishi in his last testament.

Confucius said, "A man must live in such a way that he is always prepared to die." It seems certain that both Ohnishi and Ugaki observed this dictum. Ugaki carried out his own kamikaze mission. Ohnishi committed hara-kiri. Their deaths, in themselves, are devoid of meaning. The important thing is each man's consideration of his life and his death.

Admiral Ohnishi's philosophy was summed up in a calligraphic presentation* which he gave to his staff after the organization of the Kamikaze Corps:

Kyo sakite, asu chiru;	In blossom today, then scattered;
Hana no wagami ka na.	Life is so like a delicate flower.
Ikade sono ka wo kiyoku todomen?	How can one expect the fragrance to last forever?
(Ohnishi, Kamikaze Tokkotai Ei)	(Ohnishi, of the Kamikaze Special Attack Force)

Ohnishi was human and subject to the foibles and frailties of humankind. He must have known that, since Yamamoto's death, he was Japan's leading officer in naval aviation. As such, both his life and death had

---

*A reproduction of the original writing appears on the frontispiece.

to be exemplary, in keeping with the traditions of the Imperial Navy. By the same token he would want every Navy man to meet the demands of duty until the end.

It would be wrong to think that his suicide was merely an atonement for sin. I believe that his life was dedicated from the moment he organized the Kamikaze Corps. Thereupon he had resolved to take his own life, and would have carried out that resolve even if Japan had won the war. In imagination he must have ridden with every pilot of his command as each made his final special attack.

Just before his death he wrote to a friend, Rin Masutani, a final *haiku** which read:

Suga suga shi	Refreshingly
Bofu no ato ni	After the violent storm
Tsuki kiyo shi.	The moon rose radiant.

---

*A Japanese poem form, usually of 17 syllables.

20

THE KAMIKAZE CONTROVERSY

BY INOGUCHI

JAPANESE ATTITUDES

The annals of war yield many instances of the use of death-scorning tactics. The motives and incentives have been as varied and varying as the techniques, but defiance of death has been the common ground. The history of Japan is full of examples, since the Japanese have been taught that a duty must always be performed, even at the risk of life. Why, then, did the kamikaze special attacks arouse such a storm of controversy in Japan?

What was there about these suicide actions to distinguish them from all historical precedents? The use of airplanes was a modern touch, of course, but this was only a matter of form. The fundamental difference was the protracted period—October 1944 to August 1945—during which these organized suicide attacks continued. In this respect they were without parallel in history. Suicidal military efforts of the past had always been sudden, swift, and drama-packed; from concept to conclusion in these previous instances there was not time enough for the "victim" to dwell on his prospects. Crisis, volunteer for death, death—that idea had been acceptable to the individual and lauded by his countrymen. But the idea of systematically planned suicide attacks carried out over a period of months, while acceptable to the individuals most concerned, seems to have been too much for the Japanese public. Thus the system and its leaders came in for severe criticism from the home front.

It is not strange that the *Ohka* attack method was ridiculed by the enemy, who referred to the weapon as the *"Baka"* bomb. This weapon had been invented and developed for months before it was finally called into use, out of sheer desperation, and its successes were few. No wonder it drew the scorn of the Americans, when we ourselves were skeptical about its chances of success. Our enemies, on the other hand, appear to have had real respect for kamikaze attacks, probably because these scored such telling blows.

When the war was over, some Japanese vehemently denounced the kamikazes without having given any thought or study to them. These outbursts could generally be traced and attributed to a general animosity of the civilian public toward the Army and Navy, and citing them would add nothing here.

There are, however, many responsible and informed people who, after due consideration and reflection, have expressed views on the kamikaze attacks. One of these is Admiral Kantaro Suzuki, a senior naval officer and the country's Premier at the time of Japan's surrender. In the Sino-Japanese War he had personally led a group of torpedo boats in a daring assault which truly exemplified the Japanese Navy's tradition of death-scorning tactics. In his book, *The Phases of Terminating the War,* he said:

The spirit and the deeds of kamikaze pilots naturally arouse profound admiration. But, considered from the standpoint of strategy, these tactics are a product of defeat.

An able commander would never resort to such extreme measures. The daring attempt to blockade Port Arthur during the Russo-Japanese War was not approved until it was shown that there was a fair chance of rescuing the participants. Their only aim was to sink boats at the entrance to the harbor, but the commanding officer refused his permission for the operation until he was assured that rescue boats would be provided. That is the way of a good commander.

In the midget submarine attack on Pearl Harbor at the outbreak of war we have another example. Admiral Yamamoto would not authorize that part of the operation until it was shown that there was at least some chance of retrieving the small two-man submarines.

Kamikaze attacks, on the other hand, were carried out with no possible hope of return. It is clear evidence of our fear of inevitable defeat that no other chance of turning the tide of war was visualized. The aerial operations which were begun in the Philippines left no possibility of survival. As the able pilots were expended, less experienced pilots had to be used, and finally men who had practically no training were being sent on kamikaze missions.

What Admiral Suzuki said is true. And yet it is not the way we would have liked things to be. We would have preferred to follow the precepts of what a good commanding officer should do, but the extraordinary circumstances of the war rendered conventional tactics valueless.

It is interesting to observe the parallels and the differences in comments from a non-military point of view as expressed by Dr. Daisetsu Suzuki (unrelated to Admiral Kantaro Suzuki), a noted authority and proponent of the Zen Sect of the Buddhist religion. Writing in the March 1946 issue of the *Sekai* magazine, he said:

> The recent war must be considered from many angles. Certain characteristics peculiar to the Japanese deserve our special consideration. One manifestation of these peculiarities is the special attack corps. . . .
>
> The Japanese Army was imbued with certain German ideologies, including the thought that war is destruction. The war potential of the enemy, whatever it be, must be destroyed. . . . War is the collision of two physical forces. The opposing force must be

destroyed as quickly as possible. Soldiers, therefore, should not be thought of as human beings, but merely as a means of destruction. In this concept there is no distinction between the opposing forces.

The kamikaze was born of such thinking! Shrink from nothing that may serve to destroy the war potential of the enemy. There were uttered such specious phrases as "the highest cause of our country," but thoughtful visions of the utterers never went beyond the physical realities of war. They were totally blind to the spiritual side of things.

These war professionals strove endlessly to preserve from special attacks the members of their own group who were best trained to fight. They threw into the maw of the battle the non-members of their clique— the civilian non-professionals fresh from colleges and universities.

It is most regrettable that Japanese military men have consistently been so irreligious in their outlook. Army and Navy men reiterate endlessly such Shinto ideas as "the Divine Glory of His Majesty," "the Divine Nation," "the Holy War," "the Imperial Host," and similar phrases. But they neglect or ignore such truly universal ideas as love, humanity, and mercy.

Shinto is replete with gods of war, but there are no gods or goddesses of love. These war gods, as a consequence of Japan's insularity, are totally lacking in universality. They do not give life; they only take it.

Deeming destruction the only way of war, the goal was to kill the enemy by any means at all. And the eternal thought was, "The essence of life is to die like a true samurai." Kamikaze attacks, the product of these two feudalistic concepts, provided a maximum of efficiency from man and material. And professional militarists cunningly took advantage of the situation.

Thus does Dr. Suzuki pass judgment on the "professional militarists" who organized and directed kamikaze attacks, pronouncing it a mental defect on our part. He then launches his attack against the people of Japan generally, saying that the spirit behind the kamikaze tactics is attributable to their lack of scientific spirit.

> They attempted to overcome this deficiency by means of spiritual and physical strength applied through kamikaze tactics. The unscientific mentality of the Japanese military man was common to the rest of the country as well.
>
> This compensatory tactic was bound to be suicidal. Far from being a matter of pride, it must remain a blemish on the people of Japan.

Dr. Suzuki's argument has some validity but, as he admits elsewhere in his writing that he was not familiar with kamikaze tactics in detail, it also involves some misunderstanding. He is obviously swayed as to some points by prejudice and dogmatism. Nevertheless, his views are presented here as being characteristic of certain of the thinking groups in Japan.

Another writer who expressed his opinion of kamikaze attacks and their proponents was Mr. Kazuo Watanabe, an assistant professor at Tokyo University, who wrote an article "Vacillating Youth" which appeared in the 9 September 1946 issue of *Nippon Dokusho Shimbun*. There he said:

> Among the young men of my acquaintance, several were enrolled in the Kamikaze Corps. These men had been students, and in talking with them I found no evidence that their souls were unstable.
>
> When they were dispatched to the battle front with a flourish of brass bands, or when in uniform they were roughly treated as belonging to the intelligentsia, they merely said to themselves, "Wait and see!" Or, when they were forced to volunteer for kamikaze attacks and were going through the training which they knew was preparing them to take the place of their professional comrades in arms, they consoled themselves with the inward words, "Wait and see!" Their conduct and bearing were founded on this

stoic attitude. I have great respect for this spirit, and admire the men who were able to achieve it.

These young men could not express their resentment in positive acts against the environment which we, the older generation, had created. But they instinctively protected what they believed to be right. If today's survivors of the kamikaze effort are embarrassed by the thought that the course they followed was wrong, this is an *ex post facto* consideration. At the time, everyone concerned was guided more by instinct than by reason. There really was very little chance for reflection.

Mr. Watanabe's use of the word "instinct" is interesting in that it denotes a rather skeptical or negative attitude. Although contrary to the traditional or militaristic way of thinking, his idea must still be considered because it represents another school of kamikaze critics.

I cannot help wondering, in considering these remarks, what grounds Dr. Suzuki and Professor Watanabe have for asserting that the students-turned-soldiers were offered merely as victims to preserve the professional soldiers. If there is substance to this allegation I am unaware of it.

The editorial column of the newspaper *Yomiuri* carried an article in its issue of 1 June 1946 by its president, Mr. Tsunego Baba:

> I am inclined to think that the spiritual strength of the Japanese people shows itself only in fits of passion. In the long run the Japanese people taper off and become slack. A case in point is the kamikaze attack. We must build a more tenacious race which will not have to resort to mere momentary heroism. . . .

This attitude may be construed as sympathetic to kamikaze participants, but I cannot accept his assertion that Japanese become slack in the long run. Kamikaze attacks are certainly no example of this. Those pilots had to live facing death over a long period of time, day in and day out, never knowing when it would come. And yet their spirit and determination never wavered.

In his book *Reflections upon Our National Character,* Mr. Masanori Oshima, an avowed atheist, wrote:

When confronted with a national crisis there is an urgency for immediate action. It is at such times that merits and demerits are most markedly apparent. There is no opportunity for delay or pause in which the true character may be concealed. It is then that true character is manifested; the loyalty and patriotism of the people, the real virtues of our nation, are revealed. These virtues are epitomized in the conspicuous valor of our kamikaze pilots.

It is often said that the Japanese excel in loyalty and courage. To the Japanese, death is shorn of terror. Their brave conduct on the field of battle serves as evidence of this attitude. It is a point of strength. But it is also a point of weakness, for the Japanese are prone to make light of their lives and to be too ready to die. Courage is all too often a matter of impulse rather than a matter of mature deliberation.

On the other hand, Occidentals place high value on the life of the individual. They do not die so readily, and therefore, they cannot comprehend the psychology of kamikaze pilots. It is not a question of bravery, since Occidentals display great bravery in conquering nature, hunting wild beasts, and in exploration. But when they embark upon a hazardous undertaking it is done with the utmost of individual enterprise and intellect. That approach should serve as a good lesson for us.

There have been innumerable Japanese critics of the kamikaze attacks. Most of them, however, seem to have been made by uninformed people who stood merely as spectators of the great crisis which their nation faced. The reader must understand that the criticisms chosen for inclusion here represent the more knowledgeable Japanese observers of the kamikaze phenomenon.

FOREIGN VIEWPOINTS

There is a bond of appreciation which exists among combatants, whether they be allies or enemies.

A naval officer serving on the United States Strategic Bombing Survey once told me of having been on board a ship that was hit by a kamikaze plane. He admitted to being overwhelmed at the fighting spirit exhibited by the attacking pilot. This man was not alone in being impressed by the kamikaze spirit. Many Americans have expressed their amazement, if not admiration, at the concept and execution, as well as the destructive potential, of these tactics.

Several American writers have displayed an understanding of the Japanese mind. Some, like Ruth Benedict in *The Chrysanthemum and the Sword,* reveal a deep insight as well as an understanding. She traces the kamikaze spirit far back into Japanese history and identifies it as an illustration of the power of mind over matter. Her careful analysis of Japanese thought includes not only a number of points of interest to any reader, but also a number of suggestions as to shortcomings which it would be well for all Japanese to consider. Such studies by foreigners give some indication of the impact that the deeds of kamikaze pilots had on people throughout the world.

I was interrogated by members of the United States Strategic Bombing Survey on 15 October 1945. There were present several naval officers, including a captain, as well as a United Press news correspondent. The naval captain kept asking whether some form of compulsion had not been used to recruit pilots for the kamikaze attacks. I replied that, as far as the Philippine campaign was concerned, there had never been compulsion of any sort.

He seemed to suspect that the high command in Tokyo had long been planning a resort to kamikaze attacks when the need arose, and that it was planned to put such tactics into practice on a compulsory basis. He asked if I was not aware that the *Baka* bomb had been developed in the homeland in August of

1944, preceding by two months the employment of kamikaze tactics in the Philippines.

"I heard of the *Ohka* (*"Baka"*) bomb for the first time upon my arrival in Formosa in 1945," I replied. "I was convinced that in a national crisis all of Japan would rise to the occasion, no matter what extremes were called for."

"How did you feel about the employment of these tactics in which both pilot and plane were lost, as opposed to conventional methods of aerial attack?"

"At the time, our planes and pilots were both in short supply. We had no alternative but to try for maximum effective destructiveness from their expenditure. If the pilots had entertained a hope of survival, their determination and singleness of purpose would have weakened. This would lessen their chance of success in hitting the target, and they would but die in vain.

"A world without strife will come only when every man has learned to curb his desires. Assuming that the strongest of these is man's desire to live, you may say that this desire cannot be governed. Therefore, if our wish is for a peaceful world, it would be well to study the spirit of the kamikaze pilots."

My interrogators seemed rather astonished at this.

But, after all, the arguments and criticisms of the rest of the world as to the morality of kamikaze tactics are in a way academic. They seem relatively unimportant compared to the convictions, the feelings of the kamikaze pilots themselves.

Yokosuka P1Y1 ("Frances")

21

LAST LETTERS HOME

What, then, were the thoughts and feelings of the suicide pilots themselves as they volunteered, waited their turn, and went out on their missions?

Mr. Ichiro Ohmi made a nationwide pilgrimage for four and a half years after the war to visit the homes of kamikaze pilots. The families showed him mementoes and letters of their loved ones. He has kindly provided the authors of the book with copies of these letters, some of which express more clearly than could any other words the thoughts and feelings of the pilots about to die.

In general, what little the enlisted pilots wrote was of a simple, straightforward nature. Academy graduates also wrote very little—perhaps because they were thoroughly indoctrinated in the way of the warrior and thus accepted their fate matter-of-factly. It was the reserve officers from civilian colleges and universities, who had had only a hasty military training before receiving their assignments, who wrote the most.* A few typical letters serve to convey the spirit of kamikaze pilots.

The following was written by Ensign Susumu Kaijit-

---

*It must be borne in mind that for many hundreds of years while the code of the warrior (*Bushido*), which stressed as necessary a willingness to die at any moment, governed the conduct of the samurai, similar principles were concurrently adopted by merchants, farmers and artisans, stressing the value of unquestioning loyalty to the Emperor, other superiors, and the people of Japan. Thus, the su of the Genzan (Wonsan) Air Group in Korea. Kaijitsu was born in 1923 at Omura City, Nagasaki Prefecture of northern Kyushu. He had graduated from Nagoya Technical College just before entering the naval aviation school.

Dear Father, Mother, brothers Hiroshi and Takeshi, and sister Eiko:

I trust that this spring finds you all in fine health. I have never felt better and am now standing by, ready for action.

The other day I flew over our home and bade a last farewell to our neighbors and to you. Thanks to Mr. Yamakawa I had a chance recently to have a last drink with father, and there now remains nothing but to await our call to duty.

My daily activities are quite ordinary. My greatest concern is not about death, but rather of how I can be sure of sinking an enemy carrier. Ensigns Miyazaki, Tanaka, and Kimura, who will sortie as my wingmen, are calm and composed. Their behavior gives no indication that they are momentarily awaiting orders for their final crash-dive sortie. We spend our time in writing letters, playing cards, and reading.

I am confident that my comrades will lead our divine Japan to victory.

Words cannot express my gratitude to the loving parents who reared and tended me to manhood that I might in some small manner reciprocate the grace which His Imperial Majesty has bestowed upon us.

Please watch for the results of my meager effort. If they prove good, think kindly of me and consider it my good fortune to have done something that may be praiseworthy. Most important of all, do not weep for me. Though my body departs, I will return home in spirit and remain with you forever. My thoughts and best regards are with you, our friends, and neighbors.

---

introduction of the kamikaze principle was not so shocking to these Japanese as it would be to an Occidental. In addition, the belief that one continues to live, in close association with both the living and the dead, after death, generally causes their concept of death to be less final and unpleasant in its implications.

In concluding this letter, I pray for the well-being of my dear family.

* * *

Ensign Teruo Yamaguchi was born in 1923 on Goto Island, Nagasaki Prefecture, in northern Kyushu. Brought up by a stepmother, his youth had not been a particularly happy one. He enlisted upon graduation from Kokugakuin University in Tokyo and was assigned to the Amakusa Air Group, which was based near his home. From there he was transferred to the 12th Air Flotilla for a suicide mission.

Dear Father:

As death approaches, my only regret is that I have never been able to do anything good for you in my life.

I was selected quite unexpectedly to be a special attack pilot and will be leaving for Okinawa today. Once the order was given for my one-way mission it became my sincere wish to achieve success in fulfilling this last duty. Even so, I cannot help feeling a strong attachment to this beautiful land of Japan. Is that a weakness on my part?

On learning that my time had come I closed my eyes and saw visions of your face, mother's, grandmother's, and the faces of my close friends. It was bracing and heartening to realize that each of you wants me to be brave. I will do that! I will!

My life in the service has not been filled with sweet memories. It is a life of resignation and self denial, certainly not comfortable. As a *raison d'être* for service life, I can see only that it gives me a chance to die for my country. If this seems bitter it probably is because I had experienced the sweetness of life before joining the service.

The other day I received Lieutenant Otsubo's philosophy on life and death which you so kindly sent. It seems to me that while he appears to have hit on some truth, he was concerned mostly with superficial thoughts on the service. It is of no avail to express it now, but in my 23 years of life I have worked out my own philosophy.

It leaves a bad taste in my mouth when I think of the deceits being played on innocent citizens by some of our wily politicians. But I am willing to take orders from the high command, and even from the politicians, because I believe in the polity of Japan.

The Japanese way of life is indeed beautiful, and I am proud of it, as I am of Japanese history and mythology which reflect the purity of our ancestors and their belief in the past—whether or not those beliefs are true. That way of life is the product of all the best things which our ancestors have handed down to us. And the living embodiment of all wonderful things out of our past is the Imperial Family which, too, is the crystalization of the splendor and beauty of Japan and its people. It is an honor to be able to give my life in defense of these beautiful and lofty things.

Okinawa is as much a part of Japan as Goto Island. An inner voice keeps saying that I must smite the foe who violates our homeland. My grave will be the sea around Okinawa, and I will see my mother and grandmother again. I have neither regret nor fear about death. I only pray for the happiness of you and all my fellow-countrymen.

My greatest regret in this life is the failure to call you *"chichiue"* (revered father). I regret not having given any demonstration of the true respect which I have always had for you. During my final plunge, though you will not hear it, you may be sure that I will be saying *"chichiue"* to you and thinking of all you have done for me.

I have not asked you to come to see me at the base because I know that you are comfortable at Amakusa. It is a good place to live. The mountains north of the base remind me of Sugiyama and Magarisaka on Goto Island, and I have often thought of the days when you took Akira and me on picnics to Matsuyama near the powder magazine. I also recall riding with you to the crematorium at Magarisaka as a youngster, without clearly understanding then that mother had died.

I leave everything to you. Please take good care of my sisters.

One setback in its history does not mean the destruction of a nation. I pray that you will live long. I am confident that a new Japan will emerge. Our people must not be rash in their desire for death.

Fondest regards.

> Just before departure,
> Teruo

Without regard for life or name, a samurai will defend his homeland.

* * *

The following letter is by Flying Petty Officer First Class Isao Matsuo of the 701st Air Group. It was written just before he sortied for a kamikaze attack. His home was in Nagasaki Prefecture.

> 28 October 1944

Dear Parents:

Please congratulate me. I have been given a splendid opportunity to die. This is my last day. The destiny of our homeland hinges on the decisive battle in the seas to the south where I shall fall like a blossom from a radiant cherry tree.

I shall be a shield for His Majesty and die cleanly along with my squadron leader and other friends. I wish that I could be born seven times, each time to smite the enemy.

How I appreciate this chance to die like a man! I am grateful from the depths of my heart to the parents who have reared me with their constant prayers and tender love. And I am grateful as well to my squadron leader and superior officers who have looked after me as if I were their own son and given me such careful training.

Thank you, my parents, for the 23 years during which you have cared for me and inspired me. I hope that my present deed will in some small way repay what you have done for me. Think well of me and know that your Isao died for our country. This is my last wish, and there is nothing else that I desire.

I shall return in spirit and look forward to your visit at the Yasukuni Shrine. Please take good care of yourselves.

How glorious is the Special Attack Corps' Giretsu Unit whose *Suisei* bombers will attack the enemy. Movie cameramen have been here to take our pictures. It is possible that you may see us in newsreels at the theater.

We are 16 warriors manning the bombers. May our death be as sudden and clean as the shattering of crystal.

Written at Manila on the eve of our sortie.

Isao

Soaring into the sky of the southern seas, it is our glorious mission to die as the shields of His Majesty. Cherry blossoms glisten as they open and fall.

* * *

Cadet Jun Nomoto of the Himeji Air Group was born in 1922 in Nagasaki Prefecture. He had graduated from the University of Commerce in Tokyo just before enlisting. Apparently written in great haste, the actual letter printed below is preceded by brief notes and is concluded in a hand other than that of the original writer:

Moved forward to * * * under sudden orders. Determination for success renewed upon learning that we will sortie tomorrow.

Cadet * * * was dropped from the list of those assigned to take part in the sortie, upon my arrival. Cannot help feeling sorry for him. This is a situation of mixed emotions.

Man is only mortal. Death, like life, is a matter of chance. Yet destiny, too, plays a part. I feel confident of my ability in tomorrow's action. Will do my utmost to dive head-on against an enemy warship to fulfill my destiny in defense of the homeland. The time has come when my friend Nakanishi and I must part. There is no remorse whatsoever. Each man is doomed to go his separate way in time.

Since our unit was organized at the end of February we have undergone the most intensive kind of training. Now, at last, our chance to sortie is at hand. In our last briefing the commanding officer cautioned us, "not to be rash to die." It seems to me that everything is up to Heaven.

I am resolved to pursue the goal that fate has chosen for me. You have always been good to me, and I am grateful. My 15 years of schooling and training are about to bear fruit. I feel great joy at having been born in our glorious country.

It is my firm belief that tomorrow will be successful. It is my hope that you will share this belief. The time for our departure was set so suddenly that I will not have a chance to write last letters to my relatives and friends. I shall appreciate it if you will write to these people on my behalf, at your convenience, and express my sentiments. . . .

Dearest Parents:

Please excuse my dictating these last words to my friend. There is no longer time for me to write more to you.

There is nothing special that I can say, but I want you to know that I am in the best of health at this last moment. It is my great honor to have been selected for this duty. The first planes of my group are already in the air. These words are being written by my friend as he rests the paper on the fuselage of my plane. There are no feelings of remorse or sadness here. My outlook is unchanged. I will perform my duty calmly.

Words cannot express my gratitude to you. It is my hope that this last act of striking a blow at the enemy will serve to repay in small measure the wonderful things you have done for me.

My last wish is that my brothers may have a proper education. It is certain that uneducated men have an empty life. Please see to it that their lives are as full as possible. I know that my sister is well taken care of because you have provided for her as you did for me. I am grateful for a wonderful father and mother.

I shall be satisfied if my final effort serves as recompense for the heritage our ancestors bequeathed.

Farewell!

Jun

*   *   *

Lieutenant (jg) Nobuo Ishibashi, a native of Saga City in northern Kyushu, was born in 1920. He was a member of the Tsukuba Air Group before his assignment to the special attack corps. This is his last letter home.

Dear Father:

Spring seems to come early to southern Kyushu. Here the blossoms and flowers are all beautiful. There is a peace and tranquility, and yet this place is really a battleground.

I slept well last night; didn't even dream. Today my head is clear and I am in excellent health.

It makes me feel good to know that we are on the same island at this time.

Please remember me when you go to the temple, and give my regards to all of our friends.

Nobuo

I think of springtime in Japan while soaring to dash against the enemy.

* * *

The following letter was written by Ensign Ichizo Hayashi, born in 1922, in Fukuoka Prefecture of northern Kyushu. He had been reared in the Christian faith. Upon graduation from Imperial University at Kyoto he joined the Genzan (Wonsan) Air Group, from which he was assigned to the special attack corps.

Dearest Mother:

I trust that you are in good health.

I am a member of the *Shichisei* Unit of the special attack corps. Half of our unit flew to Okinawa today to dive against enemy ships. The rest of us will sortie in two or three days. It may be that our attack will be made on 8 April, the birthday of Buddha.

We are relaxing in an officers' billet located in a former school building near the Kanoya air base. Because there is no electricity we have built a roaring log fire and I am writing these words by its light.

Morale is high as we hear of the glorious successes

achieved by our comrades who have gone before. In the evening I stroll through clover fields, recalling days of the past.

On our arrival here from the northern part of Korea we were surprised to find that cherry blossoms were falling. The warmth of this southern climate is soothing and comforting.

Please do not grieve for me, mother. It will be glorious to die in action. I am grateful to be able to die in a battle to determine the destiny of our country.

As we flew into Kyushu from Korea the route did not pass over our home, but as our planes approached the homeland I sang familiar songs and bade farewell to you. There remains nothing in particular that I wish to do or say, since Umeno will convey my last desires to you. This writing is only to tell you of the things that occur to me here.

Please dispose of my things as you wish after my death.

My correspondence has been neglected recently so I will appreciate it if you remember me to relatives and friends. I regret having to ask this of you, but there is now so little time for me to write.

Many of our boys are taking off today on their one-way mission against the enemy. I wish that you could be here in person to see the wonderful spirit and morale at this base.

Please burn all my personal papers, including my diaries. You may read them, of course, mother, if you wish, but they should not be read by other people. So please be sure to burn them after you have looked at them.

On our last sortie we will wear regular flight uniforms and a headband bearing the rising sun. Snow-white mufflers give a certain dash to our appearance.

I will also carry the rising sun flag which you gave to me. You will remember that it bears the poem, *"Even though a thousand men fall to my right and ten thousand fall to my left. . . ."* I will keep your picture in my bosom on the sortie, mother, and also the photo of Makio-san.

I am going to score a direct hit on an enemy ship

without fail. When war results are announced you may be sure that one of the successes was scored by me. I am determined to keep calm and do a perfect job to the last, knowing that you will be watching over me and praying for my success. There will be no clouds of doubt or fear when I make the final plunge.

On our last sortie we will be given a package of bean curd and rice. It is reassuring to depart with such good luncheon fare. I think I'll also take along the charm and the dried bonito from Mr. Tateishi. The bonito will help me to rise from the ocean, mother, and swim back to you.

At our next meeting we shall have many things to talk about which are difficult to discuss in writing. But then we have lived together so congenially that many things may now be left unsaid. "I am living in a dream which will transport me from the earth tomorrow."

Yet with these thoughts I have the feeling that those who went on their missions yesterday are still alive. They could appear again at any moment.

In my case please accept my passing for once and for all. As it is said, "Let the dead past bury its dead." It is most important that families live for the living.

There was a movie shown recently in which I thought I saw Hakata. It gave me a great desire to see Hakata again just once before going on this last mission.

Mother, I do not want you to grieve over my death. I do not mind if you weep. Go ahead and weep. But please realize that my death is for the best, and do not feel bitter about it.

I have had a happy life, for many people have been good to me. I have often wondered why. It is a real solace to think that I may have some merits which make me worthy of these kindnesses. It would be difficult to die with the thought that one had not been anything in life.

From all reports it is clear that we have blunted the actions of the enemy. Victory will be with us. Our sortie will deliver a *coup de grâce* to the enemy. I am very happy.

We live in the spirit of Jesus Christ, and we die in that spirit. This thought stays with me. It is gratifying to live in this world, but living has a spirit of futility about it now. It is time to die. I do not seek reasons for dying. My only search is for an enemy target against which to dive.

You have been a wonderful mother to me. I only fear that I have not been worthy of the affection you have lavished on me. The circumstances of my life make me happy and proud. I seek to maintain the reason for this pride and joy until the last moment. If I were to be deprived of present surroundings and opportunities my life would be worth nothing. Standing alone, I was good for little. I am grateful, therefore, for the opportunity to serve as a man. If these thoughts sound peculiar, it is probably because I am getting sleepy. But for my drowsiness there are many other things I should like to say.

There is nothing more for me to say, however, by way of farewell.

I will precede you now, mother, in the approach to Heaven. Please pray for my admittance. I should regret being barred from the Heaven to which you will surely be admitted.

Pray for me, mother.

Farewell,
Ichizo

(When his sortie was delayed, this flier added the following postscript to his letter.)

"Strolling between the paddy fields the night is serene as I listen to the chant of the frogs." I could not help but think of this during my walk last evening. I lay down in a field of clover and thought of home. Upon my return to the barracks, my friends said that I smelled of clover and it brought them memories of home and mother. Several of them commented that I must have been a mamma's boy.

This did not disturb me at all; in fact, I was pleased by the remark. It is an index that people like me. When I am disturbed it is good to think of the many people who have been so kind to me, and I am pacified. My efforts will be doubled to prove my appreciation of the kind-hearted people it has been my pleasure to know.

The cherry blossoms have already fallen. I wash my face each morning in a nearby stream. It reminds me of the blossom-filled stream that ran near our home.

It appears that we will go to make our attack tomorrow. Thus the anniversary of my death will be 10 April. If you have a service to commemorate me, I wish you to have a happy family dinner.

Now it is raining, the kind of rain we have in Japan rather than what I experienced in Korea. There is an old organ in our billet and someone is playing childhood songs, including the one about a mother coming to school with an umbrella for her child.

The departure was again postponed for this flier and he had a chance to add yet another bit to the letter, which was finally mailed after he had taken off on his final flight:

I have thought that each day would be the last, but just as with most things in life, one can never be certain. It is the evening of 11 April, and this was not my day.

Do hope that I was photogenic today, for several newsreel cameramen were here, and they singled me out for a special series of pictures. Later the Commander in Chief of Combined Fleet greeted us in our billet and said to me, "Please do your best." It was a great honor for me that he would speak to so humble a person as myself. He is convinced that the country's fate rests upon our shoulders.

Today we gathered about the organ and sang hymns.

Tomorrow I will plunge against the enemy without fail.

* * *

Ensign Heiichi Okabe was born in 1923. His home was Fukuoka Prefecture of northern Kyushu. Before enlisting he was graduated from Taihoku Imperial University. His first duty was in the Wonsan Air Group, and he was transferred thence to *Shichisei* Unit No. 2 of the special attack corps. He kept a diary which was sent to his family after his final sortie. The following is an excerpt from one of his last entries in that diary:

22 February 1945

I am actually a member at last of the Kamikaze Special Attack Corps.

My life will be rounded out in the next thirty days. My chance will come! Death and I are waiting. The training and practice have been rigorous, but it is worthwhile if we can die beautifully and for a cause.

I shall die watching the pathetic struggle of our nation. My life will gallop in the next few weeks as my youth and life draw to a close. . . .

. . . The sortie has been scheduled for the next ten days.

I am a human being and hope to be neither saint nor scoundrel, hero nor fool—just a human being. As one who has spent his life in wistful longing and searching. I die resignedly in the hope that my life will serve as a "human document."

The world in which I live was too full of discord. As a community of rational human beings it should be better composed. Lacking a single great conductor, everyone lets loose with his own sound, creating dissonance where there should be melody and harmony.

We shall serve the nation gladly in its present painful struggle. We shall plunge into enemy ships cherishing the conviction that Japan has been and will be a place where only lovely homes, brave women, and beautiful friendships are allowed to exist.

What is the duty today? It is to fight.

What is the duty tomorrow? It is to win.

What is the daily duty? It is to die.

We die in battle without complaint. I wonder if others, like scientists, who pursue the war effort on their own fronts, would die as we do without complaint. Only then will the unity of Japan be such that she can have any prospect of winning the war.

If, by some strange chance, Japan should suddenly win this war it would be a fatal misfortune for the future of the nation. It will be better for our nation and people if they are tempered through real ordeals which will serve to strengthen.

* * *

Like cherry blossoms
In the spring,
Let us fall
Clean and radiant.

COMPARATIVE RECORDS OF RESULTS OF SORTIES

From official United States and Imperial Japanese naval sources.

Symbols Designating Vessel Types

AGP	—Motor Torpedo Boat Tender	CL	—Light Cruiser
AGS	—Surveying Ship	CM	—Minelayer
AH	—Hospital Ship	Cr	—Cruiser
AK	—Cargo Ship	CV	—Fleet Aircraft Carrier
AKA	—Attack Cargo Ship	CVE	—Escort Aircraft Carrier
AKN	—Net Cargo Ship	CVL	—Light Aircraft Carrier
AM	—Minesweeper	DD	—Destroyer
AO	—Oiler	DE	—Destroyer Escort
APA	—Attack Transport	DM	—Light Minelayer
APH	—Hospital Transport	DMS	—High-Speed Minelayer
ARL	—Landing Craft Repair Ship	LST	—Landing Ship, Tank
		PC	—Patrol Craft
ATF	—Fleet Tug	PT	—Motor Torpedo Boat
ATO	—Ocean Tug	SC	—Submarine Chaser
Aux	—Auxiliary Vessel	SS	—Submarine
AV	—Seaplane Tender	Tr	—Transport
AVP	—Small Seaplane Tender	Unk	—Unknown
BB	—Battleship	YDG	—Degaussing Vessel
CA	—Heavy Cruiser	YMS	—Auxiliary Motor Minesweeper

Note: The Japanese data in these appendices are incomplete, based on official records available. The American data are taken from *United States Naval Chronology, World War II.*

Some ships suffered kamikaze attacks on more than one occasion. These are indicated by parenthetical numbers following the name of the ship.

APPENDIX A—Kamikaze Attack Operations in the Philippine Islands Area

DATE	TARGET	LOCATION*	SORTIE TIME/PLACE	PLANES† KAMIKAZE	ESCORTS	CLAIMED SUNK	SUNK	CLAIMED DAMAGED	DAMAGED
Oct. 1944									
13		22°55' N, 123°12' E							CV Franklin (1)
14		22°30' N, 124°50' E							CL Reno (1)
21	6 CV	90° 185 Cebu	1625/Cebu	2	1	Unk		Unk	
23	CV	Off Suluan	0500/Cebu	2					
24		10°57' N, 125°02' E					ATO Sonoma		
25	4 CV, 6 escorts	85° 90 Tacloban	1045/Mabalacat	5	4(3)	1 CVL	CVE St. Lo. 11°10' N 126°05' E	1 CVL	6 CVE: Sangamon (1) Suwannee (1) Santee 09°45' N 126°42' E White Plains Kalinin Bay Kitkun Bay (1) 11°40' N 126°20' E
	6 CV	130° 70 Badabu	?/Cebu	2	1	1 Cr			
	CV	Off Mindanao	0630/Davao	4(2)	3(2)	Unk		Unk	
	8 CV, 2 BB	90° 40 Surigao	0630/Davao	2(1)	1(1)			1 CV	
	6 CV	130° 70 Davao	1830/Davao	4(3)	2(2)	Failed to locate enemy.			
	?	Off Leyte	1030/Mabalacat	1		Unk		Unk	
26	4 CV, 7 Cr, ? DD	East of Surigao	1015/Cebu	2	1	Unk		Unk	
			1230/Cebu	3	2(1)	1 CV	0	1 CV	CVE Suwannee (2) 09°37' N 125°00' E

*90° 185 Cebu means bearing 90°, 185 miles distant from Cebu, etc.
†4(3) indicates that only 3 planes out of 4 returned from sortie, etc.

Philippine Islands Area (Cont.)

DATE	TARGET	LOCATION	SORTIE TIME/PLACE	PLANES KAMIKAZE	PLANES ESCORTS	CLAIMED SUNK	SUNK	CLAIMED DAMAGED	DAMAGED
1944 Oct. 27									
	Task Force	87° 20 Surigao	1200/Cebu	2(1)	2(2)				
	Enemy Ships	Leyte Gulf	1530/Nichols	3	8(8)			1 BB, 1 Cr, 1 Tr	
	Task Force	Leyte Gulf or Lamon Bay	1500/Nichols	3(1)	6(6)	Unk		Unk	
	Enemy Ships	Leyte Gulf	1600/Nichols	3(1)	2(2)	Unk		Unk	
	Enemy Ships	Leyte Gulf	?/Cebu	1 (on 28th)		Unk		Unk	CL Denver 10°57' N 125°02' E
29	Enemy Ships	Leyte Gulf	1600/Nichols	3	2(2)	Unk		1 Tr	
	4 CV, 3-4 BB	74° 180 Manila	1040/Nichols	3	2	Unk		Unk	
	Task Force	80° 200 Manila	?/Nichols	2	2	Unk		Unk	
	4 CV, 3-4 BB, 16 others	74° 180 Manila	1015/Nichols ?/Nichols	2 6(4)	2(1) 3(1)	Unk		1 CV Unk	CV Intrepid (1) 15°07' N 124°01' E
30	3 CV, 1 BB, DD, Cr	150° 40 Suluan	1330/Cebu	6	5(3)			3 CV (E) 1 BB	CV Franklin (2) CVL Belleau Wood 10°20' N 126°40' E
Nov. 1	Enemy Ships	Tacloban vic.	?/Nichols	6(1)	8(7)	1 BB or Cr 2 Cr	DD Abner Reed 10°47' N 125°22' E	1 DD	3 DD: Ammen Anderson Claxton in Leyte Gulf
	2 Cr, 9 Tr	Off Surigao	1100/Mabalacat	1	2(2)				
	1 BB	Off Panay	1520/Nichols	1	2(2)			1 BB	
									0

DATE	TARGET	LOCATION	SORTIE TIME/PLACE	PLANES KAMIKAZE	PLANES ESCORTS	CLAIMED SUNK	SUNK	CLAIMED DAMAGED	DAMAGED
1944 Nov. 5	2 CV, 2 BB, 4-5 Cr, 4-5 DD	90° 140 Cape Encanto	1205/Mabalacat	2	1(1)	1 CV	0	1 CVL	CV *Lexington* 16°20' N 123°59' E
	Task Force	70° 180 Cape Encanto	1215/Mabalacat	3	2(2)	Unk		Unk	
6	CV	E. of Echague	0700/Mabalacat	2	1(1)				
	Task Force	80° 120 Casiguran Airfield	?/Mabalacat	6	4(3)	Unk		Unk	
7	Task Force	E. of Luzon	?/Mabalacat	5(5)					
9	CV	Lamon Bay	?/Nichols	2	1				
11	Tr	30° 200 Suluan	?/Mabalacat	5(2)	4(2)				
12	30 Tr, 9 CV or BB	S. of Suluan	?/Mabalacat	6(2)				2 Tr	
	Tr	Leyte Gulf and off Tacloban	1115/Mabalacat	3	2(1)	Unk		Unk	
	Tr	Leyte Gulf	1230/Angeles	6	2	2 Tr		2 Tr	
	Tacloban	Tr	1300/Angeles	5	3(2)	2 Tr	0	2 Tr	2 ARL; *Egeria Achilles* 11°11' N 125°05' E
13	Convoy	Leyte Gulf	1110/Cebu	6	4(2)			3 Tr	0
	Convoy	Leyte Gulf	1645/Cebu	2	1(1)				
	Convoy	Tacloban Channel	1645/Cebu	2	1				
13	5 CV and others	60° 140 Manila	1230/Mabalacat	4	1	Unk		1 CV	0
14	Scouting	Lamon Bay	1600/Angeles	2	1	Unk		Unk	
	Task Force of 14CV	E. of Lamon Bay	1700/Clark	2					

Philippine Islands Area (Cont.)

DATE	TARGET	LOCATION	SORTIE TIME/PLACE	PLANES KAMIKAZE	ESCORTS	CLAIMED SUNK	SUNK	CLAIMED DAMAGED	DAMAGED
1944 Nov.									
17	Enemy Ships	Off Tacloban	0640/Cebu	5	4(4)				APA *Alpine* 11°07'N 125°02'E
19	Scout and Attack	E. of Manila	1600/Mabalacat	4	2(1)				
	Tr	Off Tacloban	0610/Cebu	4	2(2)			3 Tr	0
21	Scout and Attack	E. of Manila	0640/Mabalacat	6(6)	6(6)				0
23	Task Force	68° 250 Davao	?/Davao	3				1 CV	0
		10°57'N, 125°02'E							APA *James O'Hara*
25	Task Force	10° 100 Naga Pt.	?/Nichols	5	6(3)				
	Task Force	75° 150 Clark	1145/Echague	5(2)	3(1)				
	Task Force	75° 150 Clark	1130/Mabalacat	8	6(4)	1 CV 1 Cr	0	1 CV 1 CV	3 CV: *Essex* *Intrepid* (2) *Hancock* (1) 15°47'N 123°14'E CVL *Cabot* 15°45'N 123°09'E
	Tr	?	?/Davao	2					
	Task Force	E. of Lamon Bay	1143/Clark	4(2)	2				
26	Enemy Ships	South entrance of Tacloban Channel	1010/Cebu	3	2	2 Tr	0	1 Tr	0
	Enemy Ships	South entrance of Tacloban Channel	1010/Cebu	3	2	Unk		Unk	

DATE	TARGET	LOCATION	SORTIE TIME/PLACE	PLANES KAMIKAZE	PLANES ESCORTS	CLAIMED SUNK	SUNK	CLAIMED DAMAGED	DAMAGED
1944 Nov. 27	Tr	Leyte Gulf	0703/Mabalacat	5	4	Unk	SC-744 10°44' N 125°07' E		BB Colorado 10°50' N 125°25' E 2 CL: St. Louis Montpelier 10°50' N 125°25' E
29	Enemy Ships	Leyte Gulf	?/?	?	?				BB Maryland (1) 10°41' N 125°23' E 2 DD: Saufley 10°50' N 125°25' E Aulck 10°35' N 125°40' E
30	CV	Palaus	0830/Davao	3					
1944 Dec. 2	Tr	Leyte Gulf	?/Davao	1					
3	CV	Palaus	0830/Davao	3					
4	CV in port	Palaus	?/Davao	2		Unk		Unk	
5	Tr	100° 110 Surigao	1245/Cebu	3	2	1 Tr	0	1 Tr	2 DD: Drayton 10°10' N 125°20' E Mugford 10°15' N 125°20' E
6	9 Tr	Surigao Strait	0715/Cebu	3	4(3)				

Philippine Islands Area (Cont.)

DATE	TARGET	LOCATION	SORTIE TIME/PLACE	PLANES KAMIKAZE	PLANES ESCORTS	CLAIMED SUNK	SUNK	CLAIMED DAMAGED	DAMAGED
1944 Dec. 7	Crs	Camotes Sea	1220/Mabalacat	8	6(5)	1 Cr 2 DD	DD *Mahan* 10°50' N 124°30' E		DD *Lamson* 10°28' N 124°41' E
	4 Crs	Camotes Sea	1045/Cebu	4	2(1)			2 Cr	
	Enemy Ships	Camotes Sea	1600/Cebu	3	3	Unk	APD *Ward* 10°51' N 124°33' E	Unk	APD *Liddle* 10°57' N 124°35' E
	Trs	Camotes Sea	?/Clark	6		Unk		Unk	LST-737 10°09' N 124°40' E
10		10°33' N 125°14' E					PT-323		
		10°15' N 125°10' E							
11	DD	West entrance of Surigao Strait	1630/Cebu	4	7(2)	1 DD	DD *Reid* 09°50' N 124°55' E		DD *Hughes*
12		10°30' N 124°42' E							DD *Caldwell*
13	Enemy Ships	230° 20 Sequijor Is.	1630/Cebu	3	7(5)			2 Cr	CL *Nashville* 08°57' N 123°28' E DD *Haraden* 08°40' N 122°33' E
14	Tr	Mindanao Sea	?/Clark	3	2	Unk			
	Tr	240° 80 Bacolod Island	1440/?	3	2			Unk	
	Enemy Ships	near Negros Island	?/?	4	3				
	Enemy Ships	near Negros Island	0700/?	3	2(1)	1 Tr	0		

DATE	TARGET	LOCATION	SORTIE TIME/PLACE	PLANES KAMIKAZE	PLANES ESCORTS	CLAIMED SUNK	SUNK	CLAIMED DAMAGED	DAMAGED
14	Trs	South of Dumaguete	0715/Mabalacat	20(10)		Unk		Unk	CVB *Marcus Island* 2 DD: *Paul Hamilton Howorth* (1) 12°19' N 121°02' E
1944 Dec. 15	Task Force	Sulu Sea	0720/?	2		Unk		Unk	
	Trs	South of Mindoro Island	0630/Cebu	6	4	Unk		Unk	
	Enemy Ships	Vicinity of San Jose	1620/Cebu	3	3(2)		*LST-472*		
	Scout and Attack	near Mindanao	0640/Mabalacat	13		3 Tr	*LST-738* 12°19' N 121°05' E	4 Tr 1 DD	*PT-223* 12°19' N 121°02' E
	Trs	South of Mindoro Island	0655/Davao	2	3(3)			2 Tr	12°19' N 121°02' E
16	Trs	near Semiara Island	0650/Mabalacat	13		Unk		Unk	
17	CV	North Sulu Sea 12°19' N 121°04' E	1335/Davao	2	4(4)				*PT-84*
18		12°19' N 121°05' E							*PT-300*
21							*LST-460* *LST-749* 11°13' N 121°04' E		DD *Foote* 11°05' N 121°20' E
22		12°00' N 121°00' E							DD *Bryant* (1)
24	Task Force	78° 138 Manila	0710/?	8	5				
26	Scores of B-24s	over Angeles	?/Angeles	3					
27	Scores of B-24s	over Angeles	?/Angeles	3					
28	Tr	East of Sequijor Is.	0950/Cebu	3	3	3 Tr	0		
29	Tr	South of Mindoro	1600/Batangas	4	4(1)			1 Cr	0

Philippine Islands Area (Cont.)

DATE	TARGET	LOCATION	SORTIE TIME/PLACE	PLANES		CLAIMED SUNK	SUNK	CLAIMED DAMAGED	DAMAGED
				KAMIKAZE	ESCORTS				
1944 Dec. 30		12°21' N 121°02' E					Aux Porcupine		
		12°18' N 121°01' E							DD Pringle
		12°21' N 121°02' E							DD Gansevoort
		12°19' N 121°04' E							AGP Orestes
31	Task Force	88° 200 Manila	0710/Mabalacat	10	9(8)				
	Task Force	88° 200 Manila	0715/Nichols	4	3(2)				
1945 Jan. 2		08°56' N 122°49' E							AO Cowanesque
3	Task Force	Surigao Strait	1705/Sarangani	?	?	1 CV ?	CVE Ommaney Bay sunk by U.S. next day 11°25' N 121°19' E		
5	Trs	W. of Luzon	1557/Mabalacat	16	4(2)	3 Tr	0	1 Tr	2 CVE: Manila Bay 14°50' N 119°10' E Savo Island 15°50' N 119°00' E
	Trs	off Iba	?/Mabalacat	4	1(1)	1 Tr	0		CA Louisville (1) 15°00' N 119°00' E

DATE	TARGET	LOCATION	SORTIE TIME/PLACE	PLANES KAMIKAZE	PLANES ESCORTS	CLAIMED SUNK	SUNK	CLAIMED DAMAGED	DAMAGED
1945 Jan. 5	Convoy and Escort	Lingayen Gulf	1125/Mabalacat	15	2(2)			1 Cr	2 DD: *David W. Taylor* 27°04' N 142°06' E *Helm* 15°00' N 119°00' E DE *Stafford* 14°00' N 120°00' E AVP *Orca* 15°36' N 119°20' E ATF *Apache* 15°53' N 119°00' E
6	Enemy Ships	off San Fernando	1655/Mabalacat	5	1(1)			1 BB 1 Cr 8 Tr	2 BB: *New Mexico* (1) *California* 16°20' N 120°10' E
	Convoy & Escort	Lingayen Gulf	1040/Echague	8	8			1 Cr	2 CA: *Minneapolis* 16°20' N 120°10' E *Louisville* (2) 16°37' N 120°17' E
	Trs	Lingayen Gulf	1100/Angeles	5	5			4 Tr	CL *Columbia* (1) 16°20' N 120°10' E
	Trs	off Iba		9	6(1)	4 Unk	DMS *Long* 16°12' N 120°11' E	1 Tr	5 DD: *Newcomb* 16°20' N 120°10' E *Richard P. Leary* 16°20' N 120°10' E *Allen M. Sumner* 16°40' N 120°10' E

Philippine Islands Area (Cont.)

DATE	TARGET	LOCATION	SORTIE TIME/PLACE	PLANES KAMIKAZE	PLANES ESCORTS	CLAIMED SUNK	SUNK	CLAIMED DAMAGED	DAMAGED
1945 Jan. 6	CV	Mindanao Strait	?/Mabalacat	1					*Walke* 16°40' N 120°10' E *O'Brien* (1) 16°23' N 120°14' E DMS *Southard* 16°11' N 126°16' B
	CV	Lingayen Gulf	0200/Clark	1				1 CV	APA *Brooks* 16°20' N 120°10' E
7	Trs	Lingayen Gulf	1035/Echague	3	3(2)	1 BB or Cr 1 Tr	0		*LST-912* 16°20' N 120°10' E
	Trs	Lingayen Gulf	1710/Echague	3	3(2)	1 Tr	0		APA *Callaway* 17°00' N 120°00' E
	Enemy Ships	Lingayen Gulf	?/Mabalacat	1		Unk		Unk	
8	Unk	Unk	0300/Clark	1		Unk		Unk	2 CVE: *Kitkun Bay* (2) 15°48' N 119°09' E *Kadashan Bay* 15°10' N 119°08' E
	Unk	Unk	?	?	?				
9	Trs	Lingayen Gulf	0650/Nichols	3	1(1)	2 Tr	0		16°08' N 120°18' E BB *Mississippi* (1)
	Crs	Lingayen Gulf	1200/Tuguegarao	4	4(4)	1 Cr	0	2 Cr	CL *Columbia* (2) 16°08' N 120°10' E
	Anchored Ships	Lingayen Gulf	1600/Tuguegarao	2	2(1)	Unk		Unk	DE *Hodges* 16°22' N 120°12' E

DATE	TARGET	LOCATION	SORTIE TIME/PLACE	PLANES KAMIKAZE	PLANES ESCORTS	CLAIMED SUNK	SUNK	CLAIMED DAMAGED	DAMAGED
1945 Jan. 9		16°20' N 120°10' E		Suicide Boat					Tr Warhawk
10		16°20' N 120°10' E							DE Leray Wilson
		16°17' N 120°15' E							APA Dupage
		16°20' N 120°10' E		Suicide Boat					LST-610
11		16°20' N 120°10' E							APD Belknap
12		16°20' N 120°10' E							2 DE: Richard W. Suesens Gilligan
		15°23' N 119°10' E							APA Zeilin
		14°04' N 119°25' E							LST-700
13		17°09' N 119°21' E							CVE Salamaua
25	Ships	Lingayen Gulf	1415/Tugue- garao	2	2(2)	1 Unk	0		
31		14°05' N 120°30' E	Suicide Boat				PC-1129		

243

Recapitulation—Philippine Islands Area

JAPANESE NAVAL AIRCRAFT

KAMIKAZE PLANES		ESCORT PLANES	
Sortied	421	Sortied	239
Returned	43	Returned	137
Expended	378	Expended	102

Total 480

U. S. SHIPS

CLAIMED SUNK		SUNK		CLAIMED DAMAGED		DAMAGED	
CV	5	CVE	2	CV	9	CV	7
BB or CA	2	DD	3	CVL	2	CVL	2
Cr	5	DMS	1	CVE	1	CVE	13
Tr	20	SC	1	BB	4	BB	5
Unk	5	APD	4	Cr	11	CA	3
	37	LST	1	DD	4	CL	7
		ATO	1	Tr	37	DD	23
		Aux	1		68	DE	5
		PC	1			DMS	1
		PT	1			AGP	1
			16			AO	5
						APA	1
						APD	5
						ARL	3
						ATF	2
						AVP	1
						LST	1
						Tr	4
						PT	1
						Tr	2
							87

APPENDIX B—Kamikaze Attack Operations in the Formosa Area

DATE	TARGET	LOCATION	PLACE SORTIE	PLANES KAMIKAZE	PLANES ESCORTS	CLAIMED SUNK	SUNK	CLAIMED DAMAGED	DAMAGED
1945 Jan.									
15	Task Force	E. of Taito	Daichu, Formosa	8(7)	4(3)	None		None	
21	Task Force	120° 8 Sansendal	Tainan, Formosa	4	3 (3)	None		2 CV	CV *Ticonderoga* 22°40' N 122°57' E CVL *Langley* 22°40' N 122°51' E
	Task Force	E. of Taito	Tuguegarao (Phil. Is.)	7(4)	6(5)	None		None	
	Task Force	115° 60 Taito	Tainan, Formosa	8(3)	5(2)	None		2 CV	DD *Maddox* 23°06' N 122°43' E

Recapitulation—Formosa Area

KAMIKAZE PLANES			ESCORT PLANES	
Sortied	27		Sortied	18
Returned	14		Returned	13
Expended	13		Expended	5

CLAIMED SUNK None		CLAIMED DAMAGED CV	4/4	SUNK None

DAMAGED	
CV	1
CVL	1
DD	1
	3

245

1. Operations of 3rd 5th, 10th Air Fleets

DATE	TARGET LOCATION	PLACE OF SORTIE	PLANES	CLAIMED SUNK	SUNK	CLAIMED DAMAGED	DAMAGED
1945 Feb. 21	Vicinity of Iwo	Katori via Hachijo-jima	32	1 CV 4 Tr	CVE Bismarck Sea 24°36′ N 141°48′ E	1 CV 4 Unk	CV Saratoga CVB Lunga Point AKN Keokuk LST–477 LST–809 All at about 24°40′ N 142°00′ E
Mar. 2	S of Kyushu	?	12(11)	Enemy not located			
11	Ulithi	Kanoya	24(12)			2 CV	CV Randolph 10°01′ N 139°40′ E
18	SE of Kyushu	Kokubu	40(18)			1 CV	CV Intrepid (3) 30°47′ N 133°50′ E
	SE of Kyushu	Kanoya	8				
19	SE of Kyushu	Kokubu	34(20)			2 CV	0
	SE of Kyushu	Kanoya	5				
20	SE of Kyushu	Kokubu	18(11)	1 CV	0	3 CV	DD Halsey Powell 30°27′ N 134°28′ E
	25°36′ N 137°30′ E						SS Devilfish
	E of Kyushu	Oita	2	Unk		Unk	
21	160° 360 Kanoya	Kanoya	18(1)				
		Kanoya	16(1)*				
		Kanoya	55(45)				
	SE of Kyushu	Oroku Okinawa	15(3)				
24	Near Okinawa	Oroku	4(2)	Unk		Unk	
25	Near Okinawa	Oroku	2(1)	Unk		Unk	DD Kimberley 26°02′ N 126°54′ E DM Robert H. Smith 26°00′ N 128°00′ E APD Gilmer 26°00′ N 127°20′ E
26	Okinawa	TEN-GO Operation				1 BB 1 DD Others	BB Nevada CL Biloxi 3 DD: Porterfield O'Brien (2) Callaghan (1) DE Foreman DMS Dorsey AM Skirmish All at about 26°20′ N 127°20′ E

*Ohka ("Baka")—carrying bombers. Figures indicate sortie and losses of Ohka and bombers together.

DATE	TARGET LOCATION	PLACE OF SORTIE	PLANES	CLAIMED SUNK	SUNK	CLAIMED DAMAGED	DAMAGED
1945 Mar.							
27	Near Okinawa	Kikai Is.	8			1 Cr	DMS *Southard* (1) 26°00' N 127°00' E
	Near Okinawa	Miyazaki	7(2)				DM *Adams* (1) 26°17' N 127°40' E
29	S of Tane-gajima	Kokubu	4(2)			1 CV	CA *Indianapolis* (on 30th) 26°25' N 127°30' E
31	26°12' N 127°08' E						DM *Adams* (2)
	25°54' N 127°49' E						APA *Hinsdale*
	25°59' N 127°49' E						LST–724 LST–884
April 1	Near Okinawa	Kanoya	3(1) 3 *Ohka* ("Baka") bombs			1 BB 2 other	BB *West Virginia* 2 AKA: *Achernar Tyrell* APA *Alpine* All about 26°15' N 127°43' E
2	E of Ryukyus	Kanoya	45(31)			4 Unk 4	APA: *Chilton Henrico Goodhue Telfair* LST–599 All about 26°00' N 127°17' E
3	E of Okinawa	Kanoya	45(31)			1 CVE	CVE *Wake Island* 26°06' N 128°57' E DMS *Hambleton* 27°00' N 127°00' E
4	S of Okinawa	Kanoya	8(5)				APD *Dickerson* (sunk later by U.S.)
6	E and SE of Ryukyus	Kanoya	107(25)	2 BB 5 Unk 3 Cr	2 DD: *Bush Colhoun*	1 BB 10 DD 3 Unk	CL *San Jacinto* 10 DD: *Morris Bennett Hutchins Leutze Mullany Harrison Newcomb Howorth* (2) *Haynesworth Hyman* 2 DE: *Witter Fieberling* DMS *Rodman* 4 AM: *Facility Defense Ransom* (1) *Devastator* 2 YMS: *311 321*
	Near Okinawa	Kushira	45(8)	3 AM 2 DD	DMS *Emmons* LST–447		
	Near Okinawa	Kanoya	46(8)				

247

DATE	TARGET LOCATION	PLACE OF SORTIE	PLANES	CLAIMED SUNK	SUNK	CLAIMED DAMAGED	DAMAGED
1945 April							
7	E of Ryukyus	Kanoya	42(21)			2 CV	CV *Hancock* (2)
	W of Okinawa	Miyazaki	12(3)				BB *Maryland* (2) DD *Longshaw* DE *Wesson* YMS–81
8	26°18' N 127°39' E	Suicide boat					DD *Charles J. Badger* AKA *Starr*
	26°20' N 127°44' E	Suicide boat					
	27°07' N 128°39' E						DD *Gregory*
9	26°47' N 123°89' E						DD *Sterett*
11	Okinawa	Kanoya	50(30)	Unk			BB *Missouri* (1)
	Okinawa	Kokubu	9(4)	Unk			CV *Enterprise* (1)
	Okinawa	Miyazaki	5	Unk			2 DD: *Bullard* *Kidd* 26°00' N 130°00' E DE *Samuel S. Miles* 26°12' N 127°20' E
12	Okinawa	Kanoya	9 *Ohka*	3 BB	DD *Mannert L. Abele* 27°25' N 126°59' E		DD *Stanley* 27°12' N 128°17' E
	Okinawa	Kanoya	9			1 BB	2 BB: *Idaho* *Tennessee* 3 DD: *Purdy* *Zellars* *Cassin Young* 4 DE: *Riddle* *Rall* *Walter C.Wann* *Whitehurst* DM *Lindsey* DMS *Jeffers* AM *Gladiator* (1)
	Okinawa	Kushira	25(6)	about 20 Unk	0		
	Okinawa	Kanoya	49(12)				
13	26°55' N 126°46' E						DE *Connolly*
14	E of Okinawa	Kanoya	7 *Ohka*	1 BB	0		
	E of Okinawa	Kanoya	76(41)				BB *New York* 26°00' N 128°00' E 3 DD: *Sigsbee* *Dashiell* *Hunt* 27°15' N 130°25' E
15	Okinawa	Kanoya	10(8)			Unk	2 DD: *Wilson* *Laffey* AO *Taluga*
		Suicide boat					YMS–331

DATE	TARGET LOCATION	PLACE OF SORTIE	PLANES	CLAIMED SUNK	SUNK	CLAIMED DAMAGED	DAMAGED
1945 April 16	Okinawa	Kanoya	6 Ohka	1 BB	DD Pringle 27°26' N 126°59' E		CV Intrepid (4) 27°37' N 131°14' E BB Missouri (2) 20°00' N 130°00' E
		Kanoya	6(2)	1 Cr		3 Cr	DD Bryant (2) DE Bowers
		Kushira	20(5)			1 Unk	2 DMS: Hobson Harding
		Kanoya	20(10)				
	S of Kikai	Kanoya	60(17)	1 DD		1 CV	
		Miyazaki Izumi	20(8)	4 Tr			
17	Okinawa	Kanoya	45(27)			3 CV	DD Benham 24°01' N 132°32' E
		Izumi	4(3)				
22	Okinawa	Kanoya	35(3)		AM Swallow 26°10' N 127°12' E	Unk	3 DD: Hudson Wadsworth (1) Isherwood DM Shea 2 AM: Ransom (2) Gladiator (2)
27	26°00' N 128°00' E 26°40' N 127°40' E 26°26' N 127°36' E						DD Ralph Talbot DE England (1) APD Rathburne
28	Okinawa	Kanoya	4 Ohka	1 CA	0		0
	Okinawa	Kanoya	21(15)			1 CV 1 BB	4 DD: Wadsworth (2) Daly Twiggs Bennion (1)
	Okinawa	Kushira	22(2)			1 Tr 1 DD	
	Okinawa	Ibusuki	2			2 others	DMS Butler AH Comfort APH Pinkney
29	Okinawa	Kanoya	33(5)			2 Cr	2 DD: Hazelwood 27°02' N 129°59' E Haggard 27°01' N 129°40' E
	Okinawa	Ibusuki	2			2 others	2 DM: Shannon 26°00' N 127°00' E Harry F. Bauer(1) 26°47' N 128°42' E
30	27°26' N 127°51' E 26°10' N 127°18' E						DD Bennion (2) CM Terror

DATE	TARGET LOCATION	PLACE OF SORTIE	PLANES	CLAIMED SUNK	SUNK	CLAIMED DAMAGED	DAMAGED
1945 May							
3	Okinawa				3 DD: *Luce* 26°43′ N 127°14′ E *Morrison* 27°10′ N 127°58′ E *Little* 26°24′ N 126°15′ E		CL *Birmingham* 3 DD: *Bache* (1) *Ingraham* *Lowry* DMS *Macomb* DM *Aaron Ward*
		Suicide boat					MK *Carina*
		Ohka bomb					DM *Shea*
4	Okinawa	Kanoya	7 *Ohka*(1)	1 BB 1 Cr			AM *Gayety*
	Okinawa		27(7)			Unk	CVE *Sangamon* (2)
	Okinawa	Ibusuki	28(8)				DD *Cowell*
		Kushira	10(4)				DM *Gwin* DMS *Hopkins* YMS-327 YMS-331 (all ships on May 3 and 4 in Okinawa area)
5	Okinawa						AV *St. George* AGS *Pathfinder*
9	26°32′ N 127°13′ E						2 DE: *Oberrender*
	26°18′ N 127°13′ E						*England* (2)
10	26°26′ N 127°20′ E						DD *Brown*
	26°25′ N 128°31′ E						DM *Harry F. Bauer* (2)
11	Okinawa	Kanoya	4 *Ohka*(1)				DD *Hugh W. Hadley*
	Okinawa	Miyazaki	7(1)			2 CV 3 DD	DD *Evans* CV *Bunker Hill* 25°44′ N 129°28′ E
		Kushira	10				
		Ibusuki	2				
12	Okinawa	Kushira	1			1 BB	BB *New Mexico* (2) 26°22′ N 127°43′ E
13	30°23′ N 132°36′ E						CV *Enterprise* (2)
	E of Tanega-shima	Kanoya	28(6)			1 CV	
	26°01′ N 126°53′ E						DD *Bache* (2)
	26°21′ N 127°17′ E						DE *Bright*

DATE	TARGET LOCATION	PLACE OF SORTIE	PLANES	CLAIMED SUNK	SUNK	CLAIMED DAMAGED	DAMAGED
1945 May							
17	25°59′ N 126°54′ E						DD *Douglas H. Fox*
18	26°00′ N 127°00′ E						APD *Sims*
20	Okinawa						DD *Thatcher* (1) DE *John C. Butler* 2 APD: *Chase* *Register* *LST–808*
24	Okinawa	Kanoya	20(12)	1 DD		3 Cr 2 others	DD *Guest* 2 DE: *O'Neill* *William C. Cole* DMS *Butler* AM *Spectacle* 2 APD: *Barry* *Sims* (2)
25	Okinawa	Miyazaki	76(55)	1 Tr 1 other	APD *Bates* 26°41′ N 127°47′ E	1 Tr	DD *Stormes*
		Miho, Kokubu					APD *Roper*
		Kushira					
		Kanoya					
26	Okinawa						2 DD: *Anthony* (1) *Braine* DMS *Forrest* PC–1603 AGS *Dutton*
27		Kanoya	20(8)	3 DD 1 Cr 1 Tr	DD *Drexler* 27°06′ N 127°38′ E	11 others	DMS *Southard* (2) 2 APD: *Loy* *Rednour* APA *Sandoval* YDG–10
28	Okinawa	Kushira, Ibusuki	26(13)			1 Cr 1 other	DD *Shubrick* 26°38′ N 127°05′ E
29	Okinawa	Kushira	5(1)	Unk			APD *Tatum* 26°40′ N 127°50′ E
June 3	Okinawa	Kokubu	6(3)	Unk			AK *Allegan* 26°00′ N 128°00′ E
5	26°09′ N 127°35′ E						BB *Mississippi* (2)
	26°07′ N 127°52′ E						CA *Louisville* (3)
6	24°46′ N 126°37′ E						CVE *Natoma Bay*
	26°14′ N 128°01′ E						2 DM: *Harry F. Bauer* (3) *J. William Ditter*

DATE	TARGET LOCATION	PLACE OF SORTIE	PLANES	CLAIMED SUNK	SUNK	CLAIMED DAMAGED	DAMAGED
1945 June							
7	27°07' N 127°38' E						DD *Anthony* (2)
10	27°06' N 127°38' E				DD *Wm. D. Porter*		
21	26°00' N 128°00' E		19(9)				DE *Halloran*
	26°10' N 127°18' E						2 AV: *Curtiss* *Kenneth Whiting*
22	Okinawa		6 *Ohka* (2)			Unk	
	26°04' N 127°55' E		20(6)		.	Unk	DMS *Ellyson*
	26°18' N 127°49' E						LST–534
25	Okinawa	Ibusuki	11(8)			3 Tr 2 others	0
26	Okinawa	Ibusuki	18(11)			Unk	
	?	Kushira	?				
	?	Kanoya	?				
27	Okinawa	Kanoya	1			Unk	
28	Okinawa	Kanoya	1			Unk	
July 3	Okinawa	Kanoya	1			Unk	
19	26°15' N 127°50' E						DD *Thatcher* (2)
21	26°13' N 127°50' E						APA *Marathon*
24	19°20' N 126°42' E				DE *Underhill* (sunk by U.S.)		
28	25°43' N 126°55' E				DD *Callaghan* (2)		DD *Pritchett*
29	26°08' N 127°58' E						DD *Cassin Young*
	26°17' N 127°34' E						APD *Horace A. Bass*
Aug. 9	37°21' N 143°45' E						DD *Borie*
11	Okinawa	Kikai Is.	5(3)			Unk	
13	26°14' N 127°52' E						APA *Lagrange*
15		Oita	11(4)			Unk	

2. Operations of First Air Fleet

DATE	TARGET LOCATION	PLACE OF SORTIE	PLANES	CLAIMED SUNK	SUNK	CLAIMED DAMAGED	DAMAGED
1945 Mar.							
25	S of Okinawa	Taichu	6(2)	Unk			
Apr. 1	S of Miyako-jima E of Ishigaki Island	Ishigaki	20(16)			1 CV	
		Shinchiku	4(3)				
		Tainan	2				
2	Okinawa	Ishigaki	9(8)				
3	S of Okinawa	Shinchiku	19(15)				
		Tainan, Ishigaki					
4	S of Okinawa	Ishigaki	12(11)				
5	S of Miyako-jima	Ishigaki	7(5)				
6	Ishigaki Island	Shinchiku	3				
	Okinawa	Tainan	8(5)				
9	E of Miyako Island	Ishigaki	7(7)				
12	S of Yonakuni	Ishigaki	12(12)				
13	S. & E. of Yonakuni	Taichu Shinchiku	30(28) 6(6)	Unk			
14	Okinawa	Ishigaki	8(6)	Unk			
16	E of Formosa	Ishigaki	3(3)				
	S of Ishigaki	Shinchiku	10(9)				
17	E of Formosa	Ishigaki	9(7)				
18	E of Formosa	Ishigaki	6(6)				
25	S of Miyako-jima	Ishigaki	4(4)				
28	E of Miyako-jima	Shinchiku	6(5)	Unk			
		Giran	14(12)	Unk			
		Ishigaki					
30			30(30)				
May 3	Okinawa	Shinchiku	4	1 Cr		2 Cr 1 other	(See Appendix C1 for kamikaze-in-flicted damage in May and June)

253

DATE	TARGET LOCATION	PLACE OF SORTIE	PLANES	CLAIMED SUNK	SUNK	CLAIMED DAMAGED	DAMAGED
1945 May							
4	S. of Miyako-jima	Shinchiku	5(3)	Unk			
		Giran & Ishigaki	26(18)	1 CVE		1 CV 1 CVE	
	S. of Sakijima	Taito	6(6)				
9	Okinawa	Giran Shinchiku	4 1	1 DD			
	S. of Miyako-jima	Giran	10(5)			3 CV 1 DD	
13	Kerama Retto Okinawa	Giran Shinchiku	6 1			1 Cr	
15	Okinawa	Shinchiku Giran	2 8(5)	Unk			
17	Okinawa	Giran	1				
18	Okinawa	Giran	8(?)	Unk			
29	Okinawa	Shinchiku	2	Unk			
June 7	Miyako Retto	Ishigaki	9(7)	Unk			
21	Miyako Retto	Giran	15				
22	E. of Miyako Retto	Ishigaki	8	Unk			
29	Okinawa		8(4)	3 Unk			
30	Okinawa		3	Unk			

Recapitulation—Okinawa Area

(Owing to differences in administrative procedures, no breakdown between kami-kaze and escort planes is available for 3rd, 5th, and 10th Air Fleets)

PLANES

Sortied	1809
Returned	879
Expended	930

CLAIMED SUNK		SUNK		CLAIMED DAMAGED		DAMAGED	
CV	1	CVE	1	CV	25	CV	8
CVE	1	DD	10	CVE	2	CVE	4
BB	8	DE	1	BB	6	BB	10
CA	1	DMS	1	Cr	13	CA	2
Cr	7	AM	1	DD	16	CL	3
DD	8	APD	2	Tr	5	DD	63
AM	3	LST	1	Unk	32	SS	1
Tr	6		17		99	DE	19
Unk	9					DM	13
	44					DMS	14
						AGS	2
						AH	1
						AK	2
						AKA	3
						AKN	1
						AM	10
						AO	1
						APA	9
						APD	12
						APH	1
						AV	3
						CM	1
						LST	7
						PC	1
						YDG	1
						YMS	6
							198

Recapitulation—All Kamikaze Operations

JAPANESE NAVAL PLANES
(INCLUDING ESCORTS)

Sortied	2314
Returned	1086
Expended	1228

CLAIMED SUNK		SUNK		CLAIMED DAMAGED		DAMAGED	
CV	6	CVE	3	CV	38	CV	16
CVE	1	DD	13	CVL	2	CVL	3
BB	10	DE	1	CVE	3	CVE	17
CA	1	DMS	2	BB	10	BB	15
Cr	12	SC	1	Cr	24	CA	5
DD	8	AM	1	DD	20	CL	10
Tr	26	APD	3	Tr	42	DD	87
AM	3	LST	5	Misc	20	SS	1
Unk	14	ATO	1	Unk	36	DE	24
	81	Aux	1		195	DM	13
		PC	1			DMS	15
		PT	2			AGP	1
			34			AGS	2
						AH	1
						AK	2
						AKA	3
						AKN	1
						AM	10
						AO	2
						APA	14
						APD	15
						APH	1
						ARL	2
						ATF	1
						AV	3
						AVP	1
						CM	1
						LST	11
						PC	1
						PT	2
						Tr	1
						YDG	1
						YMS	6
							288

Total claimed sunk and damaged—276.
Actual sunk and damaged—322.

ABOUT THE AUTHORS

The Japanese authors of this absorbing account were with the Naval Special Attack Corps (Kamikaze) from its inception until its dissolution at the end of the war with the suicide sortie of Admiral Ugaki.

CAPTAIN RIKIHEI INOGUCHI, a graduate of the Japanese Naval Academy, served on cruisers and in the Bureau of Personnel before the war. As an air group commander, he led his unit in the campaigns at Timor, New Guinea, and Peleliu. He was senior staff officer to Admiral Ohnishi, the originator of the Kamikaze concept, and he participated in the early suicide operations from the Philippines and Formosa. In the home islands he was a staff officer with the 10th Air Fleet during the Okinawa campaign.

COMMANDER TADASHI NAKAJIMA, also a naval academy graduate, commanded air units on carriers, and ashore in China, from 1933 until the outbreak of World War II. He was an air group commander at Bali, Rabaul, New Guinea, the Solomons, Guadalcanal, and Iwo Jima. He was serving as the flight operations officer for the 201st Air Group in the Philippines when that unit was selected by Admiral Ohnishi for the initiation of suicide tactics as a deliberate weapon of policy. He served as an operations and training officer for suicide units until, in the last few months of the war, he was assigned command of the 723rd Air Group.

ROGER PINEAU, a United States Naval Reserve Officer, after service in World War II, was a member of the U. S. Strategic Bombing Survey in Japan and later assisted Admiral Samuel Eliot Morison in preparation of the authoritative *History of United States Naval Operations in World War II*. His knowledge of the Japanese and their language, together with his own naval background and extensive research experience makes him particularly well qualified as co-author of *The Divine Wind*.

BANTAM WAR BOOKS

Introducing a new series of carefully selected books that cover the full dramatic sweep of World War II heroism—viewed from all sides and in all branches of armed service, whether on land, sea or in the air. Most of the volumes are eye-witness accounts by men who fought in the conflict—true stories of brave men in action.

Each book in this series has a dramatic cover painting plus specially commissioned drawings, diagrams and maps to aid readers in a deeper understanding of the roles played by men and machines during the war.

FLY FOR YOUR LIFE by Larry Forrester
The glorious story of Robert Stanford Tuck, Britain's greatest air ace, credited with downing 29 enemy aircraft. Tuck was himself shot down 4 times and finally captured. However, he organized a fantastic escape that led him through Russia and back to England to marry the woman he loved.

THE FIRST AND THE LAST
by Adolf Galland
The top German air ace with over 70 kills, here is Galland's own story. He was commander of all fighter forces in the Luftwaffe, responsible only to Goëring and Hitler. A unique insight into the German side of the air war.

SAMURAI by Saburo Sakai with
Martin Caidin & Fred Saito
The true account of the legendary Japanese combat pilot. In his elusive Zero, Sakai was responsible for downing 64 Allied planes during the war. SAMURAI is a powerful portrait of a warrior fighting for his own cause. (May)

BRAZEN CHARIOTS by Robert Crisp

The vivid, stirring, day-by-day account of tank warfare in the African desert. Crisp was a British major, who in a lightweight Honey tank led the British forces into battle against the legendary Rommel on the sands of Egypt. (June)

REACH FOR THE SKY by Paul Brickhill

The inspiring true story of Douglas Bader. The famous RAF fighter pilot who had lost both legs, Bader returned to the service in World War II as a combat pilot and downed 22 planes in the Battle of Britain. Shot down, Bader survived the war in a German prison camp. (July)

COMPANY COMMANDER
by Charles B. MacDonald

The infantry classic of World War II. Twenty-two-year-old MacDonald, a U.S. infantry captain, led his men in combat through some of the toughest fighting in the war both in France and Germany. This book tells what it is really like to lead men into battle. (September)

Bantam War Books are available now unless otherwise noted. They may be obtained wherever paperbacks are sold.

THE SECOND WORLD WAR

The full drama of World War II is captured in this new series of books about a world on fire. In addition to paintings, there are maps and line drawings throughout the text at points where they are most informative.

- ☐ 11642 **FLY FOR YOUR LIFE** by Larry Forester $1.95
  Amazing story of R.R. Stanford Tuck, one of Britain's foremost air aces.

- ☐ 11709 **THE FIRST AND THE LAST** by Adolf Galland $1.95
  Unique view of German air war by commander of all fighter forces in the Luftwaffe.

- ☐ 11035 **SAMURAI** by Sakai with Caidin and Saito $1.95
  Sakai's own story by the Japanese combat pilot responsible for shooting down 64 allied planes.

- ☐ 11812 **BRAZEN CHARIOTS** by Robert Crisp $1.95
  Vivid story of war, of fighting in tanks in the wide spaces of the Western Desert told by Major Robert Crisp.

These large format (8½ X 11), full-color art books capture the spirit of men and machines in action.

- ☐ 01063 **THE AVIATION ART OF KEITH FERRIS** $7.95
  Canada $8.95
- ☐ 01049 **THE AVIATION ART OF FRANK WOOTON** $6.95
- ☐ 01004 **THE MARINE PAINTINGS OF CARL EVERS** $5.95
- ☐ 01029 **THE MARINE PAINTINGS OF CHRIS MAYGAR** $6.95

Buy them at your local bookstore or use this handy coupon for ordering: